KB101141

I am Independent – Beyond Mainstream: 7 Women Film Directors

자료제공 및 도움주신 분들

Archivio Cinema del reale
Albertina Carri
Barbara Loden Archives Foundation
Big Sur
Cineteca di Bologna
Diego Schipani
Erratacorrige
Fondo Mangini-Del Fra
Foundation for Filmmakers
Impact24 Public Relations
iranwire.com
Jingletown Films (Cheryl Dunye)
Malavida Films
Mariana Bomba
OfficinaVisioni (Paolo Pisanelli)
Seville European Film Festival
SND Films
Televentures Corporation
UCLA Film & Television Archive
Viennale (Eva Sangiorgi)

국립아시아문화전당(ACC)
　　시네마테크
문학의숲
서울국제실험영화페스티벌
신양섭
최종한(세명대학교)
한국영상자료원
한옥희

아이 엠 인디펜던트 — 주류를 넘어, 7인의 여성 독립영화 감독

아이 엠 인디펜던트 — 주류를 넘어, 7인의 여성 독립영화 감독

I am Independent – Beyond Mainstream: 7 Women Film Directors

아이 엠 인디펜던트 — 주류를 넘어, 7인의 여성 독립영화 감독

I am Independent – Beyond Mainstream: 7 Women Film Directors

I am Independent — Beyond Mainstream: 7 Women Film Directors

What is your favorite movie of all time?

So many people have asked me what my favorite movie is. And it is always challenging for me to come up with an answer to this question. At every moment of my life, different movies have inspired me, making it extra difficult to pick just one. Although there are so many films out there that are both great and important, I still feel hesitant to pick one out of such films and say that it is my personal favorite. It is probably because the gaze I find from many of such films reflects man's fantasy of the world. Relatedly, Barbara Hammer at DocFilm Forum 2017, said that she had similar difficulties when she started her career. Upon hearing her speak, I felt I was understood. She said that she took an introductory course on film history at college and watched so many works by male filmmakers that take their rightful places in the film canon. She found herself questioning whether the films she watched during the course were what she really aspired to make. Towards the end of the course, she watched a black and white film with fellow women students and immediately felt something radically different. It was her first time watching a film directed by a woman, which was filled with imagery and sensibility that she intuitively resonated with. Hammer wrote: "I knew for certain that I would make film." The film that paved her way to a film career was Maya Deren's *Meshes of the Afternoon* (1943).

The official history of cinema almost never leaves the following influential names unmentioned:

아이 엠 인디펜던트
— 주류를 넘어, 7인의 여성 독립영화 감독

"당신의 인생 영화는 무엇인가요?"

살면서 수없이 듣는 질문이지만 나는 쉽게 답을 찾기가 힘들다. 인생의 순간마다 영감을 받는 영화가 다양하기도 하거니와 역사적으로 훌륭한 작품이지만 남성들의 환상을 투사하여 만든 영화를 선뜻 말하기가 주저될 때도 있기 때문이다. 바바라 해머는 이런 나의 마음을 아는 듯 2017년 독필름포럼(DocFilm Forum)에서 영화 작업 초기의 어려움을 털어놓았다. 대학을 들어가서 영화 역사 첫 번째 강의 '시네마101'을 수강했지만, 수업에서 본 모든 작품이 가부장적 시선으로 만든 남성감독의 작품이었기에 영화를 할 수 있을지 고민이었다고 한다. 해머는 수업이 끝나고 여자 친구들과 조금 다른 흑백 단편영화를 봤는데 지금까지 본 것과 무언가 다르다는 걸 즉각적으로 느꼈다. 그 작품이 자신이 본 최초의 여성감독의 작업이었고 이미지를 통해 감정을 묘사하는 작품이었다. 해머는 이런 것이 영화라면 나

Lumière brothers, Georges Méliès, D. W. Griffith, and John Ford. However, as Barbara Hammer noticed, there certainly exist other ways to recount the history of film from Alice Guy-Blaché, then through Ida Lupino, Larisa Shepitko, Maya Deren, and to Claire Denis. We can take advantage of such a context to tell a history. Contexts are formed from a certain point of view. For this reason, if we have diverse points of view, we will be equipped with diverse contexts to recount the history of cinema. The more contexts we have, the richer cultural heritage of films we will discover and enjoy. This book is aimed at bringing attention to them so that we can potentially rescue them from possible oblivion. We hope this task helps us to come up with an alternative and richer history of cinema.

> I know a sad little fairy
> who lives in an ocean
> and ever so softly
> plays her heart into a magic flute
> a sad little fairy
> who dies with one kiss each night
> and is reborn with one kiss each dawn.
> – Excerpt from *Another Birth* (1963) by
>   Forough Farrokhzad

I learned about the author of this poem at an international film festival that took place at the other side of the earth. In a windy city facing the Atlantic Ocean, I gathered that a film directed by the poet had been restored and would be screened digitally. That is how I encountered the film *The House is Black* (1962), the only film that Farrokhzad directed. In this documentary, she shows us images of a leper colony. She imposed poetic imagination on them, creating an early yet fully fledged example of an essay film. It leads us to think about human dignity and

도 만들어야 한다는 걸 깨달았다고 한다. 그 영화는 마야 데렌의 〈오후의 올가미〉(1943)였다.

탄생한 지 120년이 조금 넘은 영화에는 뤼미에르 형제로 시작해 멜리에스, 그리피스, 존 포드 등의 감독으로 이어지는 일종의 공식적인 역사가 있다. 그러나 바바라 해머가 발견했듯이 우리는 앨리스 가이 블라쉬로 시작해 이다 루피노, 라리사 셰피티코, 마야 데렌, 클리어 드니까지 이어지는 맥락으로 영화의 역사를 이야기할 수도 있을 것이다. 맥락이라는 것이 어떤 시선에 의해 만들어진다는 걸 고려하면 다양한 버전이 존재할수록 우리는 더욱 풍부한 영화 문화를 가꾸어 나갈 수 있을 것이다. 이 책은 당대에 반짝이고 사라진, 영화 역사에서 중요하게 고려의 대상이 된 적이 없는 존재들을 망각으로부터 건져 내 영화 역사에 대한 새로운 착상을 하려는 시도이다.

> 나는
> 넓은 바다에 살고 있는 작고 슬픈 요정을
> 알고 있다
> 그녀는 마술 피리에 입을 대고 자신의 심장을
> 연주한다
> 부드럽게, 부드럽게
> 밤에 한 번의 입맞춤으로 죽어 가던 그 작고 슬픈 요정은
> 새벽이 되면 한 번의 입맞춤으로
> 다시 태어나리라
> ─포루그 파로흐자드의 시 '또 다른 탄생'(1963)에서 발췌

unfairness of fate, regardless of external condition. Still, *The House is Black* is regarded as one of the greatest documentaries in the Iranian film history and an important precursor to the Iranian New Wave movement. It stood out in my observation that she did not make any other films after *The House is Black*. She passed away five years after her first film came out. She was only 33 years old when she died in a car accident. Abbas Kiarostami, an Iranian master filmmaker, used the title of her poem *The Wind Will Carry Us* as the title for his masterpiece, as an homage to her. She was certainly a brilliant filmmaker. Then, why did she not make more than one film?

The House is Black reminded me of another film: *Wanda* (1970). It is an only feature film that Barbara Loden, who won a Tony Award in 1964 for her stage performance of *After the Fall*. *Wanda* is Loden's only feature film, which it is about an aimless woman who was wandering around the street and then accidentally got involved in a crime. Later, Marguerite Duras, a notable author, said, "I believe there is a miracle in Wanda." Actor Isabelle Huppert said, "She has such control," lauding Loden's talent. However, *Wanda* was acclaimed after Loden passed away from cancer, after repeatedly failing to finance her subsequent projects.

When these films were first released, not much recognition was given to them. However, now, *The House is Black* is considered to be a pioneering work in the Iranian New Wave movement. Likewise, *Wanda* is considered a masterpiece of the New American Cinema. Both of the films are reckoned a cinematic landmark for an era. Are there other women filmmakers who opened a new era like Farrokhzad and Loden? This book project started from this

이 시를 쓴 포루그 파로흐자드를 알게 된 건 지구 반대편에서 개최된 국제영화제였다. 대서양을 면하고 있어 바람이 거친 도시에서 한 시인이 연출한 영화가 복원되어 디지털로 선을 보인다는 소식을 들었다. 그렇게 만난 〈검은 집〉(1962)은 파로흐자드가 연출한 유일한 영화였다. 한센병 환자를 돌보는 폐쇄된 마을을 기록한 이미지에 시적 상상력을 가미해 에세이 영화라는 형태를 갖춘 초기 다큐멘터리로 관객에게 겉으로 드러나는 조건과 관계없는 인간의 존엄과 운명의 불공평함에 대해 생각하게 한다. 〈검은 집〉은 현재까지도 이란 영화 역사에서 가장 뛰어난 다큐멘터리이자 뉴이란시네마의 선구적인 작품으로 평가된다. 33세에 교통사고로 요절했지만 첫 작품 이후 사망하기 전까지 5년간 영화를 전혀 연출하지 않았다는 사실이 눈길을 끌었다. 이란을 대표하는 감독 압바스 키아로스타미는 포루그의 시를 영화 〈바람이 우리를 데려다 주리라〉의 제목으로 차용하며 포루그의 예술 세계에 대한 존경을 표하기도 했다. 그러한 재능에도 불구하고 왜 포루그는 단 한 편의 영화만 연출했을까?

그즈음 나는 또 다른 영화 〈완다〉(1970)를 떠올렸다. 1964년 토니상 연극 부문 최우수여우주연상을 수상한 배우 바바라 로든이 세상에 남긴 유일한 장편 극영화 연출작으로 길거리를 떠돌다 범죄에 휘말리는 한 여성 이야기를 그린 영화다. 후일 저명한 소설가 마르그리트 뒤라스가 "완다에는 기적이 있다!"라고 했고, 배우 이자벨 위페르는 "엄청난 통제력을 지닌 바바라 로든"이라며 상찬하기도 했지만, 이미 로든은 차기작을 위한 펀딩에 번번이 실패하고 암으로 세상을 떠난 후였다.

question. This book is an outcome of our endeavor to (re)discover women filmmakers who proved their presence by their films at various critical moments in film history. In this book, we would like to talk about seven pioneering women in filmmaking, here at the JEONJU International Film Festival.

Cecilia Mangini is the first Italian woman to direct a documentary film. Her first film was shot in post-war Italy. Even as a student, she was determined to stay away from fascism. She was very wary about it and even declared that she was an anarchist. As an outspoken neorealist, she took her camera to the streets and shot day-to-day life of the disadvantaged such as workers, kids, and women. She filmed them the way they were. She did not intend to chase the dark side of life and reality. Instead, she takes a non-judgmental and unprejudiced approach, leading to images full of energy, humor and insanity.

Han Okhi of Korea is a pioneering woman, who connected her identity and experimentation on cinematic formats. During the conservative 1970s when military dictatorship oppressed South Korea, she collaborated with fellow pioneering women to create an antithesis of the mainstream film industry dominated by the so-called "fallen women melodrama." Filmmaking for her was resistance, leading her to make films that are radically different. As a fearless experimenter in filmmaking, she metaphorically used avant-garde and iconoclastic images in her work, which serves as a noteworthy beginning of an era in Korean avant-garde film history.

For Han, filmmaking was a means to question and challenge the viewers' consciousness.

영화가 처음 소개될 때에는 큰 반향을 일으키지 못했지만, 지금 〈검은 집〉은 뉴이란시네마의 선구자로, 〈완다〉는 뉴아메리칸시네마의 대표작으로 손꼽힌다. 이들의 공통점은 영화 역사 속에서 새로운 시작점에 있었던 개척자라는 것이었다. 이들처럼 자신의 시대에서 새로운 지평을 열어젖힌 여성감독은 또 누가 있을까? 이 책은 영화 사조의 중요한 순간에 자신의 존재를 영화를 통해 증명했던 여성감독을 발견하고 전주국제영화제의 '스페셜 포커스: 인디펜던트 우먼'을 통해 그들을 소개하기 위한 여정의 결과물이라 할 수 있다. 여기서 우리는 모두 일곱 명의 여성감독을 소개하고자 한다.

2차세계대전 후 이탈리아에서 최초의 여성 다큐멘터리 감독으로 활동한 체칠리아 만지니는 어린 시절부터 학교를 잠식하고 있던 파시즘의 그림자를 극도로 경계하며 자신이 무정부주의자임을 선언할 정도로 당찬 인물이었다. 그녀는 네오리얼리즘의 영향 아래 카메라를 들고 거리로 나가 노동자, 아이들, 여성 등 소외된 인물과 공간의 생생한 일상을 담았다. 만지니의 영화는 현실의 어두움을 극대화시키기보다 어떤 편견이나 판단 없이 유머러스하게 때로는 광기 있게 살아가는 사람들의 에너지로 가득하다.

한국의 한옥희 감독은 여성으로의 정체성을 영화형식적 실험으로 연결한 인물이다. 그는 70년대 유신정권의 지배를 받던 보수적인 한국 사회에서 여성영화인들의 활동을 이끌었다. 기성 여성 멜로드라마와는 전혀 다른 영화를 제작하고자 급진적

It was also a means for resistance, a metaphor for her unyielding pursuit of democracy and freedom. Filmmakers from the French New Wave movement resonate with Han, in that they both worked on rethinking the conventions in their pursuit of freedom of expression. The French New Wave icon, Anna Karina quickly rose to fame as an actor. After establishing her acting career, she made her directorial debut, *Vivre Ensemble* (*Living Together*), which was premiered at the Critics' Week at the 1973 Cannes Film Festival. She became an early example of a star actor turning into an auteur. *Vivre Ensemble* is a romance film breaking all the rules of a romance film. It depicts a young woman who grows into a self-sufficient adult, reminding us of Karina herself, who did not settle for the glory of being the icon and face of an era. She wanted to move on. She pursued her dream of being an auteur who speaks in her own voice, no matter how much resistance she had to face. Her legacy, as an exceptionally courageous woman in filmmaking, continues to this day.

Speaking of exceptionally courageous women, we cannot leave Cheryl Dunye unmentioned. Her relentless search for identity and bold on-screen representations of thereof created her award-winning debut, *The Watermelon Woman* (1996). Her unique style of filmmaking, so-called "Dunyementary", makes it possible to connect issues surrounding identity, personal and social history and filmmaking. *The Watermelon Woman,* the first ever feature film directed by an African-American lesbian, is regarded as one of the best exemplifications of *Dunyementary*. Its truly honest and unprecedented way of linking different facets of identity such as race, gender and sexuality made it the first landmark of New Queer Cinema since B. Ruby Rich coined

인 영화 형식을 시도해 전위적이고 이색적인 이미지를 상징적으로 사용했다. 기성 체제에 대한 도전과 새로움을 향한 실험의 실천자로서 한옥희는 한국 아방가르드 영화사의 의미 있는 시작점을 찍은 것으로 평가받는다.

한옥희 감독이 관객들의 의식을 실험하고 도전하는 저항 정신으로 영화를 만들었다면 자유로운 영화 정신을 추구한 프랑스 누벨바그를 대표하는 인물로 안나 카리나가 있다. 카리나는 배우로 알려진 이후 1973년 칸영화제 비평가주간에서 감독 데뷔작 〈비브르 앙상블〉을 공개했다. 카리나는 이 영화로 스타 배우가 상업영화가 아닌 작가로서 감독이 된 초기 사례로 기록되었다. 고전 로맨스 영화의 질서를 뒤집는 이 작품은 해피엔딩이 아닌 사랑이 끝난 후 자립적인 주체로 변모하는 젊은 여성을 묘사하며, 누벨바그의 영광을 거쳐 나아가고 있는 감독의 정신세계를 엿볼 수 있게 한다. 카리나는 스타 배우의 삶에 안주하기보다 사회가 원하지 않는 모습일지라도 자신 본연의 목소리를 내고자 용기를 낸 특별한 창작자였다.

자신의 정체성에 귀 기울이고 이를 당당히 영화를 통해 밝힌 감독으로는 셰럴 두녜이도 빼놓을 수 없다. 그는 정체성과 역사, 영화를 연결해 일명 '두녜멘터리'라는 형식의 절정으로 꼽히는 〈워터멜론 우먼〉(1996)을 만들었다. 이 작품은 아프리카계 미국인 레즈비언이 감독한 최초의 극영화로 꼽힌다. B.루비 리치에 의해 뉴퀴어시네마라는 용어가 미국에 등장한 후 처음으로 인종, 여성, 섹슈얼리티라는 세 가지 정체성을 솔직하고도 독특

the term and introduced it to the United States.

Argentine director Albertina Carri's *Los Rubios* (*The Blonds*, 2003) is often mentioned as an example of New Argentine Cinema. Carri made this film as she traced her parents' disappearance during the regime of Argentine military junta. A dramatic enactment by an actor reminds viewers of Carri's exploration of what had happened when she was only four years old. It creates a constant clash between the worlds of facts and fiction, asking the viewers what memory really means. Although its experimental and risky style makes it difficult to categorize *Los Rubios* as a fiction or a documentary. However, it is neither esoteric nor unengaging. It shows a never-ending joy of collaboration, despite the lack of clear answers. Also, can be found is the pure joy of filmmaking even in the midst of the most arduous and emotionally charging processes.

Let me call their names once again:
Cecilia Mangini, Forough Farrokhzad, Barbara Loden, Han Okhi, Anna Karina, Cheryl Dunye, and Albertina Carri.

I am pretty certain that none of these seven women were even aware that their work would be reckoned a landmark. However, from the current perspective, they experimented with new cinematic formats and suggested new ones. They did not fear discussing taboos and controversies. They empathized with the marginalized. By doing so, they laid the groundwork for important moments in the film history.

I am Independent – Beyond Mainstream:
7 Women Film Directors is a book about seven

한 형식으로 연결한 영화다.

아르헨티나 감독 알베르티나 카리의 〈금발머리 부부〉(2003)는 뉴아르헨티나시네마 대표 주자로 꼽힌다. 카리는 군사정권에 납치된 부모의 흔적을 추적하며 영화를 만들었다. 한 명의 배우가 극적 재현을 하며 당시 네 살이던 감독에게 일어났던 실제 상황을 추적하려는 시도를 한다. 이 도전은 현실과 픽션이라는 두 세계가 지속적으로 충돌하는 형식을 선보이며 관객에게 '기억'이 무엇인가에 대한 질문을 던진다. 극영화도 다큐도 아닌 실험적인 형식이지만 영화는 난해하기보다 한 편의 영화를 만드는 어려움과 명쾌한 답이 없는 상황에도 시종일관 공동 창작의 즐거움을 잃지 않는 모습을 보여 준다.

체칠리아 만지니, 포루그 파로흐자드, 바바라 로든, 한옥희, 안나 카리나, 셰럴 두네이, 알베르티나 카리. 이들 일곱 명의 감독들은 아무도 자신이 무언가의 시초가 될지 몰랐을 것이다. 그러나 오늘의 시선으로 보면 이들의 영화는 이전에 시도하지 않던 새로운 형식을 제시하고, 당대에 금기시하던 주제를 드러내고, 소수자에 대한 공감의 상상력을 불어넣으며 영화 역사의 중요 순간에 초석을 다진 작품들이었다.

『아이 엠 인디펜던트―주류를 넘어, 7인의 여성 독립영화 감독』은 끝없이 변화하고 성장한 사람들, 독립적인 존재로 자신의 본질에 닿기를 두려워하지 않은 7인 독립영화 감독의 삶과 작품을 여성 비평가의 눈으로 소개하는 책이다. 인간 실존과 자유의

pioneering women who directed independent films. They never ceased to grow and change. They never feared to face who they really are. In this book, their life and work are introduced by women film critics. These seven filmmakers unanimously addressed questions pertaining to human existence and free will, both of which speak to universal human values. We hope to see more discussions on their work happen. We also hope to see more interpretations of their work in the present context, and inspire new spectators and filmmakers.

While I was working on this book, director Cecilia Mangini thanked us for showing interest in her work. A week after she sent us that note, on January 21st, 2021, she passed away at the age of 93. Her passing taught us a lesson: history of film is not written exclusively with the highly famous and influential names. It can be written by talking about directors whose work has not been frequently discussed in the mainstream history. There is yet another secret in the history: we notice some extraordinary talents only after they no longer exist. My utmost respect goes to the countless women filmmakers who never gave up their determination to think as women. My gratitude goes to them for giving life to novel and alternative forms of cinema. I dedicate this book to Cecilia Mangini.

> Wish you keep the eye of outsider
> Open your heart
> Awaken your mind
> Be a Rule Breaker
> As an Independent Woman

Sung Moon (Programmer of JEONJU International Film Festival)

지라는 보편적 가치를 질문하는 그들의 작품이 지속적으로 언급되고 끊임없이 현재적 의미로 해석되어 다른 독립적인 주체들의 탄생에 영감을 주길 바란다.

이 책을 준비하는 과정에서 체칠리아 만지니 감독은 한국의 영화제가 자신의 영화를 주목해 주는 것에 감사의 마음을 전해 왔고, 그 후 일주일이 지난 2021년 1월 21일 93세를 일기로 타계했다. 만지니의 죽음은 우리에게 영화의 역사가 언제나 유명하고 알려진 이름으로만 기록되는 것이 아니라, 공식적인 역사에서 충분히 이야기되지 않은 영화를 만든 감독들에 의해서도 쓰여진다는 것을 일깨웠다. 또한 특출한 재능을 더 이상 만날 수 없게 된 이후에야 그들을 주목하는 것은 또 다른 영화 역사의 비밀이기도 할 것이다. 여성으로서 생각하려는 의지를 포기하지 않고 새로운 영화의 어형을 만들어 낸 수많은 여성감독들에 대한 존경과 함께 이 책을 체칠리아 만지니에게 헌정한다.

세계와 당신과의 긴장감을 유지하길 바라며
마음을 열고
생각을 깨우고
논쟁적인 목소리를 내는
독립적인 여성이 되는데 힘이 되기를

문성경(전주국제영화제 프로그래머)

체칠리아
만지니

Cecilia Mangini
Photographer, Director

Cecilia Mangini (1927–2021) is the first woman to make a documentary film in post-war Italy. Inquisitive and rebellious, she was never hesitant to film faces of modernization after the World War II. Her groundbreaking work discussed social inequalities and human suffering, covering topics such as tradition and superstition, marginalization of the unprivileged during urban development, inequalities for women, workers' rights issues, and relationship between fascism and religion. She bravely confronted with censorship of the Italian government by her bold cinematic expression. In the history of documentary films, she is considered as a pioneer in the genre of essay documentary with the unique viewpoint and formats.

체칠리아 만지니

사진가, 영화감독

1927-2021. 2차세계대전 후 이탈리아에서
활동한 최초의 여성 다큐멘터리 감독.
타고난 호기심과 반항아적 기질로
거리로 나가 전후 이탈리아가 현대화되는
과정을 카메라에 담는 데 주저함이 없었다.
만지니의 영화는 전통의 변화, 개발되는
도시에서 소외되는 노약자, 노동자와
여성이 처한 현실, 종교와 파시즘의 결탁 등
사회적 불평등과 인간의 고통을 다루며
정부의 검열에도 한계를 두지 않는 과감한
표현법을 선보였다. 다큐멘터리 역사에서
만지니는 작품의 고유한 시선과
형식으로 에세이 다큐멘터리의 선구자로
기록된다.

©Paolo Pisanelli

Cecilia Mangini

Cecilia Mangini: Cinema of the Last ones

By Daniela Persico (Film Critic and Programmer of Locarno Film Festival)

Three images immediately come to mind when thinking about Cecilia Mangini's work.

The first one is linked to a kind of cinema that transforms itself into poetry in the act of following the limping silhouettes of dark dressed women, covered by black shawls and framed by veils. These women are transformed into entities sculpted in a timeless landscape and merged in a lament devoid of consolation.

The second image reveals itself in the fashion of a political statement. A sequence that alternates made-up faces and seductive bodies of tabloid girls, smiling bewitchingly from the pages of advertisements, and the female voices of women workers, struggling to make themselves heard over the noise of the factory, in the act of talking about a motherhood in a situation marked by the absence of rights and the presence of labor exploitation.

The third one shines bright with the spontaneity of a free and untamed cinema. It is the image of a group of young people, friends and playmates, splashing lively along a river, oblivious to a modernity that is advancing and about to destroy the carefree youth.

This handful of frames would be enough to make Cecilia Mangini's contribution to cinema unforgettable, as a creator of new forms that stem out of the opportunities offered by reality — a ritual, a fight, a game — to then reveal a deeper meaning. The search for truth, combined with an innate curiosity and an indomitable thirst for

체칠리아 만지니
— 마지막 남은 이들의 시네마

글: 다니엘라 페르시코
(영화평론가, 로카르노국제영화제 프로그래머)

체칠리아 만지니의 작품 세계를 생각하면 곧장 세 개의 이미지가 떠오른다. 첫 번째는 어두운 차림새를 한 여인들의 흐늘거리는 실루엣을 쫓다가 영화가 시(詩)로 변모하는 이미지다. 검은 숄을 두르고 베일을 쓴 채 얼굴만 내놓은 이 여인들은 시공간을 알 수 없는 풍경 속에서 조각된 실체로 바뀌고, 위안을 찾을 길이 없는 비탄으로 섞여 들어간다. 두 번째는 마치 정치적 의사를 표명하는 것과 같은 이미지다. 타블로이드지 광고에서 튀어나온 듯한 시선을 끄는 몸매에 화장한 얼굴로 매혹적인 미소를 짓고 있는 모델들, 그리고 공장의 소음을 뚫고 자신의 생각을 표현하기 위해 고군분투하는 여성 노동자들의 목소리, 권리 부재와 노동 착취로 얼룩진 현실에서 어머니로서의 역할까지, 주어진 삶을 이야기하고자 하는 그들의 목소리가 번갈아 나오는

social justice, has always led the choices of a filmmaker that is rightly considered the pioneer of Italian documentary cinema. Originally from Apuglia (she was born in Mola di Bari in 1927), but educated in Florence where she was immediately permeated by art history, she grew up in a progressive family. Despite this, while encouraging her to study and pursue a degree in political science – an uncommon fact for a woman in post-war Italy –, they also tried to keep her rebellious spirit at bay. Since she was a young girl, Cecilia smoked, wore blue-jeans and chose to cultivate her passion for photography not in the studio – as it would be recommended to girls – but out into the street. It was while shooting a reportage during a holiday on Lipari, an island of unspoiled beauty but also brutal in the living conditions of its inhabitants, that her spirit as a filmmaker was shaped. Sensitive to human suffering and social injustice, she was always willing to uncover social truths further and reveal the humanity of the last ones in glimpses of surprising beauty.

Cecilia Mangini's gaze is considered truly unique, even though it is too often linked to the

← Cecilia Mangini's portrait in 1959

1959년 체칠리아 만지니

©Fondo Mangini-Del Fra

시퀀스다. 세 번째는 자유롭고 길들여지지 않은 시네마의 즉흥성으로 환하게 빛나는 이미지다. 무리 지어 다니며 노니는 어린 친구들의 이미지가 강을 따라 선명하고 떠들썩하게 튄다. 이들은 자신의 태평한 유년 시절을 파괴할 현대성이 곧 닥칠 것이라는 사실을 깨닫지 못하고 있다.

이 몇 개의 장면만으로도 체칠리아 만지니는 영화계에 언제까지나 길이 남을 공헌을 했다. 만지니는 현실 — 의식, 투쟁, 놀이 — 이 제공하는 기회들로부터 새로운 형식을 창조함으로써 깊은 층위의 의미를 드러냈다. 그녀는 타고난 호기심과 사회 정의를 향한 끝 모를 갈증으로 진실을 찾아 나섰고, 이에 따라 행한 일련의 선택들로 한 치의 부족함 없이 이탈리아 다큐멘터리 영화의 선구자로 손꼽히게 되었다. 만지니는 풀리아 출신이나(1927년 몰라 디 바리) 피렌체에서 교육을 받았다. 미술사에 심취했고, 가정 환경은 진보적이었다. 그렇지만 만지니의 가족들은 만지니가 정치학을 공부하고 학위를 취득하도록 격려하는 한편, — 전후 이탈리아 여성에게는 흔치 않은 일이었다 — 그녀의 반항아적 기질을 억누르려고도 했다. 만지니는 어릴 때부터 담배를 피우고 청바지를 입었으며, 사진에 대한 열정을 스튜디오 — 여자아이에게 보다 적합하다고 여겨지는 곳 — 에서가 아니라 거리로 나가 발산하려 했다. 만지니가 자신의 영혼을 영화제작자로서 다잡게 된 것은 이탈리아 남부의 리파리 섬에서다. 때 묻지 않은 자연 그대로의 아름다움을 간직하고 있지만, 주민들에게는 살아가기에 혹독한 환경일 수밖에 없는 이 섬에서 휴가를 보내던 중 르포르타주 사진을 촬영했던 것이다. 사회적 불평등과 인간의 고통에 민감했던 만지니는 현대 사회의 진

word "female" and studied in the context of gender-related issues. Indeed Italian cinema, so effervescent in those years, relegated women to marginal roles on the set. At the same time Cecilia Mangini's path is totally aligned to the cultural climate of the years she lived in. She was trained in the FICC (Fédération Internationale des Ciné-Clubs) film circles, where she discovered documentary cinema by Joris Ivens and Dziga Vertov. Her first encounter to cinema was through her experience of writing for the cinephile magazine *Cinema nuovo*, but also in a more journalistic form for *Rotosei*, for which she signed and illustrated (with her own photographs) reports on the sets of René Clément's *The Sea Wall* (1957, also known as *This Angry Age*) and Jules Dassin's *La Legge* (*The Law*, 1959). It was in this context, in which her passion for cinema was intertwined with her militancy for the Italian Communist Party, that Mangini met her future husband, Lino Del Fra, a philosopher by training and future filmmaker, with him she would share a life of cultural and civil commitment. Cecilia Mangini and Lino Del Fra belong to the group of intellectuals who chose to work on the fringes of cinema as a system, bearing witness to an honest image of Italy undergoing radical mutations, caught between the reconstruction and the economic boom.

At a time when great film directors who made Italian cinema renown in the whole world (Roberto Rossellini, Vittorio De Sica, Federico Fellini, Luchino Visconti) were consolidating their role as cultural protagonists in the society of the economic boom, there was still enough space for another kind of cinema, more modest in its economic means but also freer in its approach to the honesty of life of the Italian people. Between the 1940s and the 1970s,

실을 날카롭게 밝히고, 마지막 남은 이들의 놀라운 아름다움을 슬며시 비추며 그들의 인간성을 드러내는 데 언제고 주저하지 않았다.

체칠리아 만지니의 시선은 실로 고유하다는 평가를 받고 있다. '비록' 그녀의 작품이 젠더 이슈의 맥락에서 연구되며 '여성'이라는 단어와 함께 묶이는 경우가 지나치게 잦다 해도 말이다. 그 시절 이탈리아 영화계는 굉장히 활기가 넘쳤지만, 촬영장에서 여성에게는 아주 미미한 역할만이 돌아갔다. 마찬가지로 만지니가 걸어온 길은 그녀가 살았던 세월의 문화적 풍토와 전적으로 궤를 같이한다. 만지니는 국제시네마클럽연맹(FICC)에서 기술을 익히며 요리스 이벤스, 지가 베르토프의 다큐멘터리 영화를 발견했다. 그녀가 처음 영화와 조우한 것은 시네필 매거진 '시네마 누오보'에 글을 보낸 경험을 통해서라고 할 수 있지만, '로토세이'에 한층 저널리즘적 형태를 갖춘 글을 기고하면서부터라고도 볼 수 있다. 이 매거진에 그녀는 자신이 직접 찍은 사진을 곁들이고 서명을 한 기사를 실었는데, 르네 클레망의 〈해벽 The Sea Wall〉(1957)과 줄스 대신의 〈더 로 The Law〉(1959)의 촬영 현장을 다룬 보도문이었다. 이렇듯 영화를 향한 열정과 이탈리아 공산당을 향한 투지가 뒤얽힌 가운데 만지니는 철학 전공자이자 훗날 영화제작자가 되는 미래의 남편, 리노 델프라를 만난다. 그와 함께 만지니는 문화적으로도 시민적으로도 헌신적인 삶을 꾸렸다. 두 사람은 영화계 주변부에서 새로운 계통을 형성하며 활동하고 있는 지식인 그룹에 소속돼 있었고, 재건과 경제 호황 사이에서 혼란을 겪으며 급격히 변화하고

the 'formula 10' documentary became popular. Short films around 10–11 minutes long, corresponding to a 35 mm 300-metres film roll, were dealing with the most disparate current social issues and shown in theatres before feature films. This filmic form gave filmmakers such as Michelangelo Antonioni, Florestano Vancini, Valerio Zurlini and Francesco Maselli the chance to take their first steps. It was also a context in which eccentric looks emerged, such as those of Vittorio De Seta, Michele Gandin and Luigi Di Gianni. Mangini made around fifteen short films of her own, from *Ignoti alla città* (*Unknown To The City*, 1958) to *La briglia sul collo* (*The Bridle On The Neck*, 1972), and often intervened in her husband Del Fra's work, as he did in hers. "We didn't sign them together because it seemed ridiculous to us, as they were really short works" she said, and their close collaboration is testified to by the path they followed together. Only Lino Del Fra moved on to feature-length fiction, with Mangini signing the screenplays of his films, from *La torta nel cielo* (*Cake in the Sky*, 1972) to *Antonio Gramsci – I giorni del carcere* (*Antonio Gramsci: The Days of Prison*, which won at Locarno Film Festival in 1977). Although today Cecilia Mangini's shorts are recognised as a complete body of work, in which the filmmaker's authorship and importance is clear – unlike her other "fellow travelers" – Mangini never had the chance to see her skills as a director fully expressed, paying the price – needless to say – for being a woman in times far away from any gender equality.

Now that she is not anymore with us, her documentaries, which shine with a passion for people and close observation of a clear political reading of reality, are precious testimonies not only of a piece of Italian history,

있던 이탈리아 사회의 모습을 가감 없는 이미지로 증언했다.

　이때는 이탈리아 영화를 세계에 널리 알린 위대한 감독들 (로베르토 로셀리니, 비토리오 데 시카, 페데리코 펠리니, 루키노 비스콘티)이 경제 호황기의 문화 주역으로서 자신들의 역할을 공고히 하고 있던 때로, 또 다른 종류의 시네마, 제작비 규모는 작지만 보다 자유롭게 이탈리아 민중의 솔직한 삶에 접근할 수 있는 영화를 위한 공간도 충분히 있었다. 1940년대에서부터 1970년대까지 대중화된 '포풀러 10' 다큐멘터리는 35mm 필름 300미터에 해당하는 10-11분 길이 단편영화로, 온갖 시사적인 문제를 다루며 극장에서 장편영화에 앞서 상영되었다. 이러한 영화 형식은 미켈란젤로 안토니오니, 플로레스타노 반치니, 발레리오 주를리니, 프란체스코 마셀리 등의 영화감독에게 첫걸음을 내디딜 기회를 주었고, 같은 맥락에서 비토리오 데 세타, 미켈레 간딘, 루이지 디 잔니 같은 감독들의 독특한 스타일의 영화도 등장했다. 만지니는 〈미지의 도시〉(1958)에서부터 〈목의 굴레〉(1972)에 이르기까지 약 15편의 단편영화를 만들었고, 남편 델프라의 작품에도 종종 개입했는데, 이 점은 델프라도 마찬가지였다. "공동 작품으로 내세우지 않은 건, 정말 너무 짧은 작품들이어서 그러는 게 우스꽝스럽게 느껴졌거든요." 라고 만지니는 말했다. 두 사람의 긴밀한 협업 관계는 이들이 함께 걸어온 길을 통해 증명된다. 델프라만 장편 극영화로 작업 영역을 확장했는데, 만지니는 〈하늘의 케이크〉(1972)에서부터 〈안토니오 그람시-감옥의 시대〉(1977)(로카르노국제영화제 황금표범상 수상)에 이르기까지 그의 영화의 각본을 썼다. 오늘날 만지니는 그녀의 다른 '동료 여행자들 fellow travelers' but also of a way of thinking (conveyed through a way of making cinema) that should still question our present.

The Anthropologist

One of Cecilia Mangini's best-known films is *Stendalì: Suonano ancora* (*Stendalì (Still They Toll)*, 1960), a portrait of a group of women singing a funeral litany in griko for the death of one of their sons in Salento, an area of Apuglia. The film was conceived from the suggestions developed in the writings of anthropologist Ernesto De Martino, a central figure in the social transformation taking place in Italy, whose book *Morte e pianto rituale nel mondo antico* (1958) was the inspiration for the subject's choice.

← *Stendalì (Still They Toll)*
〈스텐달리
(스틸플레이)〉

과 달리, 자신의 작품에 대해 감독이자 원작자로서 권위와 중요성을 분명히 인정받고 있다. 하지만 그녀 또한 감독으로서 자신의 기량을 충분히 발휘할 기회는 결코 얻은 적이 없다고 할 수있는데, 그야 두말할 나위 없이 그녀가 양성평등 논의가 전무했던 시대를 살아간 여성이기 때문이다.

이제 그녀는 우리 곁에 없지만, 현실을 정치적으로 명료하게 읽어 내려는 주의 깊은 관찰 정신과 사람에 대한 열정으로 반짝이는 그녀의 다큐멘터리는 이탈리아 역사의 한 조각이자 여전히 우리의 현재에 질문을 제기하는 사유 체계(그녀가 영화를 만든 방식을 통해 전달된다)의 귀중한 증언이다.

인류학자

체칠리아 만지니의 가장 잘 알려진 작품 중 하나인 〈스텐달리 (스틸플레이)〉(1960)는 풀리아의 살렌토 지역에서 아들의 죽음을 애도하며 그리스어 방언인 그리코어로 장례 기도문을 읊는 여인들의 초상이다. 이 영화는 이탈리아 사회 변혁기의 중요 인물인 인류학자 에르네스토 데 마르티노의 연구물에 나타나 있는 단서에 착안, 그의 『고대 세계의 죽음과 비탄의 의식』 (1958)으로부터 영감을 받은 것이었다. 〈스텐달리 (스틸플레이)〉는 이론적인 상부 구조로부터 벗어나 순수한 시적(詩的) 비전으로 변모한다. 이탈리아 남부에서는 가장 사적인 절망감이 의례에서 분명히 표출된다(루카니아 지역의 추수 의식을 다룬 델프라의 〈밀의 열정〉(1960)도 마찬가지다). 만지니는 기

The film frees itself up from theoretical super-structure to transform itself into pure poetic vision. The scientific nature of a cinema committed to collecting evidence of Southern Italy's customs and traditions, where the most intimate frustrations were manifested in rituals (as is also shown in Del Fra's *La passione del grano* (*The Wheat Passion*, 1960), on the harvest in Lucania), is transcended by a film heralding the immersive visual anthropology at the center of today's research. Only a few initial shots are dedicated to the specificity of the geographical location, in favour of paying attention to the details of the liturgy, isolated in gestures of singular beauty, and to the enveloping rhythm of an almost abstract montage bringing eyes and hands together. The chant was about to be lost, and what we see is a testimony based on memories on the verge of disappearance. Like Pier Paolo Pasolini's commentary, based on the reinvention of the ritual's words, this chant is putting together different orations and operating an erudite synthesis similar to the linguistic choices made by Luchino Visconti in *La terra trema* (*The Earth Will Tremble*, 1948). This type of text (developed by Mangini together with Pasolini on the occasion of *Ignoti alla città*) reflects a strong intuition on the part of the author, who felt that the commentaries in vogue were either too didactic or extremely imposing, leaving little room for interpretation to the spectator. This is why she turned to a poet like Pasolini, in order to create freer associations between images and words. Yet the commentary is perhaps the least singular aspect in a film that finds the possibility of pushing the documentary towards abstract cinema in the visual composition, conceived together with the faithful director of photography Giuseppe De Mitri. In this vein, it is certainly interesting

록이라는 영화예술의 과학적 본성을 이용해 이곳의 관습과 전통의 흔적을 수집하고 오늘날 영상인류학의 중심이 된 현장을 실감나게 잡아내는 법을 일찍이 제시한다. 지리적 위치의 특수성을 보여 주는 것은 처음 몇 쇼트들뿐으로, 영화는 두드러지게 아름다운 몸짓으로 구별되는 예배 의식의 세부사항과 눈과 손을 하나로 모으는 추상적 몽타주와 같이 에워싸는 리듬을 집중적으로 그린다. 이들의 민요(民謠)는 사라질 뻔했지만, 잊히기 직전 사람들의 기억에 기반한 증언이 영화에 담겼다. 장례곡의 노랫말을 각색한 피에르 파올로 파졸리니의 내레이션처럼, 이 민요는 여러 추도 연설을 한데 모으며 루키노 비스콘티 감독이 〈흔들리는 대지〉(1948)에서 보여 준 언어적 선택과 유사하게 지적 총체로 작동한다. 텍스트가 이러한 형태를 갖추게 된 것은 (〈미지의 도시〉 작업 당시 만지니가 파졸리니와 함께 개발한 형태이다) 당시 유행하던 내레이션 양식이 극히 설교적이거나 지나치게 돋보여서 영화를 보는 사람에게 독자적 해석의 여지를 거의 남기지 않는다고 생각했던 만지니의 작가로서의 통찰이 강하게 반영된 결과다. 그리고 이러한 연유에서 이미지와 언어 사이의 자유로운 연상을 이루고자, 파졸리니 같은 시인에게 도움을 구했던 것이다. 그런데 〈스텐달리 (스틸플레이)〉는 시각적 구성 면에서도 만지니가 믿음직한 촬영감독 주세페 데미트리와 함께 그 가능성을 발견해 다큐멘터리를 추상적 시네마로까지 밀어붙인 작품으로, 특별한 점을 꼽자면 내레이션에 앞서 열거해야 할 것들이 무수히 많은 영화다. 이러한 맥락에서 〈신성한 사랑〉(1961)도 살펴보고 넘어가는 것이 흥미로울 것 같다. 라치오 지방에서 촬영되었으며 독실한 가톨릭 신자들

to mention *Divino amore* (1961), on a nocturnal
pilgrimage to a sanctuary in the Lazio region,
in which the faithfuls' journey, culminating in
a moment of devotion at dawn, is transformed
into a moment of pagan celebration. The short film
has no commentary but shows a clear point of
view by using editing in a strongly expressive
manner – the scene with faces distorted by the

← *Unknown To The City*
〈미지의 도시〉

의 성소(聖所)를 향한 밤의 순례길을 담았다. 이들의 여정은 새벽녘의 기도로 절정에 이르고, 어느 순간 토속 신앙적 축전으로 완전히 바뀐다. 이 단편 작품은 상당히 표현적인 편집 방식 — 특히 종교적 환상으로 일그러진 얼굴을 보여 주는 장면이 인상적이다 — 과 대위법과 감산(減算)의 원리로 작동하며 아이러니하고 문답체적인 분위기를 형성하는 에지스토 마키의 음악 덕분에 내레이션이 없음에도 감독의 관점이 분명히 전달된다.

이미 수많은 것을 조사하고 기록한 데 마르티노로부터 받은 영향 — 이 때문에 만지니는 이 대학자가 전개한 이론의 해설자에 불과하다는 오해의 시선을 자주 받는다 — 을 제쳐 놓고도, 여성감독 체칠리아 만지니는 인류학을 도시화의 중심부에 침투시키고 산업화가 가져온 개인, 부부, 가족의 기능 변화를 소상히 알린, 도시 지리학의 진실한 탐사가이다.

만지니는 카를로 레비의 대표작『그리스도는 에볼리에 머물렀다』(1945)에 극명히 묘사돼 있는 연민의 감정으로부터 영감을 받았고, 피에르 파올로 파졸리니에서 바스코 프라톨리니까지 위대한 작가들과 협업했다. 〈미지의 도시〉에서는 로마 교외의 젊은이들을 탐구했다. 이들은 더 나은 미래의 약속을 위해 그날그날의 고된 일상을 살아가지만, 오락과 유희로 가득한 삶에 대한 열정으로 충만하다. 〈프라톨리니의 피렌체〉(1959)에서는 버려진 노인들의 삶을 찾아 나섰다. 영화는 피렌체 산 프레디아노 구역의 발전과 활기 이면에 감춰진 자본주의 사회의 어두운 모습을 들추고, 온 나라가 경제 발전에만 목을 매느라 뒤에 남겨진 마지막 이들을 잊었다는 사실을 일깨운다.

sacred vision is impressive – and leaving free space for Egisto Macchi's music, which works by subtraction and counterpoint, creating an ironic and interlocutory atmosphere.

Apart from the Demartinian influence, on which much has been already written and which often – and wrongly – sees Mangini as merely a brilliant interpreter of the great intellectual's theories, the woman filmmaker is a true explorer of urban geographies, pushing anthropology into the heart of urbanisation and recounting how industrialisation has changed the role of individuals, couples and families.

In collaboration with great writers, from Pasolini to Vasco Pratolini, and inspired by that feeling of pity so accurately described by Carlo Levi in the novel *Cristo si è fermato a Eboli* (*Christ Stopped at Eboli*, 1945), his founding work, Mangini explores young people in Roman suburbs (*Ignoti alle città*), amidst promises of a better future and day-to-day drudgery in a crescendo of zest for life and dissipation. She also explores the lives of the abandoned elderly in Florence (*Firenze di Pratolini*, 1959), in which progress and liveliness of San Frediano's area of the city reveal the dark side of capitalist society, also showing a country so busy chasing progress that it is bound to forget the last ones behind.

The Militant

Cecilia Mangini's cinema is also and above all the place where the outcasts of modernity gain visibility, and the strong political imprint is to be found first and foremost in the attention devoted to the elderly, women and children. Even the workers, when they enter the field, are never portrayed in their position of workers,

투쟁자

체칠리아 만지니의 영화는 무엇보다도 현대화로부터 소외되고 추방당한 이들에게 가시성을 부여하는 공간이자, 노인, 여성, 어린이에게 최우선으로 관심을 쏟으며 견고한 정치적 의도를 새겨 놓은 공간이다. 나아가 노동자들도 다루는데, 이들에 대해서는 노동자로서 일하는 모습은 한사코 등장시키지 않고, 더 나은 미래를 꿈꾸고(〈토마소〉(1965)) 잃어버릴 위기에 처한 일자리의 안정성을 지키기 위해 투쟁하는(〈내 가슴속의 트리에스테〉(1964)와 〈브린디시 '65〉(1966)) 민중으로서의 모습만 묘사하는 식이다. 내레이션이 다소 교훈적으로 느껴지는 경우라도, 화면에는 만지니의 시선과 그녀의 호기심을 강하게 사로잡았을 사회적이고도 영화적인 생동감이 있다. 소비사회의 노동 생산성 향상을 위한 스타하노프 운동에 반기를 든 만지니가 새로운 정치 모델의 등장을 내다보며 만든, 시골길 12km를 행군하는 이야기(〈체리에서 람푸르스코 와인까지〉(1973))는 그녀가 시대를 한참 앞섰다는 것을 보여 준다.

만지니 영화의 정치적 견해는 그녀가 자신의 작품을 '신념 투쟁의 한복판에 있는 것'으로 규정한 데서 각별히 드러난다. 만지니는 시네마라는 공간을 통해 보이지 않는 이들을 조명했을 뿐 아니라, 소비에트식 편집 기법을 활용해 새로운 사상을 정교하게 표현함으로써 아카이브 다큐멘터리, 넓게는 에세이 영화의 중심인물로 우뚝 섰다. 1962년에는 리노 델프라, 리노 미치케와 함께, 정치 영화사에 큰 획을 긋게 되는 〈우리는 무장 파시스트!〉(프랑코 포르티니 내레이션)를 만들었다. '벤텐

but in that of people dreaming of a better future
(*Tommaso*, 1965) or fighting for a stability they
are about to lose (*O Trieste del mio cuore*, 1964;
Brindisi '65, 1966). Even when the commentary
appears to be didactic, the liveliness lies in
the movement, both social and cinematographic,
capturing the interest of her curious eye, very
ahead of her time when she recounts a 12km

← *Being Women*
〈여자-되기〉

니오'라 불리는 이탈리아의 파시스트 치하 20년을 다룬 장편 작품으로, 파시즘의 부상에 바티칸 교회의 책임이 있다는 사실을 신랄히 고발함으로써 현재에 물음을 던지고, 이탈리아에서 우파의 관행이 여전히 작동되고 있음을 폭로했다. 그런데 오늘날에는 여성의 현실을 고스란히 꼬집은 그녀의 영화 〈여자-되기〉(1965)가 더욱 상징적이며 투쟁적인 영화로 평가받고 있다. 이는 원래 이탈리아 공영 방송 RAI의 의뢰로 제작되었으나 당시 RAI는 이 영화가 급진적 정치 성향의 작품으로 완성된 것에 유감을 표했다. 〈여자-되기〉를 기점으로, 창의적이며 열정적인 형태의 이탈리아 여성 해방 운동 역사를 회고하는 알리나 마라치의 〈장밋빛 인생을 원했던 여자〉(2007)와 같은 다큐멘터리들이 등장할 수 있었다.

〈여자-되기〉는 2세대 페미니즘이 대두하기 전인 1965년, 만지니가 미디어에 비치는 여성의 이미지와 여성이 실제로 처해 있는 환경을 섬세하게 포착해 내놓은 두폭화(diptych)다. 그녀는 공장에 최초로 카메라를 들고 들어가 공장 노동자들의 생생한 모습을 채집했다. 한편으로 만지니는 '자매들'처럼 느껴지는 이 여성 노동자들을 더 알고 싶었다. 그녀가 생각하기에 경제적 독립은 여성 해방의 선결 조건이었기 때문이다. 다른 한편으로 만지니는 상상력이 풍부한 잡지 속 여성의 이미지에도 이끌렸다. 그녀는 이 실제 상황과 이상적 상부 구조 사이의 간극에서, 여성이 사회에서 자리를 찾지 못하고 자기실현으로부터 멀어지게 만드는 문제를 인식한다. 모델들의 마스카라를 짙게 바른 눈, 그리고 공장 노동자와 어머니들의 흐릿한 눈(경제적으로 부유한 북부 롬바르디아와 빈곤한 남부 풀리아의

march in the countryside (*Dalla ciliegia al lambrusco*, 1973) which, with its revolt against the stakhanovism of consumer society, heralds a new political model.

Politics, in Cecilia Mangini's work, is above all the way she thinks of her films as "at the centre of the battle of ideas". Cinema as a place where to give non only visibility to the invisible, but also where to elaborate a new thought through the use of Soviet-style editing, which makes her a central figure for the archive documentary and more generally for the essay film. In 1962, together with Lino Del Fra and Lino Micciché (with the addition of a commentary by Franco Fortini), she made *All'armi siam fascisti!*, a feature film on Fascism "Ventennio", destined to remain a milestone in political cinema, capable of questioning the present by harshly denouncing the Church's responsibility for the rise of Fascism and showing how right-wing practices were still at work in the country. Today, however, her film *Essere donne* (*Being Women*, 1965) is even more emblematic, a militant film on the condition of women – commissioned by RAI, which later regretted it, given the radical political force of the operation. This was the departing point for later documentaries like *Vogliamo Anche Le Rose* (*We Want Roses Too*, 2007) by Alina Marazzi, which recounts the women's liberation movement retrospectively with creativity and passion. In 1965, before the great feminist demonstrations, Mangini developed a sophisticated diptych between the media's image of women and the real situation of their lives, entering a factory for the first time with a camera to collect the testimonies of factory workers. On the one hand, she wanted to get to know these workers she felt they were like her "sisters", as for her, women's liberation always meant economic independence. On the other, she was attracted

구별 없이)을 오가는 극단적 몽타주는 이탈리아 여성들이 의식 증진을 위해 전개한 실제 행진 장면을 마지막으로 끝이 나며, 마르크스주의적 변증법을 훌륭하게 성취한다. 만지니는 사상에서뿐 아니라 자신의 영화 세계를 펼치는 방식에서도 투쟁적이었고, 심지어 크리스마스 시즌에 백화점에서 쇼핑을 즐기는 가족들과 무균실에서 깃털이 잡아 뽑히고 도축되는 닭들을 번갈아 등장시키는 편집 전략을 과감히 구사하며 관객을 충격과 전율에 빠뜨린다(〈해피 크리스마스〉(1965)). 게다가 이 영화가 극장에서 달콤한 미국식 코미디 영화에 앞서 상영된 적이 있을지 누가 알까. 만약 그랬다면 어떤 코미디 영화인지는 몰라도 관객들은 그 영화를 봐도 아무런 소비 욕구를 느끼지 못했을 것이다.

휴머니스트

내게 있어 체칠리아 만지니는 특히 영화제에서 어린 동료들의 다큐멘터리를 아이러니와 호기심 가득한 눈으로 관람하던 이탈리아 영화계의 나이 지긋한 여성의 모습으로 각인돼 있다. 그녀가 그곳에 있었던 것은, 오랜 시간이 흐른 후—다시금 카메라를 든 모험을 떠나러 돌아왔기 때문이었다—이번에는 카메라 앞으로도 나섰다. 만지니는 조카뻘 영화제작자 마리안젤라 바르바넨테와 함께 자신의 출신지인 풀리아 지방을 여행했고, 이를 통해 완성된 〈체칠리아와 함께한 여행〉(2013)은 만지니의 영화 인생에 새로운 전기를 일으켰다. 지안프랑코 로시, 피

by the imaginative magazine image of women.
In this hiatus between the real condition and the
ideal superstructure, the director recognises
the problem that leads women away from self-
fulfillment, unable to find their place in society.
In a fierce montage between the mascara-laden
eyes of the models and the misty eyes of
the factory workers and mothers (without any
distinction between Apuglia and Lombardia), we
find the admirable enactment of a Marxist
dialectic, composing a veritable march for the
awareness of Italian women in the ending scenes.
Militant not only in her ideas but also in the way
she conceived her cinematic universe, even
daring in the use of alternate editing to connect
families in department stores during Christmas
shopping and chickens plucked and slaughtered
in an aseptic room: the title *Felice Natale*
(*Happy Christmas*, 1965) makes one shudder.
And who knows if it has ever been programmed
in a theatre before a sugary American comedy,
defusing that desire for consumption encouraged
by a certain film product.

The Humanist

For me, discovering Cecilia Mangini was first
and foremost about getting to know this elderly
lady of Italian cinema, who watched the
documentaries of her young colleagues at a
festival with great irony and curiosity. She was
there because, after so many years, she had
returned behind – and above all in front of – the
camera adventuring on a trip to her native
Apuglia together with her filmmaker niece,
Mariangela Barbanente. *In viaggio con Cecilia*
(2013) inaugurates a new season for Mangini.
One in which the importance of her cinema is
rediscovered, at least in Italy, at a time when the

에트로 마르첼로 같은 감독을 필두로 현실을 다루는 영화의 새로운 시론이 전개되는 시점에, 적어도 이탈리아에서는 만지니 영화의 중요성이 재발견되었다. 그리고 93세의 만지니는 남다른 아량을 발휘해 젊은 영화제작자들의 이야기를 경청하며 그들과 함께 서슴지 않고 자유롭게 일했다. 한편, 큐레이터이자 영화제 관계자인 파올로 피자넬리가 만지니의 경력 중 소실됐던 기억들을 되살리는 데 중심 역할을 했다. 1960년대 중반, 만지니는 베트남의 참상을 담은 영화를 제작하고자 했으나 폭격이 심화돼 촬영이 돌연 중단됨에 따라 완성할 수 없었고, 당시의 기록은 잊힌 채 잠들어 있었다. 그가 만지니와 함께 이 프로젝트를 소생시킨 영화가 〈베트남은 자유로울 것이다〉(2018)와 〈두 개의 잊혀진 상자〉(2020)다. 이 작품들에서 만지니는 여전히 자신에게 영화로 담기로 한 이들을 신뢰하고 경청할 힘이 있음을, 그리고 그녀가 여타 지식인들과 다른 견지를 대표하고 있음을 확고히 보여 준다.

만지니의 초기작 중 한 편인 〈마리아와 나날들〉(1960)과 포뮬러 10 다큐멘터리에 해당하는 후기작 〈목의 굴레〉를 함께 살펴보면, 그녀의 영화가 언제나 정치적 표현을 넘어 다른 이들을 이해하려는 열망에서 비롯되었으며, 카메라를 매개로 그녀와 촬영 대상 간에 강렬한 교감의 순간이 창조되곤 했음을 뚜렷이 알 수 있다. 만지니가 늘 자신의 작품 세계를 통해 입증한 사실이지만 유달리 이 두 영화에 잘 드러난 점이 있다면, 바로 그녀가 자신을 풀리아에서 살아가는 연로한 소작인이나 로마 변두리 산 바실리오에서 어렵게 자란 아이와 같은 지위에 위치시킨다는 것이다. 애당초 그녀는 이탈리아 남부 지역과 명백한

poetics of the new authors of the cinema of
reality – from Gianfranco Rosi to Pietro Marcello –
are developing, and one in which the woman,
aged 93, freely opened up to collaborations with
younger filmmakers, demonstrating a rare
generosity and ability to listen. Paolo Pisanelli,
a curator and festival organiser, plays a central
role in this project, recovering part of the memory

Maria's Days
〈마리아와 나날들〉

The Bridle On The
Neck
〈목의 굴레〉

아이 엠 인디펜던트 — 체칠리아 만지니

of the documentary filmmaker's career, bringing out of oblivion the project, never completed, for a film on Vietnam in the mid-1960s, which was abruptly interrupted when the bombings worsened. The result was *Le Vietnam sera libre* (2018) and *Due scatole dimenticate – Un viaggio in Vietnam (Two Forgotten Boxes – a trip to Vietnam*, 2020) in which Mangini is the symbol of a different position of the intellectual, still capable of listening and trusting those who she decides to film.

If we compare one of her first experiments, *Maria e i giorni (Maria's Days*, 1960), and one of the last from the period of the "formula 10" documentaries, *La briglia sul collo*, it is clear that, beyond political dictates, her work has always come from a desire to understand others, creating an intense moment of exchange during filming. Mangini has always demonstrated this, but in these two works it becomes particularly emblematic, putting herself on the same level as an elderly sharecropper from Apuglia or a difficult child who has grown up amidst the hardships of San Basilio, on the outskirts of Rome. From the outset, the director has a frank relationship with Southern Italy, and in particular with Apulia, where her family comes from and where she spent her childhood. She builds it by portraying the archaic rituals, which mix Christian beliefs and pagan rites of elderly Maria gives the filmmaker an opportunity to reveal a bridge between intellectuals and people, creating assonances between those ancient gestures and the woman's isolation, with the magic of cinema as an instrument of dialogue and understanding. It is not the anthropologist's eye that emerges, but rather that of the woman who searches for a prophetess, a mother nature figure behind this ancient femininity. Cecilia and Maria look at each other at the same height, even though one

관계를 맺고 있었다. 특히 풀리아는 만지니 가족의 출신지이며, 그녀가 어린 시절을 보낸 곳이다. 마리아의 하루에는 고대 의례뿐 아니라 기독교 의식, 토착 신앙이 뒤섞여 있다. 만지니는 지식인들과 민중 사이에 가교를 놓고 대화와 이해의 도구인 시네마의 마법으로 이 오래된 의식들과 마리아가 느끼는 고독의 관계를 모음운(assonance)으로 빚어냈다. 〈마리아와 나날들〉에서 발견되는 것은 인류학자의 시선이 아니라 고대 여성성을 지닌 마리아가 예언자, 그리고 어머니 대자연의 현현(顯現)임을 알아차린 한 여성의 시선이다. 만지니와 마리아는 같은 높이에서 서로를 바라본다. 여기에는 한 사람은 젊은 여성이고 다른 한 사람은 나이 든 여성이라는 사실이 끼어들 여지가 없다. 이는 〈목의 굴레〉를 찍을 때 만지니가 어린아이와 같은 높이에 섰던 것과 마찬가지다. 〈목의 굴레〉는 주의력이 약한 남자아이 파비오를 둘러싼 작은 사회의 초상으로, 교사들은 파비오를 다시 무리 안으로 데려오기 위해 노력한다. 그러나 본래 성자(聖者)와 혁명가는 통제될 수 없는 법으로, 그들은 누구든 자유롭고 가만히 있지 않는다. 마치 파졸리니의 시구를 따르듯, 〈습지의 노래〉(1961)에 나오는 하루 종일 강가에서 한가롭게 노는 별난 소년들처럼 말이다. 이 소년들과 다름없이 파비오는 자기 자신을 찾고, 사랑을 찾고, 안식처를 찾고 있을 따름이다. 한 순간, 단 한 순간, 파비오는 이 모든 것을 발견한다, 카메라를 든 여성과 어린아이 사이가 빈틈없는 관계를 이루었던 〈목의 굴레〉에서... 그 여성은 파비오의 존재를 큰 소리로 외칠 준비가 돼 있는 여성이었다.

is a girl and the other an old woman, just as it is at child height that the director shoots *La briglia sul collo*, a sociological portrait of the hyperactive Fabio, whom the teachers try to bring back into the flock. But saints and revolutionaries cannot be harnessed, they are free and darting, like the extraordinary boys portrayed on a day of leisure by the river in *La Canta delle Marane* (*The Marshes' Chant*, 1961), following in the footsteps of Pasolini's poetry. Just like them, Fabio is in search of himself, of love, of a space where to feel at home. For a moment – just one – he finds it in the film that welds a relationship between a child and a woman, ready to shout out loud he is.

(Translated in English by Ludovica Fales)
out loud his freedom.

Daniela Persico
Daniela Persico (Treviso) is film critic and programmer, based in Milan. She is the Head of special events and she is part of the selection committee of Locarno Film Festival. She's founder and editor in chief of the online quarterly *Filmidee* (www.filmidee.it) and she manages the Filmidee Summer School. She's in the selection's committee of International Film Festival Mannheim Heidelberg (Germany), she is consultant for Nara Film Festival (Japan), Festival dei Popoli (Florence, Italy) and IsReal – Festival di cinema del reale (Nuoro, Italy). She wrote essays for various collective books and edited books on the work of Claire Simon (2008), Wang Bing (2010), Ross McElwee (2013) and Emmanuel Carrère (2014).

↑ *The Marshes' Chant*
〈습지의 노래〉

(루도비카 팔레스 영역)

파비오의 자유를 크게 외치며.

다니엘라 페르시코

이탈리아 트레비소 출생. 밀라노를 중심으로 활동하는 영화
비평가이자 프로그래머이다. 로카르노국제영화제의 여러 특
별 행사를 이끌고 있으며 현재 당 영화제의 선정위원회에 참
여하고 있다. 온라인 계간지 '필미데'(www.filmidee.it)를 창
간하고 편집장으로 활동 중이며, 필미데여름학교도 운영한
다. 만하임-하이델베르크국제영화제(독일) 선정위원회 위
원이며, 나라국제영화제(일본), 포폴리국제다큐멘터리영
화제(이탈리아 피렌체), 이스레알영화제(이탈리아 누오로)
의 고문이기도 하다. 다양한 공동 집필 도서에 에세이를 실었
고, 영화감독 클레르 시몽(2008), 왕빙(2010), 로스 맥켈위
(2013), 에마뉘엘 카레르(2014)의 작품을 다룬 서적들을 편
집한 바 있다

아이 엠 인디펜던트 — 체칠리아 만지니

53

Cecilia Mangini

1927 + Born between a mother from a gentry family from north
Tuscany and a socialist father from southern Apulia.
She spends her childhood in southeastern Italy in Mola
di Bari. The southern region was suffering from poverty
after World War I, so superstitions and customs were
prevalent. Mangini grows up while observing different
conditions that would've been otherwise hard to coexist.

1933 – 1951 + When her father's leather business goes under, the family
moves to Florence to find work. When Mangini turns
7 or 8, she goes to the museum with her mother every
Sunday, and this naturally becomes a learning experience
about images. While attending school, she recognizes
that fascism is prevalent in the education system and
everywhere in life, and she raises her guard. She takes
in the precepts of leftists and classifies herself as an
anarchist. She studies in Political Science at the University
of Florence (without graduation). She finds work at the
Florence Cinema Club and founds the movie club
"Controcampo".

1952 – 1955 + After World War II, major Italian cities were destroyed.
Mangini moves to Rome during the Cold War, when part
of the city was in ruins. While working at Fédération
Internationale des Ciné-Clubs (FICC), she meets her
future husband and work partner, Lino Del Fra. Years later,
Mangini says, "There are things I fall in love with in life
without knowing the reason why, and to me, those things
are nature and photography," while explaining why
she started photography.[1] Through Roberto Rossellini
and Vittorio De Sica's works, Mangini gets influenced by
neorealism and she starts to walk around the streets
taking pictures and making movies.

+ She takes a vacation with a diver friend to
an island called Lipari in southern Italy,
surrounded by the Mediterranean Sea.
She goes around the island with a Zeiss
Ikon Super Ikonta 6×6 camera, taking
reportage photography. She records the
faces and gestures of factory laborers
quarrying white volcanic pumice as well as

1
Cecilia Mangini:
There Are Many
Things I Love About
Iranian Culture
(2018.4.20),
Fajr International
Film Festival
Official Website

체칠리아 만지니 연보

1927년 + 북부 토스카나 귀족 출신의 어머니와 남부 풀리아의
사회주의자인 아버지 사이에서 출생. 이탈리아 남동부
몰라디바리(Mola di Bari)에서 어린 시절을 보냄.
제1차 세계대전 후 가난으로 고생하던 남부 지역은 종교와
미신풍습이 만연했고 만지니는 공존하기 힘든 여러
조건을 관찰하며 어린 시절을 보냄.

1933년–1951년 + 아버지의 가죽 사업이 실패하자 일자리를 찾아 가족 모두
피렌체로 이사. 만지니가 7–8세였을 당시 매주 일요일
어머니와 박물관을 다녔고 이 경험은 자연스레 이미지에
대한 교육으로 이어짐. 학교를 다니는 동안 교육과
생활 곳곳에 만연한 파시즘을 인식하고 경계함. 좌파의
계율을 받아들여 자신을 무정부주의자로 분류함.
피렌체대학교에서 정치학을 수료. 피렌체 시네마클럽에서
일했고, 영화클럽 '콘트로캄포(Controcampo)'를 창설함.

1952년–1955년 + 2차 대전 후 이탈리아의 주요 도시가 일부 파괴되고
폐허로 남은 냉전 상황에 로마로 이동.
국제시네마클럽연맹(FICC)에서 일하며 미래 남편이자
작업 파트너가 되는 리노 델프라를 만남. 훗날 만지니는
"삶에는 이유를 모르고 사랑에 빠지는 것들이 있는데 내게는
자연과 사진이 그러했다"고 이미지 작업에 발을 들인
이유를 설명함.[1] 로베르토 로셀리니와 비토리오 데 시카의
작품을 통해 네오리얼리즘에 영향을 받아 목에 카메라를
걸고 거리를 돌아다니며 사진과 영화를 촬영함.

+ 다이빙을 하던 친구를 따라 지중해를 둘러싼 이탈리아 남부
섬 리파리로 휴가를 떠남. 만지니는 자이스이콘 슈퍼이콘타
6×6 카메라를 들고 섬을 돌아다니며
르포르타주 사진을 촬영함. 백색의
화산 경석을 채석하는 공장
노동자들의 일하는 얼굴과 몸짓, 섬에
사는 사람들의 일상을 기록했으나
세상에 알려지지 않았고 이 사진들은
2017년이 되어서야 공개됨.

1
파즈르국제영화제
공식 사이트
(2018.04.20):
'체칠리아 만지니:
내가 이란 문화를
사랑하는
수많은 이유'

the faces of the residents on the island, but these pictures are not known to the world until 2017.

1956–1957 + Mangini publishes a photo series in the weekly magazine, *Rotosei*. Her shots of writers Elio Viittorini and Riccardo Bacchelli's lives in Milan show the traditional trends of Italian literature and the influence of modernism at the time. While shooting reportage photography, Mangini sees the dark shadows and contradictions of a post-war city, and this leads to the production of her first film.

1958 + Mangini calls Pier Paolo Pasolini, who is known to be a controversial writer, and requests for a short text. Pasolini, who had not yet directed any of his films yet, talks to Mangini for two hours, then he prepares his poem and runs over to the editing room. Through writing and reading the voiceover, Pasolini participates in *Ignoti alla città* (*Unknown To The City*).

1959 + Completes *Firenze di Pratolini*.
Completes *Vecchio regno* (co-directed with Lino Del Fra).

1960 + *Stendalì: Suonano ancora (Stendali (Still They Toll))* is Mangini's second work with Pasolini, and it documents the funeral culture and mourning rituals of southern Italy that date back more than 3,000 years. Pasolini writes the screenplay referencing a famous poem written in Griko, a regional dialect of the Salento region that was influenced by ancient Greek. The film observes the mourning rituals that have been handed down from ancient times to the present, transcending the cycles of human life, while showing that language and culture act as tools to maintain memories.
+ Films *Maria e i Giorni (Maria's Days)* in her hometown. It tells the story of an elderly named Maria who continues to live with rural customs that are gradually disappearing.
+ Reveals *La Passione del Grano (The Wheat Passion)* (co-directed with Lino Del Fra), which shows a ritual in Basilicata, southern Italy, where a goat becomes a symbolic sacrifice while praying for a good harvest.

1961 + *La Canta delle Marane (The Marshes' Chant)* is her third project with Pasolini as well as the last. It wins the Gold Medal at the Festival dei Popoli.

1956년-1957년 + 주간잡지 '로토세이'에 사진 연작을 실음. 작가 엘리오
비토리니와 리카르도 바켈리의 밀라노 생활을 촬영해 당시
이탈리아 문학계의 전통적인 사조와 모더니즘의 영향을
드러냄. 르포 촬영 중 전후 도시의 그늘과 모순을 발견하고
첫 번째 영화제작으로 이어지는 계기가 됨.

1958년 + 만지니는 논쟁적인 작가로 유명하던 피에르 파올로
파졸리니에게 전화를 걸어 짧은 텍스트를 부탁함. 당시 아직
자신의 영화를 연출하지 않았던 파졸리니는 만지니와 두
시간에 걸친 통화 후 자신의 시를 준비해 편집실로 달려왔고
내레이션을 쓰고 읽는 것으로 〈미지의 도시〉에 참여함.

1959년 + 〈프라톨리니의 피렌체〉 제작 완료.
〈오래된 왕국〉(리노 델프라 공동연출) 제작 완료.

1960년 + 파졸리니와의 두 번째 작업 〈스텐달리 (스틸플레이)〉는
이탈리아 남부에서 3천 년 이상 내려오는 장례 문화와
애도 의식을 기록함. 고대 그리스어의 영향을 받은 살렌토
지역에서 방언인 그리코로 쓰인 유명한 시를 참고해
파졸리니가 글을 씀. 영화는 고대에서부터 현대까지
인간 생의 주기를 뛰어넘어 구전되어 오는 애도 의식을
관찰하며 언어와 문화가 기억을 간직하는 도구로
작동한다는 사실을 보여 줌.
+ 고향 마을에서 〈마리아와 나날들〉 촬영. 점점 사라져 가는
농촌 풍습 속에서 살아가는 노년의 마리아를 담음.
+ 이탈리아 남부 바실리카타에서 추수를 기원하며 염소를
상징적 제물로 바치는 의식을 보여 주는 〈밀의 열정〉(리노
델프라 공동연출) 공개.

1961년 + 〈습지의 노래〉는 파졸리니와의 세 번째 작업이자
마지막 작업임. 포폴리국제다큐멘터리영화제에서
금메달 수상.
+ 당시 주세페 페라라, 지안프랑코 민고지, 루이지 디지아니,
리노 델프라 등이 결성한 네오리얼리즘 영화인 모임의
유일한 여성감독이었음. 이탈리아 사람들에게
자신들의 현실을 어떤 판단과 선입견 없이 보여 주는
작업을 목표로 함.

+ At the time, she was the only woman director in the Neorealist filmmaker gathering composed of Giuseppe Ferrara, Gianfranco Mingozzi, Luigi Di Gianni and Lino Del Fra. Their goal was to make films that show reality without being judgmental or biased.

+ *Divino amore* captures a night procession of the people in a remote region for a religious anniversary. It is edited like a thriller despite it being a documentary, and this new format receives a lot of attention. Receives the Gold Medal at Festival dei Popoli.

+ Anti-fascist movie *All'armi siam fascisti!* (co-directed with Lino Del Fra and Lino Micciichè) premieres at the 22nd Venice International Film Festival in 1961. It becomes controversial for depicting an image that the Vatican Church conspired with Mussolini's fascist regime.

1962 + The Italian government stops all screenings of *All'armi siam fascisti!*, and after it goes through a censorship process, the film is allowed to be released in theaters by March, 1962. The film's controversial theme and the process of censorship it went through causes a great sensation. Wins a special jury award at the International Leipzig Festival for Documentary and Animated Film.

1963 + Completes *La statua di Stalin* (co-directed with Lino Del Fra), but the directors did not sign the film due to the cuts imposed by the production.

1964 + Completes *O Trieste del mio cuore.*

1965 + Completes *Essere donne* (*Being Women*), the first depiction in the history of documentaries about the reality of Italian women. However, in accordance with the Italian government's "Obligatory Programming" standards, *Essere donne* was judged to be a film with excessive radicality, making it difficult to be distributed domestically. But Joris Ivens, John Grierson, and Jerzy Toeplitz mention the value of *Essere donne* at the International Leipzig Festival for Documentary and Animated Film in Germany, and it receives the special jury award despite the political pressure from Italy.

+ Completes *Tommaso and Felice Natale* (*Happy Christmas*).

+ 〈신성한 사랑〉은 지방 사람들이 종교기념일을 맞아
  야간 행렬을 하는 모습을 촬영함. 다큐멘터리임에도
  스릴러처럼 편집한 새로운 형식으로 주목을 받음.
  포폴리국제다큐멘터리영화제에서 금메달 수상.
+ 반파시스트 영화 〈우리는 무장 파시스트!〉(리노 델프라,
  리노 미치케 공동연출)가 1961년 제22회
  베니스국제영화제에서 공개됨. 바티칸 교회가 무솔리니의
  파시스트 정권과 공모했다는 이미지를 묘사한 영화로
  논란이 됨.

1962년 + 이탈리아 정부는 〈우리는 무장 파시스트!〉 상영을
  중지하고 검열을 거쳐 1962년 3월이 되어서야 극장 개봉을
  허용. 영화의 논쟁적 주제와 검열의 과정으로 인해 사회에
  큰 반향을 일으킴. 라이프치히다큐멘터리영화제에서
  심사위원특별상 수상.

1963년 + 〈스탈린의 조각상〉(리노 델프라 공동연출) 제작 완료.
  제작사가 편집에 관여하자 개봉을 거부함.

1964년 + 〈내 가슴속의 트리에스테〉 제작 완료.

1965년 + 다큐멘터리 사상 최초로 이탈리아 여성들의 현실을 그린
  〈여자-되기〉가 제작 완료됨. 그러나 이탈리아 정부의
  '의무적 편성' 법률기준에 의거해 〈여자-되기〉가 과도한
  급진성을 지닌 영화로 판단되어 자국 내 배급의 어려움을
  겪음. 독일에서 개최된 라이프치히다큐멘터리영화제에서
  요리스 이벤스, 존 그리어슨, 예르지 퇴플리츠가
  〈여자-되기〉의 가치를 언급하며 이탈리아의 정치적
  압박에도 불구하고 심사위원특별상을 수여함.
+ 〈토마소〉, 〈해피 크리스마스〉 제작 완료.

1966년 + 〈브린디시 '65〉 제작 완료.

1967년 + 〈선택〉 MEC에서 최우수유럽단편상 수상.

1969년 + 〈내일은 내가 이길 거야〉 제작 완료. 이탈리아
  RAI 방송국 방영.

1966 + Completes *Brindisi '65*.

1967 + *La Scelta* receives the top European short award at MEC.

1969 + Completes *Domani Vincerò* which gets broadcasted through the television service Rai Italia.

1972 + Completes *L'altra faccia del Pallone*, *La torta in cielo* (*Cake in the Sky*) (participated in the screenplay) and *La Briglia sul collo* (*The Bridle On The Neck*, released in 1974).

1973 + Completes *Michiamo Claudio Rossi*, *Dalla ciliegia al Lambrusco* and *La villeggiatura* (*Black Holiday*) (participated in the screenplay).

1977 + *Antonio Gramsci – I giorni del carcere* (*Antonio Gramsci: The Days of Prison*) (participated in the screenplay) is awarded the Golden Leopard at the Locarno International Film Festival.

1982 + *Comizi d'amore '80* (participated in the screenplay) gets broadcasted through the television service Rai Italia.

1980s + Due to the economic recession and political pressure, filmmaking becomes difficult. Starting from the 1970s, a policy with government censorship is implemented to reduce awards from film festivals and film institutions by more than 80% a year. Broadcasting on television, one of the most important ways of distributing documentaries, is reduced in number, so completed works have no places to show their films and are shelved. Also, due to the technological changes at the time, filmmaking comes to a halt.

1994 + Completes *Klon* (participated in the screenplay).

1997 + On July 19, husband Lino Del Fra passes away.

1999 + Completes *Regina Coeli* (participated in the screenplay).

2004 + Completes *Uomini e voci del congresso socialista di Livorno*.

1972년 + 〈공의 이면〉, 〈하늘의 케이크〉(각본 참여) 제작 완료.
〈목의 굴레〉 제작 완료 후 1974년 공개됨.

1973년 + 〈내 이름은 클라우디오 로지〉, 〈체리에서 람푸르스코
와인까지〉, 〈휴가〉(각본 참여) 제작 완료.

1977년 + 〈안토니오 그람시−감옥의 시대〉(각본 참여),
로카르노국제영화제에서 황금표범상 수상.

1982년 + 〈사랑의 집회〉(각본 참여), 이탈리아 RAI 방송국 방영.

1980년대 + 경제적 궁핍과 정치적 압박으로 영화제작에 어려움을
겪음. 1970년대부터 정부의 검열로 영화제와 영화기관의
시상 내역을 매년 80% 이상 축소하는 정책이 시행됨.
다큐멘터리 배급의 가장 중요한 방법 중 하나이던
텔레비전 방송사 프로그램 역시 그 규모가 축소되어 완성된
작품들조차 선보일 자리가 없어져 서랍 속에 묻힘. 또한
당시 기술의 변화로 작업의 휴지기가 찾아옴.

1994년 + 〈클론〉(각본 참여) 제작 완료.

1997년 + 7월 19일, 남편 리노 델프라 사망.

1999년 + 〈코엘리 여왕〉(각본 참여) 제작 완료.

2004년 + 〈리보르노 사회주의 의회의 사람들과 목소리〉 제작 완료.

2009년 + 이탈리아 대통령 훈장 솔리나스상 수상. 1950−60년대
이탈리아의 가장 아름다운 이미지를 다큐멘터리로 담아내
다음 세대에 전한 활동을 높이 평가.

2013년 + 〈체칠리아와 함께한 여행〉(마리안젤라 바르바넨테
공동연출) 제작 완료.

2017년 + 마드리드이탈리아영화제에서 공로상 수상
+ 9월 21일−10월 22일, 리파리에서 촬영했던 비공개 사진

2009 + Awarded the Solinas Award by the Italian president and highly praised for capturing and documenting the most beautiful images of Italy in the 1950s and 1960s for the next generation.

2013 + Completes *In viaggio con Cecilia* (co-directed with Mariangela Barbanente).

2017 + Receives the Career Award from the Festival de Cine Italiano de Madrid.
     + From September 21 to October 22, Mangini puts together 46 unreleased photographs she took in Lipari and holds an exhibition in Nuoro called *Islands, a trip to Panarea and Lipari*, as well as publish a photograph collection called *Isole*.
     + Completes *Un viaggio a Lipari* (*A trip to Lipari*) (co-directed with Paolo Pisanelli)

2018 + Completes *Le Vietnam sera libre* (co-directed with Paolo Pisanelli)

2019 + Completes *Facce* (co-directed with Paolo Pisanelli)
     + Gets invited as the guest of honor to the Vienna International Film Festival.

2020 + *Due scatole dimenticate – un viaggio in Vietnam* (*Two Forgotten Boxes – a trip to Vietnam*) (co-directed with Paolo Pisanelli) gets its world premiere at the International Film Festival Rotterdam. Following that, Seville European Film Festival holds a special programming to screen her earlier shorts, her feature, as well as an online photo exhibition to honor her achievements.
     + Becomes the winner of the achievement award, Premio Maria Adriana Prolo alla carriera 2020, by the Torino Film Festival and the l'Associazione Museo Nazionale del Cinema (AMNC).

2021 + She dies on January 21 in Rome.

46점을 모아 누오로 지역에서 '섬, 파나레아와 리파리로의 여행' 전시 개최 및 『섬 Isole』 사진집 출간.

+ 〈리파리로의 여행〉(파올로 피자넬리 공동연출) 제작 완료.

2018년 + 〈베트남은 자유로울 것인가〉(파올로 피자넬리 공동연출) 제작 완료.

2019년 + 〈얼굴〉(파올로 피자넬리 공동연출) 제작 완료.
+ 비엔나영화제에 특별 게스트로 초청됨.

2020년 + 〈두 개의 잊혀진 상자〉(파올로 피자넬리 공동연출)가 로테르담국제영화제에서 전 세계 최초로 공개됨. 이후 세비아유럽영화제에서 특별전을 마련해 초기 단편과 함께 장편 상영, 업적을 기리는 추모 온라인 사진전 공개.
+ 토리노영화제와 국립영화박물관(AMNC)이 수여한 '마리아 아드리아나 프롤로' 공로상의 주인공이 됨.

2021년 + 1월 21일, 로마에서 영면.

필모그래피

1958년 + 미지의 도시
1959년 + 프라톨리니의 피렌체
1959년 + 오래된 왕국 (리노 델프라 공동연출)
1960년 + 스텐달리 (스틸플레이)
1960년 + 마리아와 나날들
1960년 + 밀의 열정 (리노 델프라 공동연출)
1961년 + 습지의 노래
1961년 + 신성한 사랑
1962년 + 우리는 무장 파시스트!(리노 델프라, 리노 미치케 공동연출)
1963년 + 스탈린의 조각상 (리노 델프라 공동연출)
1964년 + 내 가슴속의 트리에스테
1965년 + 여자-되기
1965년 + 토마소

Filmography

1958 + Ignoti alla città (Unknown To The City)
1959 + Firenze di Pratolini
1959 + Vecchio regno (co-directed with Lino Del Fra)
1960 + Stendalì: Suonano ancora (Stendali (Still They Toll))
1960 + Maria e i giorni (Maria's Days)
1960 + La Passione del grano (The Wheat Passion) (co-directed with Lino Del Fra)
1961 + La Canta delle Marane (The Marshes' Chant)
1961 + Divino amore
1962 + All'armi siam fascisti! (co-directed with Lino Del Fra, Lino Micciichè)
1963 + La statua di Stalin (co-directed with Lino Del Fra)
1964 + O Trieste del mio cuore
1965 + Essere donne (Being Women)
1965 + Tommaso
1965 + Felice Natale (Happy Christmas)
1966 + Brindisi '65
1967 + La Scelta
1969 + Domani Vincerò
1972 + L'altra faccia del pallone
1972 + La torta in cielo (Cake in the Sky) (participated in the screenplay)
1972 + La Briglia sul collo (The Bridle On The Neck)
1972 + Michiamo Claudio Rossi
1973 + Dalla ciliegia al lambrusco
1973 + La villeggiatura (Black Holiday) (participated in the screenplay)
1977 + Antonio Gramsci – I giorni del carcere (Antonio Gramsci: The Days of Prison) (participated in the screenplay)
1982 + Comizi d'amore '80 (participated in the screenplay)
1994 + Klon (participated in the screenplay)
1999 + Regina Coeli (participated in the screenplay)
2004 + Uomini e voci del congresso socialista di Livorno
2013 + In viaggio con Cecilia (co-directed with Mariangela Barbanente)
2017 + Un viaggio a Lipari (A trip to Lipari) (co-directed with Paolo Pisanelli)
2018 + Le Vietnam sera libre (co-directed with Paolo Pisanelli)
2019 + Facce (co-directed with Paolo Pisanelli)
2020 + Due scatole dimenticate – un viaggio in Vietnam (Two Forgotten Boxes – a trip to Vietnam) (co-directed with Paolo Pisanelli)

1965년 + 해피 크리스마스

1966년 + 브린디시 '65

1967년 + 선택

1969년 + 내일은 내가 이길 거야

1972년 + 공의 이면

1972년 + 하늘의 케이크(각본 참여)

1972년 + 목의 굴레

1972년 + 내 이름은 클라우디오 로지

1973년 + 체리에서 람푸르스코 와인까지

1973년 + 휴가(각본 참여)

1977년 + 안토니오 그람시-감옥의 시대(각본 참여)

1982년 + 사랑의 집회(각본 참여)

1994년 + 클론(각본 참여)

1999년 + 코엘리 여왕(각본 참여)

2004년 + 리보르노 사회주의 의회의 사람들과 목소리

2013년 + 체칠리아와 함께한 여행(마리안젤라 바르바넨테 공동연출)

2017년 + 리파리로의 여행(파올로 피자넬리 공동연출)

2018년 + 베트남은 자유로울 것인가(파올로 피자넬리 공동연출)

2019년 + 얼굴(파올로 피자넬리 공동연출)

2020년 + 두 개의 잊혀진 상자(파올로 피자넬리 공동연출)

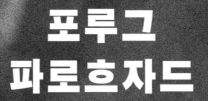

포루그
파로흐자드

Forough Farrokhzad
Poet, Film editor, Director

Forough Farrokhzad (1934–1967),
a controversial poet and pioneer in Iranian New
Wave movement, directed only one documentary
film *The House is Black* (1962) in her lifetime.
In this film, she shows the life in a leper colony
and talked about human dignity and the unfairness
of fate. By showing everyday life of lepers, she
implicitly criticized the closed Iranian society and
religious ideology of her time. Even nowadays,
many critics consider *The House is Black* as one
of the best Iranian documentary films. Abbas
Kiarostami used the title of her poem as the title
for his masterpiece, *The Wind Will Carry Us*,
as an homage to her.

포루그 파로흐자드
시인, 영화편집자, 영화감독

1934-1967. 이란의 논쟁적인 시인이자
뉴이란시네마의 선구자인 파로흐자드
감독은 한센병 요양원의 삶을 기록한 〈검은
집〉(1962)이라는 단 한 편의 다큐멘터리
영화를 남겼다. 감독은 이 작품에서 겉으로
드러나는 조건과 관계없는 인간의 존엄성과
운명의 불공평함에 대해 이야기하고자
했으며, 한센병 환자의 일상을 통해 당시
폐쇄적인 이란 사회와 종교 이데올로기를
비유적으로 비판했다. 지금까지도 〈검은
집〉은 이란 최고의 다큐멘터리 중의 한 편으로
평가되고 있으며, 압바스 키아로스타미
감독은 파로흐자드에 대한 존경으로 그녀의
시 '바람이 우리를 데려다 주리라'를 자신의
영화 제목으로 사용했다.

THE WIND WILL TAKE US

Forough
Farrokhzad

In my small night, ah
the wind has a date with the leaves of the trees
in my small night there is agony of destruction
listen
do you hear the darkness blowing?
I look upon this bliss as a stranger
I am addicted to my despair.

listen do you hear the darkness blowing?
something is passing in the night
the moon is restless and red
and over this rooftop
where crumbling is a constant fear
clouds, like a procession of mourners
seem to be waiting for the moment of rain.
a moment
and then nothing
night shudders beyond this window
and the earth winds to a halt
beyond this window
something unknown is watching you and me.

O green from head to foot
place your hands like a burning memory
in my loving hands
give your lips to the caresses
of my loving lips
like the warm perception of being
the wind will take us
the wind will take us.

바람이   나의 작은 밤 안에, 아
우리를   바람은 나뭇잎들과 밀회를 즐기네
데려다   나의 작은 밤 안에
주리라   적막한 두려움이 있어

포루그   들어 보라
파로흐자드   어둠이 바람에 날리는 소리가 들리는가
               나는 이방인처럼 이 행복을 바라보며
               나 자신의 절망에 중독되어 간다

               들어 보라
               어둠이 바람에 날리는 소리가 들리는가
               지금 이 순간, 이 밤 안에
               무엇인가 지나간다
               그것은 고요에 이르지 못하는 붉은 달
               끊임없이 추락의 공포에 떨며 지붕에 걸쳐 있다
               조문객 행렬처럼 몰려드는 구름은
               폭우의 순간을 기다리고 있다

               한순간
               그 다음엔 무
               밤은 창 너머에서 소멸하고
               대지는 또다시 숨을 멈추었다
               이 창 너머 낯선 누군가가
               그대와 나를 향하고 있다

               오, 머리부터 발끝까지 온통 푸르른 이여
               불타는 기억처럼 그대의 손을
               내 손에 얹어 달라
               그대를 사랑하는 이 손에
               생의 열기로 가득한 그대 입술을
               사랑에 번민하는 내 입술의 애무에 맡겨 달라
               바람이 우리를 데려다 주리라
               바람이 우리를 데려다 주리라

『바람이 우리를
데려다 주리라』
(2012),
신양섭 옮김,
문학의숲

Forough
Farrokhzad

Women in Window

By Nicole Brenez (Professor of Film Studies
at the University of Sorborne Nouvelle)

One window for the moment
Of realization, revelation, contemplation
—*Window*[1]

Like some other masterpieces, such as *Hôtel des
Invalides* (1951) by Georges Franju, which also
deals with corporal mutilation, or *Le rapport Darty*
(1989) by Jean-Luc Godard and Anne-Marie
Miéville, *The House is Black* (1962) by Forough
Farrokhzad subverts and sublimates its conditions
of production. Among other films, these three
films are the results of official requests (public or
private) and, attacking their own sponsors without
the slightest hesitation, they each create a
pamphlet film that varies from all social, political
and aesthetic standards.

Forough Farrokhzad makes her film in the
framework of a triple cultural and economic
constraint: since its inception, the Golestan Film
Studio has been financed by an oil company;
The House is Black deals with a leper colony,
Behkadeh Rādschi, at the request of the Society
For Assisting Lepers, then chaired by Farah
Pahlavi, third wife of the Shah[2]; and the poetess
goes there as a single woman, losing custody of
her son, in an oppressive patriarchal society
where her divorce state makes her a reprobate.

Forough Farrokhzad has never made a film
nor led a team before. But she transforms all of
these constraints, of this collective and
intimate suffering, into a blaze of intelligence,
despair and love in the fire of which a unique
visual poem has been forged.

1
Window (Panjareh,
1974): translation from
the Persian by Meetra
A. Sofia (2009.7–8),
World Literature Today
Vol. 83, N° 4, p. 15.

2
Mohammad Hossein
Azizi, Moslem
Bahadori (2011.11),
"A history of leprosy
in Iran during the 19th
and 20th centuries",
*Archives of Iran
Medicine*,14(6),
p. 425–430: https://
pubmed.ncbi.nlm.nih.
gov/22039850/

창가의 여자
포루그 파로흐자드의 〈검은 집〉

글: 니콜 브르네
(누벨소르본느대학 영화학과 교수)

인식, 폭로, 응시
그 순간을 위한 창문 하나
— "창문"[1]

포루그 파로흐자드의 〈검은 집〉(1962)은 신체 훼손이라는 주제를 다루는 조르주 프랑주의 〈앵발리드 호텔〉(1951)이나 장 뤼크 고다르와 안느 마리 미에빌의 〈다티 리포트〉(1989)와 같은 걸작들처럼 주어진 영화제작 조건을 전복시켜 이상적인 것으로 바꾸어 버린다. 이 세 편의 영화는 사실 공공기관이나 사기업의 공식적인 의뢰를 받아 제작된 것이지만, 시작부터 주저함 없이 스폰서 측을 공격하면서 기존의 모든 정치, 사회, 미학의 규범에서 벗어난 팸플릿 형식의 영화를 만들었다.

1. Realization

Ten years earlier, on October 28, 1953 in New York, Amos Vogel, programmer of Cinema 16, organized a roundtable devoted to "Poetry and Film."[3] Among the most interesting proposals, filmmaker, writer and activist Maya Deren characterized the nature of film poetry: it consists in exploring a situation, "to probe the ramifications of the moment, and to be concerned with its depth and its qualities."[4] And, explains Maya Deren, the main means of such in-depth work is film editing: to combine two distinct phenomena that only a consciousness can reunite. The example given by the author of *Meshes of the Afternoon* (1943) resonates, in a disturbing way, with the windows that constellate Forough's poems: "you stand by the window and have a sense of afternoon, which is neither the children in the street nor the women talking behind you but a curious combination of both, and that is your resultant image."[5]

2. Revelation

The House is Black is structured with such a

3
The roundtable is rehosted in Scott MacDonald. – Scott MacDonald (2010), *Cinema 16: Documents Toward History Of Film Society*, Temple University Press, p. 200

4
It is a "vertical" investigation of a situation, in that it probes the ramifications of the moment, and is concerned with its qualities and its depth. Scott MacDonald (2010), *Cinema 16: Documents Toward History Of Film Society*, Temple University Press, p.204

5
Scott MacDonald (2010), *Cinema 16: Documents Toward History Of Film Society*, Temple University Press, p. 209.

← Farrokhzad in the Play of *Six Characters in search of a write* 루이지 피란델로의 희곡 '작가를 찾는 6인의 등장 인물' 연극에 출연한 파로흐자드 ©iranwire.com

파로흐자드 감독은 문화적이고 경제적인 관점에서 세 가지 제약 아래 〈검은 집〉을 제작해야 했다. 우선, 이 영화의 제작사인 골레스탄필름스튜디오는 설립 초부터 석유 회사로부터 재정적인 지원을 받아 왔다. 게다가 〈검은 집〉은 한센병환자후원협회 의뢰를 받아 한센병 요양원의 이야기를 다루는 작품인데, 당시 후원협회의 회장이 이란국왕 샤의 세 번째 부인인 파라 파흐라비였다.[2] 마지막으로, 시인이기도 한 이 여성감독은 그녀의 이혼을 비난하는 억압적인 가부장적 사회에서 아들의 양육권까지 박탈당한 채 독신여성으로 촬영에 임했다.

파로흐자드는 〈검은 집〉 이전에 영화를 만든 적도 촬영 팀을 이끌어 본 적도 없었지만, 이 모든 제약들을, 그리고 집단적이고 사적인 모든 고통을 지성과 절망과 사랑의 불꽃으로 바꾸어 버렸으며, 바로 그 불 속에서 독특한 '비주얼 포엠'을 창작해 낸다.

1. 인식

〈검은 집〉이 제작되기 10년 전인 1953년 10월 28일, 뉴욕의 시네클럽 '시네마 16'의 프로그래머인 아모스 보겔은 '시와 영화'에 대한 좌담회를 개최했다.[3] 매우 흥미로운 발제가 많이 이루어졌는데, 이때 영화감독이자 작가인 마야 데렌은 '영화 시(film poetry)'의 본성을 설명했다. 그녀에 따르면, 영화 시는 하나의 상황을 탐구함으로써 "그 순간의 파급 효과를 추적하고, 순간의 깊이와 특질에 대해 연구하는 것이다."[4] 그녀의 설명

fusion of phenomena, but in three terms rather than two.

First of all, the film fulfills its contract with great seriousness: it shows the ravages of leprosy and the daily life in the colony, it shows, through the male voice of Ebrahim Golestan, the medical information on the pathology, the clinical actions to remedy leprosy and the social injustice that determines the disease: "leprosy is a disease of the poor."

But, secondly, the editing between the images and the female voice, that of Forough, brings the film into another dimension: the injustice of the fate striking the sick is a lever to denounce the lies of religious ideology. Forough's sense of revolt here does not retreat before any blasphemy, any visual irony. A patient reads the Koran: "Lord, I praise you for giving me hands to work"; but the shot, in a low angle, insists on the fact that the young man only has stumps of his hands in order to hold the sacred book. Great despair runs through the film, the narrator speaks from hell, and each word points to an inevitable and precipitous death. Behind the objective description, it is the second dimension of this documentary, the most controversial: collective confinement in an intolerable human condition. It allows Iranian audiences at the time to receive *The House is Black* as a metaphor for Iran crushed under monarchical precepts, religious dogmas, and even those who, under the Shah regime, were allied with the capitalist powers – the very ones who financed the Golestan Film Studio. Ebrahim Golestan, sympathetic to Communist, declared publicly in 2016 that the film wanted to show how "Iranian society was then locked up and sick".[6]

6
"Lezione di Cinema. Golestan Film Studio, tra poesia e politica" (2016.6.28), *Il Cinema Ritrovato 2016*, Meeting with Ebrahim Golestan led by Ehsan Khoshbakht and Mehrnaz Saeed-Vafa(25min): https://www.youtube.com/watch?v=rKSFKce83qg&list=PLwg8VB64LkBKuVV1qFIlkpggfKllLjcs&index=194&ab_channel=CinetecaBologna

에 의하면, 이러한 심층 탐구의 주요 수단이 바로 영화 편집이며, 편집은 의식만이 결합할 수 있는 두 개의 개별 현상을 연결하는 작업이다. 〈오후의 올가미〉(1943)의 감독인 마야 데렌이 제시하는 예는 파로흐자드의 시를 뒤덮고 있는 '창문'들을 바로 떠올리게 한다. "당신은 창가에 서서 오후의 감각을 느끼고 있다. 그 감각은 거리의 아이들이나 당신 뒤에서 수군대는 여성들로부터 오는 것이 아니라, 이 두 가지의 기묘한 결합, 그 결과로 생긴 이미지다."[5]

2. 폭로

〈검은 집〉은 여러 현상들의 결합으로 구성되어 있는데, 이 결합은 둘을 넘어 무려 세 가지 차원에서 이루어진다.

먼저, 이 영화는 제작상의 계약을 매우 성실하게 이행한다. 한센병의 피폐함과 수용소의 일상을 보여 주고, 에브라힘 골레스탄이라는 남성의 목소리를 통해 이 병의 병리학적 정보와 치료를 위한 임상 행위에 대해 들려주는 한편, "한센병은 가난한 사람들의 질병"이라고 규정하면서 사회의 불평등을 시사한다.

그러나 두 번째 차원에서, 이미지들과 파로흐자드의 여성 목소리를 결합한 편집은 이 영화를 또 다른 국면으로 이끌게 되는데, 환자들에게 닥친 부당한 운명은 종교 이데올로기의 거짓말을 고발하기 위한 수단이 된다. 파로흐자드의 저항 의식은 신성모독이나 시각적인 아이러니도 서슴지 않고 시도한다. 한 환자가 코란을 읽는다. "신이시여, 제게 일할 수 있는 손을 주셔서

3. Contemplation

What combines these two dimensions, factual and pamphleteering, is not only a political analysis and a humanist empathy for the victims, but a sense of belonging of the entire film to the leper community. This is the third dimension of the film: the transformation of a documented writing into a love poem. Sister of the sick woman putting make-up

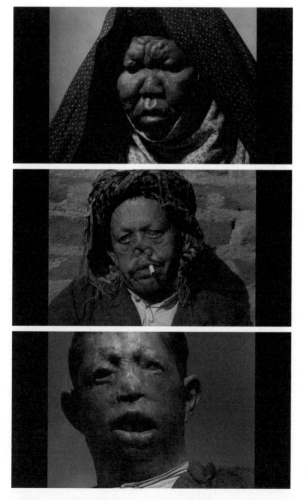

← *The House is Blac*
〈검은 집〉

감사합니다." 그러나, 하이 앵글로 촬영된 쇼트는 코란을 든 청년의 손가락이 모두 잘려 나가서 뭉툭한 손만 남았다는 사실을 강조한다. 영화 전반에 화자의 목소리는 지옥에서 들려오는 듯하다. 화자가 읊조리는 매 단어들은 피할 수 없이 서둘러 다가오는 죽음을 환기시킨다. 객관적인 묘사에 이어지는 이 다큐멘터리에서 가장 논쟁적인 두 번째 국면은 인간으로서 견디기 어려운 조건 아래 행해지는 집단 감금에 대해 이야기한다. 이를 통해 당시의 이란 관객들은 〈검은 집〉을 군주제의 계율과 종교적 교리로 억압당하던 이란에 대한 은유로 받아들일 수 있었다. 게다가 샤 왕정하에서 정치와 종교는 자본주의 세력과 결탁을 했는데, 바로 이들이 골레스탄필름스튜디오를 재정적으로 지원했던 세력이었다. 공산주의 동조자인 에브라힘 골레스탄은 이 영화를 통해 얼마나 "이란 사회가 폐쇄적이고 병적인지"를 보여주고 싶었다고 2016년도에 공개적으로 밝히기도 했다.[6]

3. 응시

사실 전달과 비판적 팸플릿의 두 국면을 결합하는 것은 정치적 분석이나 피해자에 대한 인본주의적 공감을 불러올 뿐 아니라, 〈검은 집〉이라는 작품 전체가 한센병 환자 공동체의 일부라는 소속감을 보여 준다. 이것이 이 영화의 세 번째 국면으로, 기록으로서 글쓰기가 사랑의 시로 전환되는 지점이다. 여성 환자가 짓무른 눈가를 화장하는 장면에서, 파로흐자드 감독은 자신의 고독과 슬픔을 분명히 드러낸다. "기억해, 먼 사막에서 들려오

on her ravaged eyes, Forough explains her own loneliness and grief: "Remember you made yourself beautiful for nothing / for a song from the faraway desert"; the concrete loneliness of the lover every evening abandoned by the beloved, which she made the subject of her many poems, and that Golestan will describe the following year in his feature film *Khesht va Ayeneh* (*Brick and Mirror*, 1964). To this fusion between image and sound responds an economy of images between them which organizes a mentalization: the repetitions of shots, which come back in clusters and loops, transform the shots into musical motifs, rhymes and refrains. The entire film appears as an extension of the mental image evoked by the little boy, who is asked by the schoolteacher to write a sentence with the word "house" on the board. The boy contemplates, an image appears, a black image ostensibly staged like a nightmare: the entire population of the colony moves towards the camera, and this image, by its terrible collective force, allows the boy to finally write "The house is black" on the blackboard. Synthesis, allegory, summary, fantasy, living picture, the image reflected by the boy is an active image, an image that leads to writing. At the end of the film, the whole credits are written in the same way with white chalk on the blackboard: thus, through these purely cinematographic processes of play between the regimes of images, the film indicates itself as being born of the imagination of this boy inspired by the energy of his community. The film is in a way produced by leprosy as much as against it.

It is in this way that *The House is Black* is most reminiscent of another film masterpiece, just as unique, by another great writer who also lived as an outcast: *Un Chant d'Amour* (*A Song of Love*, 1950) by Jean Genet, a tale of the circulation of desires between prisoners and

는 노래로 인해/ 네가 헛되이 아름답게 꾸몄던 것을". 매일 저녁 연인에게 버림받던 여성의 깊은 고독은 파로흐자드 감독이 여러 편의 시를 통해 표현했던 주제이며, 골레스탄도 그 이듬해에 만들었던 장편영화 〈벽돌과 거울〉(1964)에서 다루었던 것이다. 이와 같은 이미지와 사운드의 결합에 대해 일종의 정신화(mentalization)를 조직하는 이미지의 경제학이 작용한다. 즉 묶음이나 모음으로 된 쇼트들의 반복이 그 쇼트들을 음악적 모티프나 운율과 후렴구로 변환시킨다. 이 영화 전체는 선생님으로부터 "집"이라는 단어를 포함한 문장을 칠판에 쓰라고 지시받은 한 소년이 불러일으킨 정신적 이미지에서 뻗어 나온 것처럼 보인다. 소년이 생각에 잠기자, 이미지가 나타난다. 수용소의 사람들이 카메라를 향해 몰려오는 악몽처럼 노골적인 검은 화면이 연출되고, 이 이미지는 무시무시한 집단의 힘에 의해 결국 소년이 "그 집은 검다"라고 칠판 위에 쓰게 만든다. 합성, 풍자, 요약, 판타지, 리빙 픽처와 같은, 소년이 떠올린 이미지는 살아 있는 그림으로 글을 쓰도록 인도한다. 마찬가지로, 이 영화의 끝에 나오는 크레디트도 칠판 위에 하얀 분필로 기록된다. 그래서 이미지의 체제들 간의 작용이라는 순수한 영화적인 방식을 통해, 〈검은 집〉은 공동체로부터 영감을 받은 이 소년의 상상력 속에서 태어난 것처럼 보인다. 어떤 의미에서 보면 이 영화는 한센병에 대항하기 위해 제작되었을 뿐 아니라 한센병에 의해 제작됐다고 할 수 있을 것이다.

　바로 이 지점에서 〈검은 집〉은 역시 추방자로 살아야 했던 또 한 명의 위대한 작가의 영화 한 편을 떠올리게 한다. 그것은 감옥을 배경으로 죄수와 교도관 간의 욕망의 순환을 이야기했

guards in a prison. *Un Chant d'Amour* intertwined three figurative regimes: realistic approximation (the prison, treated in sketches and pieces); fantasy as a catalyst of scenarios (the idyllic reverie of a prisoner); fantasy as a fetishization of a phenomenon (the monumental erotic visions of a prison guard). Like *Un Chant d'Amour*, *The House is Black* is the site of a thorough investigation into the differential substances and powers of the image. Cinema has a vital need for writers to elucidate what it is and what it can be.

4. Autonomization

But in contrast to Jean Genet's exclusively psychical tale, here it is not at all concerning a subjective appropriation of the condition of the sick by a compassionate poetess. On the contrary, the film elaborates many ways to not only listen to the lepers themselves, but to autonomize them as subjects.

After a preamble spoken on a black background, the first visual initiative brings us closer, by virtue of a tracking shot, to a veiled

↓ *The House is Black*
〈검은 집〉

던 장 주네의 〈사랑의 찬가〉(1950)다. 이 영화에서는 거의 사실적인 재현(스케치와 조각조각으로 묘사되는 감옥)과 시나리오의 촉매제로서의 환상(죄수의 목가적인 몽상), 그리고 현상에 대한 페티쉬로서의 환상(교도관의 거대한 성애적 상상)과 같은 세 가지 이미지의 형상적 체제들이 얽혀져 있다. 〈사랑의 찬가〉처럼 〈검은 집〉도 이미지의 변별적인 실체와 힘을 근본적으로 탐구하는 영화이다. 영화는 영화가 무엇인지, 무엇이 될 수 있는지를 밝히기 위해, 작가들을 반드시 필요로 한다.

4. 자율성

장 주네의 심리적인 이야기와는 달리, 〈검은 집〉은 동정심을 품은 시인이 환자의 상황을 주관적으로 전유하는 그런 작품이 아니다. 오히려 환자들의 이야기를 직접 듣고, 그들에게 주체로서 자율성을 부여하기 위해 여러 가지 방법을 동원한다.

검은 화면 위 도입의 말에 이어 나오는 이 영화의 첫 시각적 이미지는 트래킹 쇼트를 통해 베일을 쓴, 짓무른 눈을 지닌 여성에게 우리가 다가가게 해 준다. 그 여성은 꽃으로 장식된 거울 속의 자신을 들여다보고 있다. 관객은 그녀도 보고 있는 거울 속에 비친 그녀의 모습을 우선적으로 보게 된다. 관객이 보게 될 것을 그녀가 조율하는 것이다. 이 계획된 쇼트는 에브라힘 골레스탄이 조연출로 참여했던 베르트 한스트라 감독의 〈거울 속 네덜란드〉(1950)를 참조한 것으로 보인다.[7] 네덜란드 운하의 물속에서 전체를 촬영한 이 영화는 오늘날에는 다소

woman with damaged eyes who is looking at herself in a mirror decorated with flowers: from her, we first see the reflection that she also sees. She controls what she gives us to see. This programmatic scene has probably referred to the know-how of Bert Haanstra's masterpiece, of which Ebrahim Golestan had been the assistant[7], *Spiegel van Holland* (*Mirror of Holland*, 1950): entirely filmed in the water of the Dutch canals, the film, a little forgotten today but very famous at the time, gave a lesson on the plastic and symbolic importance of reflections. Contrary to Jean Cocteau's famous statement in *Le sang d'un poète* (*The Blood of a Poet*, 1930), "Mirrors should reflect a little before sending back images", *Mirror of Holland* showed just how rich the reflections were with plastic propositions on a reality that they enriched with all the mobility of their nuances. Whether intentionally or not, the visual opening of *The House is Black* is included in the same lineage of trust in the reflection: by virtue of this shot, the film looks like a story of images; it finds a way to affirm that the filmed beings are the sources of their own representations and that they remain the owners of these representations; and therefore, simultaneously, that the film comes back to them, that it is made first by and for them.

In the register of other means which allow the film to autonomize the filmed beings, to affirm them as subjects of their representations: the fact of filming their reflections, that is to say the overwhelming graffiti drawn on the walls: "Heaven closed and I fell down here"; "I am going to leave. My heart is full of tears. O my brothers, I am sad tonight"… The great writings seem to be the direct source of inspiration for the poems read by Forough on the soundtrack – if they were not, they are in any case the scriptural and fraternal echo of them. Another means of autonomization

7
Bert Haanstra was also the president of the jury which, during the 1964 edition of the International Short Film Festival Oberhausen, awarded the Documentary Grand Prix to *The House is Black*. The other members of the jury were Jerzy Bossak, Walter Buhrow, Fedor Chitruk, Paul Haesaerts, Hristo Kovatschev, Walter Lasselly, Michael Lentz, Pierre Rémont, Karl Schedereit, Haro Senft, Amos Vogel, Dusan Vukotic and Karel Zeman. Thanks to Lars Henrik Gass and Cartsen Spicher for this information.

잊힌 작품이지만, 당시에는 반사체가 지닌 조형성과 상징성의 중요함을 알려 준 것으로 유명했다. "거울은 이미지를 되돌려 보내기 전에 좀 더 숙고하는 게 좋을 것이다"라는 〈시인의 피〉(1930)에서 들려주었던 장 콕토의 유명한 말과는 반대로, 〈거울 속 네덜란드〉는 뉘앙스의 모든 가능성을 열어 줌으로써 반사체들이 현실에 대해 얼마나 풍부한, 유연한 제안을 할 수 있는지 보여 주었다. 의도적이든 아니든, 〈검은 집〉의 오프닝 이미지는 반사체를 신뢰하는 바로 그 계보에 속하게 된다. 이 장면 덕분에 이 작품은 이미지들의 이야기처럼 보인다. 촬영된 존재들이 그 재현물의 원천이자 소유자임을 단언하기 위한 방법을 찾는다. 동시에 이 영화는 다시 돌아와서 무엇보다 그들에 의해서, 그리고 그들을 위해서 만들어졌다는 것을 확인하고자 한다.

〈검은 집〉이 촬영된 존재들에게 자율성을 부여하고, 그들이 재현물의 주체인 것을 확인해 주기 위한 또 다른 방법들 중의 하나는 그들의 사유를 촬영하는 것이었다. 이를 위해 이 영화는 벽 위에 남겨진 아주 경이로운 낙서들을 필름에 담는다. "천국은 닫혀 버렸고, 나는 이 세상에 떨어졌다." "나는 떠날 거야. 내 심장은 눈물로 가득 찼다. 오 형제들이여, 오늘 밤 나는 슬프다." 참으로 아름다운 이 글들은 사운드트랙 위로 낭송되는 파로흐자드의 시에 직접적인 영감을 준 것으로 여겨지는데, 만약 그렇지 않다 하더라도, 이 글들은 그녀의 시에 대해 경전적이고 형제애적인 공명을 불러일으킨다. 그들에게 자율성을 부여하기 위한 또 다른 방법으로 신체를 다루는 방식이 있다. 대부분 파편화된 형식으로 포착된 신체들은 예상치 못한 각도

is that of the treatment of bodies: most often
captured in the form of fragments, these are
taken at unexpected angles, in elaborate
low-angle shots, whose main effect is not only
to monumentalize them but also to contribute
to making them overflow from the frame.
We find here the manner of the "plan-éperons
(spurs-shots)" precious to S.M. Eisenstein,
that is to say of the shots which seek to tear
the visible surface and get out of their two
dimensionality, that seek to abolish the distance
between the screen and the spectator's
gaze. In *The House is Black*, filmed in total
low-angle shooting, the palms of hand strangely
pressed against a glass pane seem to bend
over our brain to penetrate it, and all the feet,
hands and stumps that reach out to the
camera seem to menace the surface to open
a path to our heart. We can describe these
shots as "haptics", according to their learned
name, but they are above all "organic", in the
sense that the framing and the panting
repetitions of the shots (especially the one of
the flatten palms which comes back several
times) come to be imprinted on our retina with
force and thus, to be grafted onto our neurons.

5. Confrontation

"You see these men: the dreadful disease has
metamorphosed them into beasts; instead of
nails, it put pieces of wood on their hands and
feet. Strange footprints left on our roads!
Who would recognize a human step there?
Those people who yesterday stood upright and
looked up at the sky, here they are today bent to
the ground, walking on all fours, and almost
changed into beasts: listen to the raucous breath
that comes out of their chests; that is how they

인 정교한 로우 앵글로 촬영되며, 이러한 방식은 신체들을 엄청난 것으로 표현할 뿐 아니라 그것들이 프레임 앞으로 넘쳐 나올 것 같은 효과를 만든다. 여기에서 세르게이 에이젠슈쩨인이 좋아하던 "박차-쇼트"의 방식이 발견되는데, 이 쇼트는 가시적인 표면을 찢으면서 평면적인 2차원성에서 벗어나고, 또한 스크린과 관객의 시선 사이의 거리를 없애고자 한다. 예를 들어, 완전히 로우 앵글로 촬영된 〈검은 집〉에서, 기이하게 유리창에 기대는 손바닥은 마치 유리창을 통과하여 우리 뇌에 침투하려는 것 같다. 또한, 카메라를 향해 뻗어 오는 발과 손, 손가락이 잘려 나간 뭉툭한 손은 우리의 심장에 길을 내기 위해 표면을 위협하는 것만 같다. 이러한 쇼트들을 과학 용어를 사용하여 "햅틱"으로 분류할 수도 있겠지만, 프레이밍과 숨 가쁘게 전개되는 쇼트(특히 여러 차례 등장하는 평평한 손바닥 쇼트)의 반복이 우리의 망막에 힘을 가해 흔적을 남기고 신경에 접목되는 점에서 특별히 "유기적"이라 할 수 있다.

5. 대면

"이 사람들을 보십시오. 무서운 질병이 그들을 짐승으로 변하게 했습니다. 손톱과 발톱 대신, 그 병은 그들의 손과 발에 나뭇조각을 남겨 놓았습니다. 이 길 위에 남겨진 이상한 자국을 보십시오! 누가 이것을 사람의 발자국이라 생각하겠습니까? 어제는 똑바로 서서 하늘을 바라보던 이 사람들이 오늘은 땅을 향해 구부린 채 네 발로 걸으면서 거의 짐승처럼 변했습니다. 그

breathe. [...] To these men, everything happens as if they changed their nature and lost the features of their species to turn into monsters. Their hands serve as their feet. Their knees ecome heels, and their ankles and toe, and if they have not been completely ravaged, they drag them miserably like the boats that pull ships. [...] Let us respect the sickness that comes with holiness and pay tribute to those whose suffering has brought them to victory."[8] From *Gregorio di Nissa* to *Francesco, giullare di Dio* (*The Flowers of St. Francis*, 1950) by Roberto Rossellini, from the *New Testament* to *Il Vangelo secondo Matteo* (*The Gospel according to St. Matthew*, 1964) by Pier Paolo Pasolini, the figure of the Leper offers the opportunity of a face to face with the very condition of the human being: the most disfigured, the most excluded, the most humble and destitute being, denudes the very principle of humanity, its mortality. To accomplish face to face is to immediately get to its opposite, to the glorious body of universal goodness, of universal brotherhood. Nothing of the kind in *The House is Black*: the ordeal of encountering the disfiguration does not lead to a transfiguration; because in the encounter, the two parts are equivalent, one is neither healthy nor the other sick, one is neither learned nor the other ignorant, they are all immersed in the work of everyday survival. Big or small, men, women, children, residents of the colony are always active as do all other humans: spinning wool, playing, eating, dancing, learning at school ... They register in life, in this ephemeral terrible which is exactly the same as that of the narrator.

"Alas, for the day is fading,
the evening shadows are stretching.
Our being, like a cage full of birds,
is filled with moans of captivity.

8
Gregorio di Nissa, *De pauperibus amandis* II, 342: quoted by Dionysios Stathakopoulos (2011.12), *Preaching embodied Emotions. Bishops, Beggars and their Audience in Late Antiquity*, Médiévales – Presses universitaires de Vincennes, p. 28

들의 가슴에서 나오는 거친 숨소리를 들어 보십시오. 이렇게 그들은 숨을 쉽니다. (…) 이 사람들에겐, 마치 그들이 괴물로 변하기 위해 자신의 본성을 바꾸고 인간의 특성을 잃어가는 것처럼 모든 일이 일어납니다. 그들의 손은 발의 역할을 합니다. 그들의 무릎은 발꿈치가 되고 발목과 발이 됩니다. 그것들이 아직 완전히 침식되지 않았다면, 마치 큰 선박을 이끄는 작은 배처럼 비참하게 그들을 땅 위로 끌고 다닙니다. (…) 거룩함을 지닌 이 질병을 존중합시다. 그리고 고통을 승리로 승화시키는 이들에게 경의를 표합시다."[8] 인용된 '니사의 그레고리우스'에서부터 로베르토 로셀리니의 〈프란체스코, 신의 어릿광대〉(1950)까지, 그리고 신약성서에서 피에르 파올로 파졸리니의 〈마태복음〉(1964)에 이르기까지, 한센병 환자의 형상은 인간의 조건을 대면할 기회를 제공한다. 가장 훼손되어 소외되고, 보잘것없이 비천한 존재는 인류의 근원인 죽음이라는 운명을 노출시킨다. 이와 같은 직접적인 대면은 그 즉시 반대 지점에 있는 영광스런 신체를 바라보게 한다. 그것은 보편적 선, 즉 보편적인 동지애에 다가가는 것이다. 그러나 〈검은 집〉에는 그런 대면이 없다. 즉 훼손된 형상과 마주하는 시련이 형상의 변모로 이어지지는 않는다. 왜냐하면 이 만남에서는 두 부분이 모두 동등하기 때문이다. 한쪽이 건강하거나 다른 쪽이 아픈 것도 아니고, 한쪽이 유식하거나 다른 쪽이 무지한 것도 아니다. 그들은 모두 살아남기 위해 일상의 노동에 몰두하고 있다. 크든 작든, 남자, 여자, 아이 할 것 없이 수용소의 모든 거주자들은 다른 인간들과 똑같이 살아간다. 양털을 잣고, 놀고, 먹고, 춤추고, 학교에서 공부한다… 그들은 이 영화의 화자와 똑같이 끔찍하고 덧없는

And none among us knows how long he
will last.
The harvest season passed,
The summer season came to an end,
and we did not find deliverance.
Like doves we cry for justice …
and there is none.
We wait for light
and darkness reigns."

One of the most subtle montages in this regard
is also the simplest: it juxtaposes the poetic

↓ *The House is Blac*
〈검은 집〉

인생을 살아간다.

> "아아, 하루가 저물어 가고,
> 저녁 그림자는 길게 뻗는다.
> 우리 존재는, 새들로 가득 찬 새장처럼,
> 포로의 신음으로 가득 차 있다.
> 그리고 우리 중 누구도 그가 얼마나 버틸 수 있는지 모른다.
> 수확기가 지나고,
> 여름이 끝나도,
> 우리는 구원을 찾지 못했다.
> 비둘기처럼 우리는 정의를 외치지만…
> 아무도 없다.
> 우리는 빛을 기다리지만
> 어둠이 지배한다."

이러한 관점에서, 가장 섬세한 편집은 가장 단순한 편집이다. 그 편집은 화자의 시적 언어와 한 주의 요일을 나열하는 환자의 목소리를 병치시킨다. "토요일, 일요일, 월요일, 화요일"… 파로흐자드 시의 여러 특징 중 하나는 단순하고 구체적인 언어를 사용하여 대중성을 지니는 것이다. 그 시는 가장 보편적이고 말 그대로 가장 일상적인 언어들을 시적 아름다움으로 물들인다. 그런데, 그 반대 역시 진실이다. "화요일, 수요일…" 끊임없이 반복되는 일상어를 아무도 없는 창문 앞에서 목적 없이 서성이는 환자의 이미지와 연결하면, 그 일상어는 갑자기 고통스러운 괴물로 변하고, 세상의 불길한 덧없음에 대해 이야기하는 파로

words of the narrator with the ginning of the days
of the week provided by a leper: "Saturday,
Sunday, Monday, Tuesday" ... It is often said that
one of the characteristics of Forough's poetry is
to use simple and concrete words, to remain
popular; here, it contaminates with its beauty the
most common and the most literally everyday
words ; but the converse is also true: everyday
words, "Tuesday, Wednesday ...", to be set in
litany, associated with the image of a leper who
aimlessly comes and goes before empty windows,
suddenly become monsters of anguish and
underpin Forough's statements about sinister
fugitivity of the world:

"The universe is pregnant with inertia,
and has given birth to time."

The House is Black belongs to the great realism
of immanence, of corruptible flesh without the
slightest promise of redemption, of salvation.
In a museum gallery, Forough Farrokhzad's film
can be placed following the paintings by
Francisco de Goya, Théodore Géricault, and
Gustave Courbet. Just after *The House is Black*,

↓ *The House is Blac*
〈검은 집〉

흐자드 감독의 진술을 뒷받침해 준다.

> "우주는 무력감을 수태하여
> 시간을 낳았다."

〈검은 집〉은 어떠한 속죄와 구원의 약속도 없이 썩어 가는 육체의 내재성에 대한 사실주의 작품이다. 박물관 전시실에 파로흐자드의 영화를 걸게 된다면 프란시스코 고야나 테오도르 제리코, 구스타브 쿠르베의 작품 옆에 배치할 수 있을 것이며, 〈검은 집〉 옆에는 장 다니엘 폴레의 에세이 다큐멘터리 〈질서〉 (1973)를 걸 수 있을 것이다. 이 작품 역시 크레타 해안가의 스피나롱가섬에서 벌어졌던 한센병 환자의 감금 문제를 다루고 있다. 〈질서〉는 극장의 관람석에서 에파미논다스 레문다키스라는 한센병 환자들의 대표 역할을 하는 사람과 만남을 갖는다. 뛰어난 지식인인 레문다키스는 스피나롱가섬에서의 수용소 경험을 전해 줄 뿐 아니라, 문학, 사진, 영화에 나타난 한센병 환자에 대한 재현의 문제도 유려하게 비판한다. "애통합니다! 지금까지 그들은 우리 모두를 배신했으며, 어느 누구도 우리가 원했던 그리고 그들이 세상에 보여 주겠다고 약속한 것을 전해주지 않았습니다. 결국, 속임수와 사진과 그 아래의 설명문으로 우리와의 약속을 저버리고 우리를 기만했습니다. 이것으로 인해 우리는 상처를 입었는데, 어떤 이는 동정심을 어떤 이들은 거부감을 보여 주었기 때문입니다. 그러나, 우리는 사람들이 우리를 미워하거나 동정하기를 원치 않습니다. 단지 사랑이 필요할 뿐입니다."[9] 레문다키스 덕분에, 우리는 〈검은 집〉의 고유한 특징

we can display *L'Ordre* (*The Order*, 1973) by
Jean-Daniel Pollet, an essay documentary film on
the incarceration of lepers on the island of
Spinalonga off the coast of Crete. *L'Ordre* is above
all a meeting with Epaminondas Remoundakis,
in a way the deputy of the lepers in the cinema
amphitheater. One of brilliant intellectuals,
Remoundakis eloquently articulates the analysis of
the concentration camp experience in Spinalonga,
but also the criticism of literary, photographic
and cinematographic representations devoted to
lepers. "Alas, until today, they have betrayed us all,
none of them has given what we wanted, and
what he had promised to show to the world.
Finally, a deception, a photo, and the legend below
that changed the promises and betrayed us. And
this hurt us because some wanted to show
compassion, and others wanted to show repulsion,
but we didn't want people to hate us or pity us,
we just needed love."[9] Thanks to Remoundakis,
we understand even better the uniqueness of
The House is Black: it is by facing the lack of love
that Forough enters the colony and is able to
symbolically sign her film with the writing of the
lepers. Such are the last words of the film, against
a black background: "O overrunning river driven
by the force of love, flow to us, flow to us."

6. Experimentation

We know of course that, from Behkadeh Rādschi,
Forough will bring back not only a masterpiece
but also a new son, Hossein Mansouri, the little
boy who answers the question on "beautiful
things": "The moon, the sun, flowers, recreation."
The poetess is her own river all to herself.

In an interview with Bernardo Bertolucci,
Forough defines the artist's work as follows:
"An intellectual is someone who, besides trying

9
In 1972, Maurice Born
conducted a long
interview, which was
published later in 201
Epaminondas
Remoundakis (2015),
*Vies et morts d'un
Crétois lépreux*:
translated from Greek
by Maurice Born and
Marianne Gabriel (20°
édition Anarchasis

을 더 잘 이해할 수 있다. 사랑의 결핍을 직시함으로, 파로흐자드 감독은 수용소에 동화될 수 있었고, 검은 화면 위로 들리는 마지막 구절처럼, 한센병 환자들의 글로 이 영화에 상징적인 서명을 남길 수 있었다. "오, 사랑의 힘으로 넘쳐흐르는 강물이 우리에게 흘러온다, 우리에게 흘러온다."

6. 실험

파로흐자드 감독이 한센병 수용소로부터 걸작 영화 한 편만을 탄생시킨 것뿐 아니라, 호세인 만수리라는 소년을 입양해 데려왔다는 이야기는 이미 잘 알려져 있다. 만수리는 이 영화의 교실 장면에서 "아름다운 것"에 대한 질문에 "달, 태양, 꽃, 놀이 시간"이라고 대답했던 소년이다. 시인 파로흐자드는 스스로 자신을 위한 강(江)이 된다.

베르나르도 베르톨루치와의 인터뷰에서, 파로흐자드 감독은 예술가의 작업을 다음과 같이 정의했다. "지식인은 삶의 외적인 발전 이외에도, 윤리적 문제를 개선하기 위해 정신적인 발전을 시도하는 사람입니다. 그리고 그 사람은 문제를 발견하고 스스로 해결합니다."[10] 포루그 파로흐자드는 타인의 경험을 어떻게 정확히 전달할 수 있는가, 라는 다큐멘터리의 가장 어려운 문제를 해결하기 위해, 영화적 묘사를 풍부하게 하는 시청각적 글쓰기 양식을 확장시키고, '영화 시'를 스스로 창조해 냄으로써 여성으로서 자신의 인생 속에 이미지와 사운드의 묶음이 흘러 들어오게 하는 방법을 택했다. 그녀의 이러한 방법들은 결코

for the external development of life, tries for the spiritual advancement for the improvement of the moral issues. And he looks at these issues and solves them for himself."[10] The way Forough Farrokhzad solved the most difficult problem of documentary filmmaking – how to convey the experience of others with accuracy –, the way she was able to use a variety the modes of visual and sound writing to enrich the film description, the way she invented a film poem all by herself, the way she made a block of images and sounds in her own life as a woman, will never cease to inspire. *The House is Black* exemplifies Maya Deren's proposal: "Poetry, to my mind, is an approach to experience".[11]

Nicole Brenez

Nicole Brenez is Professor of Film Studies at the University of Sorbonne Nouvelle, Director of the Analysis & Culture Department at the Femis since 2017, curator of the Cinémathèque française's avant-garde film series since 1996. With the filmmaker Philippe Grandrieux, she produces the film collection *It May Be That Beauty Has Strengthened Our Resolve* (2011), devoted to revolutionary filmmakers forgotten or neglected by the histories of cinema. Her most recent book is *Manifestations* (De l'Incidence, 2020). She worked with Chantal Akerman – *Almayer's Folly* (2011) –, Jocelyne Saab, Marylène Negro, Jean-Gabriel Périot, and is currently working with Jean-Luc Godard (2015–present, *Le Livre d'Image* (*The Image Book*, 2018), awarded Special Golden Palm), Jacques Kebadian (2016–present).

10
Forough Farrokhzad interviewed by Bernardo Bertolucci (1965): https://www.youtube.com/watch?v=L_DVYmrm7Do&ab_channel=Koyaanisqats

11
Cinema 16: Documentary Toward History Of Film Society (2010), Scott MacDonald, Temple University Press, p. 204.

멈추지 않고 영감을 불러일으킬 것이다. "내 생각에, 시라는 것은 경험에 접근하는 방식이다."[11]라고 마야 데렌이 제안했던 명제를 〈검은 집〉이 증명한다.

니콜 브르네

니콜 브르네는 누벨소르본느대학 영화학과 교수이자, 영화학교 페미즈에서 '영화 분석과 문화'학과의 학장을 맡고 있으며, 1996년 이후 시네마테크 프랑세즈에서 아방가르드 영화시리즈의 큐레이터로 활동하고 있다. 영화감독 필립 그랑드리외와 함께 영화사에서 잊혔던 혁명적인 영화감독들을 다룬 영화 선집 『우리의 결의를 다진 것은 아름다움이었으리라』(2011)를 제작했고, 최근 출판물로는 『선언들』(2020)이 있다. 또한 샹탈 아케르만(〈알마이에르가의 광기〉, 2011), 조슬린 사브, 마릴렌 네그로, 장 가브리엘 페리오 등의 감독들과 함께 작업하였으며, 현재는 장뤼크 고다르(〈이미지북〉, 2015-), 자크 케바디앙(2016-)의 작품제작에 참여하고 있다.

← The cover of Foroug
Farrokhzad's
collection of poems
Tavallodi Digar, 196
『또 다른 탄생』(196
시집 표지

1   '창문'(1974): 페르시안 번역 ─ 미트라 A. 소피아(2009.7-8), 세계 문학의 오늘, 83판 4권, p.15

2   마호마드 호세인 아지지, 모슬렘 바하도리(2011), 『19, 20세기 이란의 한센병 환자 역사』, 이란 의학 아카이브, 11월 14(6), p. 425-430

3   '시와 영화' 좌담회는 책으로 출판되었다. (출처: 스콧 맥도널드(2010), 『시네마 16: 영화 사회의 역사를 향한 문서』, 템플대학교 출판사, p.200)

4   "이것은 상황에 대한 '수직적' 탐구라 할 수 있다. 순간의 영향을 조사하고 그것의 성질과 깊이를 고려한다는 점에서 말이다."스콧 맥도널드, 앞의 책, p. 204

5   스콧 맥도널드, 앞의 책 p. 209.

6   '영화 강의. 시와 정치 사이, 골레스탄필름스튜디오'(2016.6.28), 2016년 시네마 리트로바토 고전영화제, 에산 코스바트와 메라나즈 사이드-바파의 진행으로 성사된 에브라힘 골레스탄과의 만남 영상(25분): https://www.youtube.com/watch?v=rKS FKce83qg&list=PLwg8VB64LkBKuVV1qFIlkpgg_fKIlLjcs&index=194&ab_channel=CinetecaBologna

7   베르트 한스트라 감독은 〈검은 집〉에 그랑프리를 수여한 1963년 오버하우젠 국제단편영화제의 심사위원장이었다. 당시 심사위원은 예르지 보삭, 월터 버로우, 표도르 키트럭, 폴 해서츠, 흐리스토 코바체프, 월터 라셀리, 마이클 렌츠, 피에르 레몽, 칼 쉬데라이트, 하로 센프트, 아모스 보겔, 듀산 뷰코틱, 그리고 카렐 제만이었다. (정보를 확인해 준 라스 헨릭 게스와 칼슨 스피셔에게 고마움을 전한다.)

8   '니사의 그레고리우스, 가난한 이들을 사랑하는 이들 II, 342' 중 인용: 디오니시오스 스타타모풀로스(2011.12), 『구체화된 감정에 대한 설교, 후기 고대 시대의 주교, 거지, 그리고 청중』, 메디에발-벵센느대학 출판사, p. 28

9   에파미논다스 레문다키스는 1972년 인터뷰를 토대로 『크레테섬 사람, 어느 한센병 환자의 삶과 죽음』(2015, 모리스 본과 가브리엘 번역, 아나르샤니스 출판사)을 집필했다.

10 베르나르도 베르톨루치와 파로흐자드의 인터뷰 영상(1965): https://www.youtube.com/watch?v=L_DVYmrm7Do&ab_channel=Koyaanisqatsi

11 스콧 맥도널드, 앞의 책, p.204

Forough Farrokhzad

1934 + On December 29, Farrokhzad is born in Tehran,
a metropolitan city in northern Iran, as the third child of
seven children under mother Touran Vaziri-Tabar and
father, Mohammad Farrokhzad Araghi, a military colonel.
She is registered on the birth registry as Foroughzama
Farrokhzad Araghi.
(*There is a lot of speculation surrounding her date of
birth, but according to the government records, it is 1934.
Farzaneh Milani, an Iranian scholar from the University of
Virginia personally checked her birth certificate.)

1935 + A year after she's born, they move to Noshahr in
northern Tehran for her father's work. Farrokhzad grows
up surrounded by the beautiful forests and the sea for
six years.

1950 + Spends her childhood in Amirieh. After completing
her elementary, middle, and high school education up
to the ninth grade, Farrokhzad attends Kamal-ol-Molk
Art School where she learns painting and sewing.
+ At the age of 16, she falls in love and quits school,
wanting to marry the man next door. Despite the family's
severe objection, she marries her distant relative Parvis
Shapour (1923–2000) who is 11 years her senior and
gets disowned by her family. After she gets married,
she moves to a small town in southwestern Iran called
Ahvaz with her husband who worked as a treasurer and
a satire cartoonist.

1952 + On June 19, the protagonist of *A Poem for You* and her
son, Kāmyār Shapour, is born.
+ Farrokhzad's first poem, *Gonah*, is published in the
Roshanfekr magazine which introduced innovative
literary works. Despite having split opinions internally, the
unprecedented poem about a woman's love and desires
gets to see the world thanks to the support from the
editor in charge and renowned poet, Ferreydoon Moshiri.
This poem not only gets Farrokhzad's name known in the
literary world, but she becomes a controversial figure
at the same time. However, when the magazine sales go
up and many readers ask for more of her poems, her

포루그 파로흐자드 연보

1934년 + 12월 29일, 이란 북부 대도시 테헤란에서 어머니
투란 바지리타바르와 군 대령이었던 아버지
모하마드 파로흐자드 아라기 사이에서 7남매 중 셋째로
태어남. 출생신고서상 이름은 포루그자만 파로흐자드
아라기로 기록됨.
(*출생일에 관한 정보가 난무하나 정부 기록상
1934년으로 되어 있음. 버지니아대학교 이란 학자
파르자네 밀라니가 직접 출생신고서를 확인함.)

1935년 + 태어난 지 1년 후 아버지의 근무 지역을 따라 테헤란
북부 노샤르(Noshahr)로 이주해 6년간 숲과 바다를
둘러싼 아름다운 자연환경에서 성장함.

1950년 + 아미리에(Amirieh) 지역에서 유년기를 보냄.
9학년까지 초중등 교육을 마친 파로흐자드는 카말올몰크
미술학교(Kamal-ol-Molk Art School)에 진학해
회화와 재봉을 배움.
+ 16세에 사랑에 눈을 뜨면서 학업을 중단하고 옆집
남자와 결혼을 원함. 집안의 극심한 반대에도 불구하고
먼 친척이자 열한 살 연상의 파르비즈 샤푸르(1923-
2000)와 결혼.
재무부 직원이자 풍자만화가로 활동하던 남편을 따라
결혼 후 이란 남서부 소도시 아바즈(Ahvaz)로 이주함.

1952년 + 6월 19일, '너를 위한 시'의 주인공인 아들 캄야르
샤푸르가 태어남.
+ 파로흐자드의 첫 시 '죄'가 혁신적인 문학작품을
소개하던 '로샨페흐' 잡지에 실림. 내부 편집진의
찬반이 분분했음에도 책임 편집자이자 저명한 시인이던
페리둔 모시리의 지지로 당시 접할 수 없던 여성의
사랑과 욕망을 표현하는 시가 세상에 나옴.
이 시는 파로흐자드를 문학계에 알림과 동시에 논쟁적
인물로 지목하는 계기가 되었지만, 잡지의 판매 부수가
늘어나고 독자들의 요청이 쇄도하자 그녀의 시는

works are introduced more actively. Her father and husband saw this poem as a disgrace, and did not step outside the house for a while. The more she got famous, the more pressure she got from her family. Farrokhzad starts writing under various pseudonyms.

1954 + Upon her divorce, she loses the custody and the rights to see her son. She is labeled as a divorced woman. After moving around friends' houses, she gets herself a single room and settles in Tehran.

1955 + *Asir*, her first poetry collection of 44 works gets published. It is seen as the first collection of poems in Iran by a woman without any literary background in the family. Since Farrokhzad's poems deal with the female gender and existence, no one dares to write recommendations for her in fear of ruining their reputation in the poetry world. So Farrokhzad takes her book to the renowned Iranian writer Shojaeddin Shafa in person to get the recommendation.

+ In September, the social accusations, the poverty, and the inability to see her son makes her suffer, and she tries to commit suicide. She's transferred to a psychiatric clinic for an electric shock treatment.

1956 + Publishes her second book, *Divar*. The 25 poems written like short lyrics plead about the social prejudices and distorted notions on divorcees. The book is dedicated to her ex-husband.

+ Farrokhzad who had to give up studying abroad due to financial reasons goes on her first trip abroad after her discharge. She travels in Italy and Germany for 16 months and makes travel expenses through sewing and short-term dubbing jobs.

+ Upon her return, she immediately publishes her European travel book, *In the Eternal Sunset*. Despite it being a self-reflective essay, it was attacked and seen as a diary of a hedonist when the travel journal was serialized in a magazine.

1958 + Publishes the third book, *Esian*. It contains 17 poems with the will to resist the immoral society that is male-centered. Farrokhzad becomes known as a talented

더 활발히 소개됨. 시가 발표된 후 친부와 남편은
집안을 망신시켰다는 인식에 한동안 외출을 못 했으며
그녀가 유명해질수록 집안의 압박이 심해짐.
파로흐자드는 다양한 필명으로 글을 쓰고 기고함.

1954년 + 이혼과 동시에 아들 양육권과 접근권을 상실함.
이혼녀라는 꼬리표가 붙음. 친구 집을 전전하다
테헤란에 단칸방을 얻어 정착.

1955년 + 마흔네 편의 시가 담긴 첫 시집 『포로』 출판. 이란에서
처음으로 문학적 배경이 없는 집안 출신의 여성이
쓴 시집으로 평가받음. 여성의 성과 존재에 대한 사유를
다룬 파로흐자드의 시 세계에 대한 평판이 두려워
추천사를 써 주는 이가 없자 자신의 책을 들고 이란의
저명한 저술가 쇼자에딘 샤파의 집으로 찾아가
직접 글을 받음.
+ 9월, 사회적 비난, 아들을 볼 수 없는 괴로움, 빈곤의
문제로 자살을 시도하고 정신과 진료소로 옮겨져
전기 충격 치료를 받음.

1956년 + 두 번째 시집 『벽』 출판. 이혼 후 사회적 편견과
왜곡으로 인한 고통을 호소하는 시로 스물다섯 편의
짧은 가사처럼 구성됨. 전남편에게 헌정함.
+ 경제적인 이유로 외국 유학을 포기했던 파로흐자드는
퇴원 후 생애 첫 외국 여행을 떠남. 16개월간
이탈리아와 독일을 여행했고 바느질과 단기 더빙
일로 여비를 마련함.
+ 귀국 직후 유럽 기행문 『영원의 석양에서』 출판.
자기 성찰적인 에세이였음에도 불구하고 여행기가
잡지에 연재됐을 당시 쾌락주의자의 일기라는
공격을 받음.

1958년 + 세 번째 시집 『저항』 출판. 남성 중심의 부도덕한
사회에 저항하는 의지가 느껴지는 17편의 시 수록.
재능이 있으나 악명 높은 시인으로 알려짐.
+ 학력이 좋지 못해 일자리를 구하기 힘들었으나 경제적

and notorious poet.

+ Due to her low level of education, she finds it difficult to get a job, but she tries hard to become financially independent. She gets a receptionist job at the Golestan Film Studio, where more than 40 filmmakers work. Soon after, her talent is recognized and she gets to expand her work to film editing and directing. She started a relationship with writer and cinematographer Ebrahim Golestan, but receives social criticism as Golestan was a married man.

1960 + Attempts her second suicide. After waking up, Golestan supports her to live an independent life and she devotes herself to filmmaking.

1961 + Participates as the editor in *Yek Atash* (directed by Ebrahim Golestan), a documentary about oil wells in southern Iran, and participates in *Courtship* (co-directed by several directors along with Ebrahim Golestan) as the assistant director of the part titled *Iran*. She plays an active part in various films and commercials by the Golestan Film Studio.

1962 + While spending 12 days in Bababaghi Hospice located in the leprosy town of central Iran, she directs the documentary *The House is Black*. Although it receives harsh criticism domestically, she received international acclaim including a recognition as the best documentary at the International Short Film Festival Oberhausen. She adopts Hossein Mansouri, whom she meets in the ward while filming the movie. She does not hesitate to become a single-parent which was a concept that did not exist in Iran at the time. Mansouri later moves to Germany to translate Farrokhzad's poems.

1963 + On May 6, the Cannes Film Festival invites *The House is Black* to the competition category, and informs the producer Golestan that the screening will take place on May 20. For an unknown reason, Golestan replies that they would like to cancel their submission to the film festival. On May 14, the Cannes Film Festival announces through an official letter that it will accept the cancellation of the screening of *The House is Black*.

독립을 실천하기 위해 노력함. 40여 명의 영화제작자들이
일하는 골레스탄필름스튜디오의 접수원으로 취직.
이후 재능을 인정받아 영화 편집, 연출로 영역을 확대해 감.
작가이자 영화감독이던 에브라힘 골레스탄과의
만남이 시작됐으나 골레스탄이 유부남이었기에 사회적
비난을 받음.

1960년 + 두 번째 자살을 시도함. 병원에서 깨어난 후 독립적인
존재로 살라는 골레스탄의 후원 아래 영화제작에 몰두함.

1961년 + 이란 남부 유정(油井)에 대한 다큐멘터리
〈불〉(에브라힘 골레스탄 연출)에 편집자로 참여하고,
다큐멘터리 〈교제〉(에브라힘 골레스탄 외 공동연출)
중 '이란' 에피소드에 조감독으로 참여하는 등
골레스탄필름스튜디오의 다수 영화 및 광고에서 활약함.

1962년 + 이란 중부 한센병 환자 마을 바바바기 병동에서 12일간
머물며 다큐멘터리 〈검은 집〉 연출. 자국 내에서는
혹평을 받았지만, 오버하우젠단편영화제에서 다큐멘터리
부문 대상을 받는 등 국제적으로 찬사를 받음.
영화 촬영을 하며 병동에서 만난 호세인 만수리를 입양함.
당시 이란에 존재하지 않던 개념인 한부모 가정을
꾸리는 데 주저하지 않음. 만수리는 이후 독일로 건너가
파로흐자드의 시를 번역함.

1963년 + 5월 6일, 칸영화제는 경쟁 부문에 〈검은 집〉을 초청했으며
상영 일정은 5월 20일로 결정되었다고 프로듀서인
골레스탄에게 전달함. 알 수 없는 이유로 골레스탄은
영화제에 작품 접수를 취소하겠다고 답장함. 5월 14일,
칸영화제는 공문을 통해 〈검은 집〉의 상영 취소를
받아들인다고 공지함.
+ 베르나르도 베르톨루치가 파로흐자드와 만나기 위해
이란을 방문했으며 짧은 인터뷰를 진행함.
+ 루이지 피란델로의 희곡 〈작가를 찾는 6인의
등장인물〉(1922)이 이탈리아 문화청의 협력으로 테헤란
무대에서 선을 보였고, 포루그는 의붓딸 역으로 출연함.

+ Bernardo Bertolucci visits Iran to meet Farrokhzad and conducts a short interview.
+ With the cooperation of the Italian Ministry of Cultural Heritage and Activities and Tourism, Luigi Pirandello's play *Six Characters in Search of an Author* (1922) is introduced on a stage in Tehran. Farrokhzad appears in the role of the stepdaughter.
+ It is said that UNESCO produced a 30-minute film about Farrokhzad, but there is no evidence of this project in UNESCO's official records.
+ Her fourth poetry collection, *Tavallodi Digar*, gets published. The 35 poems written over five years contain a variety of topics such as the state, social issues, and gender. Critics see this collection as one of the best works of Farrokhzad.

1965 + Her fifth book, *Let Us Believe in the Beginning of the Cold Season*, goes into print. Consisting of poetries and essays, this book gets published in 1972 after Farrokhzad's death.
+ Plays a supporting role (a mother) in *Khesht Va Ayeneh* (directed by Ebrahim Golestan).

1967 + Was preparing to play Joan of Arc in the play *Saint Joan* by playwright George Bernard Shaw.
+ On February 14, Farrokhzad gets into a car accident after having lunch with her mother. When her Jeep Station Wagon switches directions to dodge an oncoming car, she crashes into a stone wall. She gets a head injury and is transferred to a hospital, but she dies on the way. On a snowy day, Farrokhzad gets buried in a small cemetery named Zahir-od-dowleh in Tehran.

+ 유네스코가 포루그에 관한 30분 길이의 영화를
제작했다고 알려졌으나 유네스코 공식기록에는
이 프로젝트에 대한 흔적이 없음.
+ 네 번째 시집 『또 다른 탄생』 출판. 5년이 넘는 기간
동안 쓴 서른다섯 편의 시에는 국가, 사회문제, 젠더 등
다양한 주제가 담김. 평단은 파로흐자드 최고의
작업으로 손꼽음.

1965년 + 다섯 번째 시집 『추운 계절의 시작을 믿어보자』가
인쇄에 들어감. 시와 에세이로 구성된 이 책은 포루그의
사후인 1972년에 출판됨.
+ 영화 〈벽돌과 거울〉(에브라힘 골레스탄 연출)에
단역(어머니 역)으로 참여.

1967년 + 극작가 조지 버나드 쇼의 연극 '성녀 잔다르크'에서
잔다르크 역을 준비 중이었음.
+ 2월 14일, 어머니와 점심을 먹고 집으로 돌아오던 중
차 사고가 남. 그녀의 지프 스테이션왜건이 다가오는
차량을 피하기 위해 방향을 틀다 돌벽과 충돌함.
머리 부상을 입고 병원으로 후송되었지만 이동 중 사망함.
눈이 오던 날 테헤란의 작은 공동묘지
자히르오도레(Zahir-od-dowleh)에 묻힘.

바바라 로튼

Barbara Loden
Actor, Director

Barbara Loden (1932–1980). After about
a decade of career as a lesser known actor,
in 1964, she won a Tony Award for Best
Featured Actress for her performance of
Arthur Miller's *After the Fall*. Even after winning
a Tony Award, her career as an actor was
not smooth sailing. After 11 years after she
started the project, she finally finished
making her only film, *Wanda* (1970). It was
inspired by a woman who took part in a bank
robbery. Although the film was invited to
Venice International Film Festival and
Cannes Film Festival, it failed in making
commercial success. *Wanda* became more
widely and extensively discussed after
Loden's death, and now regarded as one of
the greatest American independent films
of the 1970s.

바바라 로든
배우, 영화감독

1932–1980. 십 년이 넘는 무명 생활을
견디고 1964년 아서 밀러 극본의
'추락 이후'로 토니상 최우수여우주연상을
수상하며 연기력을 인정받았다. 그럼에도
배우로 경력을 이어 가는 데 어려움이
있었고, 우여곡절 끝에 유일무이한 영화
〈완다〉(1970)를 연출한다. 은행 강도 사건에
휘말린 실제 여성에 영감을 받아 11년
만에 완성된 〈완다〉는 베니스국제영화제,
칸영화제에 초청되었지만 흥행에는 실패한다.
로든이 사망한 후 더욱 활발히 논의되고 있는
〈완다〉는 오늘날 1970년대 제작된 최고의
미국 독립영화 중 한 편으로 손꼽힌다.

Barbara
Loden

Don't try to tame me

By Sung Moon (Programmer of JEONJU
International Film Festival)

When a pedestrian scramble light turns on,
people swarm from all directions, passing each
other busily. At that moment, there are people
whose eyes meet intensely for an unknown
reason. Soon, they disappear from our view.
The movie *Wanda* (1970) also disappeared in a
flash only after letting a small number of people
know about its existence. The director of the
film, Barbara Loden, was an artist who came to
this world to make miracles as an actress and a
director, albeit only for a short amount of time,
just like her character, Wanda.

Barbara Loden died of cancer on September 5,
1980 at the age of 48, while preparing for her
next film after a long break since *Wanda*. She first
debuted on a theater stage on Broadway, and
occasionally played small roles in television and
films, but she was an unknown actress for
10 years. In 1964, she played Maggie in Arthur
Miller's play, *After the Fall*, which got her the
Tony Award for Best Actress in a Play. That was
what she accomplished as an actress. As a
director, she's faintly remembered for her debut
film, *Wanda*, which was invited at the 31st Venice
International Film Festival and awarded the
Pasinetti Award in 1970, and also invited to the
Cannes Film Festival the following year. What
the media never fails to mention about Loden's
life is her marriage to Elia Kazan. At the time,
Kazan was an established theater director, and
he was on his way to success after moving over
to Hollywood and making films like *A Streetcar*

나를 길들이려 하지 마세요
바바라 로든의 〈완다〉

글: 문성경
(전주국제영화제 프로그래머)

사거리 교차로에 동시 보행 신호가 떨어지면 인파가 사방에서 몰려온다. 바쁘게 교차하는 사람들. 그때 알 수 없는 이유로 강렬하게 눈이 마주치는 사람들이 있다. 곧 그들은 시야에서 사라진다. 영화 〈완다〉(1970)도 스쳐가듯 짧은 시간 동안 소수의 사람들에게 자신의 존재를 알리고 사라졌다. 이 영화를 만든 감독, 바바라 로든 또한 자신이 만든 캐릭터 완다처럼 짧은 시간 이 세상에 배우로, 감독으로 그리고 기적을 만든 한 명의 예술가로 나타났다 사라졌다.

바바라 로든은 첫 장편영화 〈완다〉의 연출 이후 오랜 시간 차기작을 준비하던 중 암에 걸려 1980년 9월 5일 48세를 일기로 타계했다. 그녀는 브로드웨이 연극무대를 통해 데뷔한 배우였고

Named Desire (1951). The marriage seemed like it would give Loden psychological stability while opening her up to more opportunities and social activities, but every time she expanded her acting career or tried something new, the media was fast to write columns asking, "what more could she want?" On top of that, Kazan exposed personal information about his relationship with Loden in his autobiographical novel called *The Arrangement* (1967), damaging Loden's public image. The stereotypes placed on Loden were clear. When she received the Tony Award for playing Maggie (a character who represents metaphorically Marilyn Monroe), gossipers saw it as the birth of a blonde sexy queen rather than the rise of a rookie

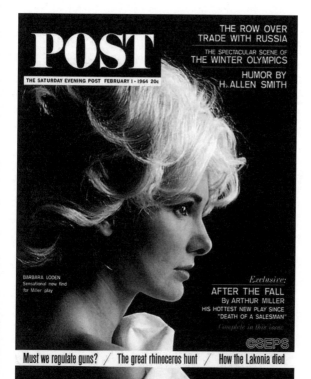

← Barbara Loden
on the cover of
*Saturday Evening
Post* in occasion of
the release of
play *After the Fall*
1964년 2월 1일,
연극 '추락 이후'로
'새터데이 이브닝
포스트'의 표지로
등장한 바바라 로든

간혹 텔레비전과 영화의 단역을 맡기도 했지만 10년이 넘는 무명 세월을 거쳤다. 1964년 아서 밀러 극본의 연극 '추락 이후'에서 매기 역을 연기하고 토니상 연극 부문 최우수여우주연상을 수상한 것이 배우로서 그녀가 이룬 성취다. 감독으로서는 데뷔작 〈완다〉로 1970년 제31회 베니스국제영화제에서 파지네티상을 받고 이듬해 칸영화제에 초청된 것으로 흐릿하게 기억된다. 언론이 로든의 삶에서 빼놓지 않고 언급하는 개인적 이력은 엘리아 카잔과의 결혼이다. 당시 카잔은 성공한 연극 연출가였고, 할리우드로 옮겨 〈욕망이라는 이름의 전차〉(1951) 등 영화감독으로도 성공 가도를 달리는 유명 인사였다. 이 결혼은 그녀에게 정서적 안정과 사회 활동 면에서 더 많은 기회를 열어 줄 수 있을 것처럼 보였지만 로든이 연기 활동을 넓히고, 새로운 분야에 진출할 때마다 언론은 '그녀는 무엇을 더 원하는가' 따위의 칼럼을 내곤 했다. 심지어 카잔은 자전 소설 『열망』(1967)에서 로든과의 관계에 대한 과도한 사적 정보를 노출해 그녀의 이미지에 타격을 입혔다. 로든에게 씌워진 고정 관념은 완고한 것이었다. 그녀가 마릴린 먼로를 은유적으로 표현하는 매기 역으로 토니상을 받았을 때 호사가들은 새로운 연기자의 부상보다는 금발 섹시퀸의 탄생에 더 주목했고, 베니스국제영화제 수상 소식을 알리는 기사에도 엘리아 카잔의 아내로 먼저 소개했다. 따라서 개봉 당시 〈완다〉의 예술적 성취를 진지하게 논의할 여지는 별로 없었다. 그러나 이런 악조건에도 불구하고 바바라 로든 자신은 창작 경험을 통해 자존감을 회복하는 한편 나아가 한 명의 주체적인 인간으로서 자신의 목소리를 발산하는 '어떤 사람(somebody)'으로 변모할 수 있었다.

performer. Even in an article about her award from Venice International Film Festival, she was introduced as Kazan's wife before anything. That's why there was no room for serious discussions on the artistic successes of *Wanda* at the time of its release. But despite these unfavorable conditions, Barbara Loden was able to recover her self-esteem through the creative experience of filmmaking and was able to transform into an independent "somebody" with a voice.

Wanda is the only feature film directed by Barbara Loden. This film is meaningful, but not because Loden only got to make one feature in her lifetime. It's important because it uses a completely different film format and techniques from mainstream films. In addition, the production was finished through an independent funding system, while the theme and characters also make *Wanda* important. When it was invited to the Cannes Film Festival, it received the attention of some critics. It was released on a single screen at New York's Cinema II, but it was soon forgotten. In many ways, it is one of the most unique films in the history of American independent cinema, but until it was digitally restored, revisited, and recognized in 2010 at film festivals, it only resurfaced momentarily time and again by a handful of supporters over the last few decades.

"Why would this girl feel glad to be put away?"[1]

Wanda is the story of a woman named Wanda who gets roped into a crime while wandering the streets after turning her back on her family. Loden wrote, directed, and starred in the film, playing three different roles. Initially, Loden didn't have a great ambition. But because the

1
Quoting an Interview with Barbara Loden – Kate Taylor (2010.8.2? "Driven by Fierce Vision of Independence", *The New York Times*

〈완다〉는 배우로 경력을 쌓아 가던 바바라 로든이 남긴 유일한 장편 극영화 연출작이다. 물론 로든이 단 한 편만 만들었기 때문에 이 영화가 의미 있는 것은 아니다. 주류 영화와 완전히 다른 영화 형식과 촬영 기법, 독립적인 자금 조달 방식으로 영화를 완성했다는 점, 영화 주제와 캐릭터 성격이라는 측면에서도 〈완다〉는 중요하다. 칸영화제에 초청되자 잠시 비평가들의 관심을 받았지만 관객을 빨아들이는 할리우드 스타일 영화도, 영웅이 등장하는 것도 아닌 이 영화는 뉴욕 Cinema II에서 단관 개봉 했지만 이내 잊혀졌다. 여러 측면에서 미국 독립영화 역사상 가장 유니크한 영화 중 하나였지만 2010년 이후 디지털 복원을 통해 영화제를 중심으로 재평가될 때까지 〈완다〉는 수십 년 동안 소수 지지자들에 의해 잠시 수면 위에 오르고 사라지기를 반복할 뿐이었다.

"이 여자는 사회에서 내쳐진 게 왜 기쁠까요?"[1]

〈완다〉는 가족을 등지고 길거리를 떠돌다 범죄에 휘말리는 동명 여성의 이야기로 로든이 시나리오, 연출, 연기까지 1인 3역을 맡은 영화다. 처음부터 로든에게 대단한 야망이 있었던 것은 아니다. 저예산으로 영화를 완성해야 했기에 최소 규모의 스태프를 꾸릴 수밖에 없었다. 많은 감독에게 연출을 제안했지만 모두 거절당한 끝에, 스스로 연출을 맡게 된 것이다.

한 여성에 대한 내밀한 이야기와 생생한 연기 때문에 〈완다〉는 로든의 자전적 이야기가 반영된 것이라는 짐작이 나왔다. 영화

film had to be shot on a low budget, she had no choice but to put together the least number of staff. After being rejected multiple times by several directors, she decided to direct it herself.

Because of its intimate story about a woman and Loden's vivid acting, it was speculated that *Wanda* is a reflection of Loden's autobiography. The background of the film and the character's family have traces of Loden's childhood in them, but the story actually started from an article that was published in the *Sunday Daily* newspaper on March 27, 1960. This article was about Alma Malone, a woman who was caught on site while robbing a bank. Malone, who was wandering the streets after leaving her family, was roped into becoming an accomplice of a crime. When her partner Ansley was shot to death, Malone was left to stand in court alone on charges of armed robbery and planned abduction, giving her a sentence of 20 years. Instead of pleading innocence or complaining that she wasn't the one who took the lead in the crime, she thanked the judge for allowing her to spend 20 years in jail where she'll get food and a place to sleep. Loden could not understand Malone. After a background check, she requests to visit Malone, but gets refused. In a 1974 interview, Loden says to the journalist, "Why would this girl feel glad to be put away?... I was fascinated by the kind of girl who would be that passive and dumb."

To some, it was just an ordinary bank robbery and someone else's story. One could read Malone's behavior as an act of atonement, so why did Loden find her strange? Why did Loden try so hard to understand Malone? Loden immediately felt something about this woman, and it wasn't because it was a crime case.

배경, 가족 캐릭터 등 로든의 어린 시절 흔적이 묻어나는 부분은 많지만 실상 이 영화는 1960년 3월 27일 '선데이데일리' 신문에 실린 어느 기사에서 시작되었다. 그것은 은행 강도를 벌이다 현장에서 잡힌 알마 멀론이란 여성의 이야기다. 가족을 떠나 떠돌다 만난 남자 안슬리에게 얽혀 범죄에 가담한 멀론은, 남자는 총에 맞아 죽고 홀로 법정에서 무장강도, 계획에 의한 납치 등의 죄목으로 20년 형을 선고받는다. 그녀는 자신이 주도한 범죄가 아니라는 점 등을 내세워 억울함을 호소하는 대신, 잠자리와 음식이 제공되는 감옥에 20년 동안 가게 해 준 판사에게 감사를 표했다. 로든은 이런 멀론을 이해할 수 없었다. 배경 조사를 하고 교도소 면회 신청까지 하지만 거절당한다. 1974년 어느 인터뷰에서 로든은 기자에게 되묻는다. "이 여자는 사회에서 내쳐진 게 왜 기쁠까요? 어떤 여자가 그렇게 수동적이고 바보 같을 수 있죠?"

누군가에게는 그저 흔한 은행 강도 사건이었을 뿐이고, 자신과는 상관없는 다른 세계의 이야기였을 것이다. 멀론의 행동이 속죄하는 것으로 보일 수도 있는 상황에서 왜 유독 로든은 그녀를 이상하다고 생각했을까? 왜 로든은 멀론을 이해하고자 노력했을까? 로든은 이 여성에게 즉각적인 뭔가를 느꼈다. 범죄 사건이어서가 아니었다. 로든이 멀론의 이야기를 하고 싶던 강렬한 이유가 있었다. 〈완다〉는 이렇게 실화를 토대로 시작되었지만 온전히 바바라 로든의 해석과 창작이 더해져 탄생한 이야기다. 그렇기에 알마 멀론과 바바라 로든은 완다라는 인물 속에서 교차점을 가지며 만난다. 로든은 정체성에 대한 고민이 전혀 없

There was a strong reason why Loden wanted to tell Malone's story. Like so, *Wanda* started from a true story, but it was solely through Barbara Loden's interpretations and creativity, that the story was born. This is why Alma Malone and Barbara Loden meet at a cross point through the character of Wanda. At a time when Loden didn't question her identity, she tried to become the person other people wanted her to be. She didn't deny the fact that this side of her past was reflected in Wanda.

"I made Wanda as a way of confirming my own existence. I was like the living dead. I lived like a zombie for a long time, until I was nearly thirty."[2]

After reading the news article in 1960, Barbara Loden could start filming in 1969. The film took 10 years of preparation.

Discomfort from having no place to belong

The film begins with uncomfortable screeching noises. In a mining village full of black stones and ashes, an excavator runs fiercely while a baby cries in discomfort. The uncomfortable air inside and outside the house seem to tell us that an unwelcome person is here. When a man slams the door behind him and leaves, Wanda says her first line, buried in the sofa. "He's mad because I'm here." Wanda knows her existence alone causes discomfort. With hair rollers in her hair, she leaves the house she was staying at temporarily. The whole village is ashen, and it's hard to differentiate the sidewalk from the construction site. It's as if the whole world is made out of coals. Wanda, who is dressed in light colors, looks overly innocent as she walks

2
Nathalie Léger (2012
Supplément à la vie (
Barbara Loden (Suite
for Barbara Loden),
Paris: P.O.L – quotin(
FILM Magazine (197

던 시절, 사람들이 되길 바라는 모습대로 되려 했던 자신의 과거 모습을 완다에게 투영시켰음을 부인하지 않았다.

> "나는 서른이 되기 전까지 아주 오랜 시간 좀비처럼 살았어요. 완다처럼 어떤 정체성도 없고, 그저 사람들이 원하는 나를 살아가며 수동적으로 삶을 대했습니다. 친구도 없고, 재능도 없고, 학교에서 배운 것도 없었어요. 여전히 셈도 못해요. 그래서 감정적으로 완다 캐릭터에 친밀함을 느꼈어요."[2]

바바라 로든은 1960년 신문 기사를 읽은 후 1969년에야 촬영에 들어갈 수 있었다. 준비에만 10년이 걸린 셈이다.

어디에도 속하지 않는 존재의 불편함

영화는 신경을 긁는 소음으로 시작한다. 검은 돌과 재로 가득 찬 광산 마을에서 맹렬히 돌아가는 굴착기와 뭔가 불편해 울어 대는 아기는 집의 안팎으로 불편한 공기를 조성하고 반갑지 않은 존재의 등장을 알린다. 소파에 파묻혀 있던 완다는 거칠게 문을 닫고 나가는 남자를 뒤로하고 첫 대사를 한다. "내가 여기 있어서 화났어." 자신의 존재 자체가 불편을 일으킨다는 걸 알고 있는 완다는 헤어롤을 머리에 올린 채 잠시 머물렀던 집을 나선다. 마을은 보행로와 공사장이 구분이 안 될 정도로 새까맣게 그을려 있고, 세상은 거대한 석탄산으로만 이루어진 듯 보인다. 그 속

through, to a point she might disappear from this black world if she were a bit more transparent.

In an interview with *Positif* in 1975, Loden says that if she had stayed in the coal mine village with her family whom she had no affection for, she would've led a life just like Malone. She said, "If I had stayed there, I would have gotten a job at Woolworth's, I would've gotten married at 17 and had some children, and would have got drunk every Friday and Saturday night. Fortunately, I escaped."[3] In fact, Alma Malone got married at a young age of 14 and was divorced by her husband. While divorcing her on the grounds of desertion, Malone's husband said, "She was there, Your Honor, but she was not there."[4]

Right from the start, *Wanda* seems to declare that the main character is a complete oddball. At the divorce trial, her husband furiously complains that Wanda was always in a daze on the sofa. While listing the reasons why she's not qualified to be a mother, he also says that she's horrible at cleaning and that she doesn't look after the children. What's unexpected is the scene where the woman says that the children would be better off with their father. It's uncommon to see a mother character who does not want her children in a film. Usually, the mother would go through all kinds of hardships to keep her children, while making the audiences cry with a life full of sacrifices. At the time when the film was released, some feminists criticized how passive Wanda is, but this scene in particular shows that not all passiveness is the same. Instead of accepting everything she's told to do, Wanda understands very well what she's not good at and what she doesn't like, and she responds accordingly. She's passive because the divorce

3
Michel Ciment (1970)
"Entretien avec
Barbara Loden
(Interview with Barbara
Loden)", published in
Positif (1975.4), n°1

4
Nathalie Léger (2012)
Supplément à la vie
de Barbara Loden
(*Suite for Barbara
Loden*), Paris: P.O.L
quoting *The Sunday
News* (1960.3.27)

을 걸어가는 옅은 색 옷을 입은 완다는 지나치게 순수해 보인다. 조금 더 투명하다면 그 까만 세상에서 사라져 버릴 존재처럼.

1975년 '포지티프' 잡지와의 인터뷰에서 로든은 만약 자신이 애정 없는 핏줄을 떠나지 않고 탄광촌에 머물렀다면 멀론의 삶을 살았을 거라 말했다. 17세에 결혼을 하고, 몇 명의 자녀가 있었을 것이고, 울월스에 취직해 매주 주말 술을 마시는 게 낙인 삶을 살았을 것이라고.[3]

실제로 알마 멀론은 14세에 결혼했고 곧 남편에게 이혼당했다. 사유는 그녀가 황폐하다는 것. 법정에서 남편은 이혼을 요구하며 말했다고 한다. "재판장님, 그녀는 그곳에 있었지만, 그녀는 거기에 없었어요."[4]

〈완다〉는 도입부에서 주인공이 완전히 별종임을 선언하는 듯하다. 이혼 재판에서 남편은 완다가 항상 소파에 멍하니 널부러져 있다고 화를 낸다. 그녀가 얼마나 청소를 못하는지, 아이들을 돌보지 않는지, 아내로서 엄마로서 자격이 없음을 나열한다. 반전은 아이들은 아버지와 함께 사는 게 나을 거라고, 여자가 말하는 장면이다. 영화에서 아이를 원치 않는 엄마 캐릭터는 흔치 않다. 관습적인 영화였다면 어머니는 아이를 지키기 위해 온갖 고난을 극복하고 희생하는 삶으로 눈물을 자아냈을 것이다. 영화가 개봉했을 당시 일부 페미니스트들이 완다 캐릭터의 수동성을 비난했는데, 이 장면은 그런 수동성에도 결이 있음을 보여 준다. 타인이 시키는 대로 모든 것을 받아들이는 것이 아니라 완다는 자신이 무엇을 못하는지, 좋아하지 않는지 분명히 알

isn't up to her decision, but through her actions, we can see that she's not the woman with the personality her husband and family want.

From the beginning of the movie, Wanda continuously gets rejected. She gets kicked out by her family for being an unqualified mother, and the sewing factory doesn't want to keep her because she's too slow. Even the man she meets at a bar tries to abandon her after spending a single night together. Oftentimes, Wanda stares at the other person, but it's hard to read her. Even when male characters insult her violently, she doesn't run away and remains helpless. Her unconfident voice and slow and weak movements make her seem like she's passive, but actually, she's rejecting and resisting the preexisting social order with her actions. Her husband complains about how she doesn't clean or take care of the children. From the start, it's possible to see that by not playing the role of women the society wants, she is resisting. This is why the divorce court scene can be seen as her declaration and refusal to be tamed by the society. This is the moment she refuses to be a good mother, a sincere worker, and a subject of sexual sacrifices, and decides to break away from the system. Instead of becoming a "normal" person tamed by the social system, she chooses to go out onto the streets where she's unprotected.

Unconventional anti-heroine and ending

In the 1960s to the 1970s, it was nearly impossible for a woman character like Wanda to become a protagonist of a film. Wanda is someone who does not belong to any of the categories in what defines protagonists in films.

고 그대로 반응한다. 이혼이 자신의 결정이 아니라는 점에서 수동적이지만, 그녀는 행동으로 남편과 그 가족이 원하는 성격의 여성이 아니라는 것을 보여 준다.

영화 초반부터 그녀는 계속 거절을 당한다. 가족으로부터 자격이 없다고 쫓겨나고, 봉제공장은 느리다고 그녀를 써 주지 않는다. 바에서 만난 남자도 한 번의 잠자리 후 그녀를 버리고 떠나려 한다. 그녀는 대부분 속을 알 수 없을 정도로 상대방을 빤히 쳐다보고, 남성 캐릭터의 폭력과 모욕적 언사 앞에서도 도망치지 않고 속수무책이다. 자신 없는 목소리, 느린 움직임, 기운이 없는 몸짓은 완다의 수동성을 보여 주는 듯하지만 그녀의 행동에는 오히려 기존 질서에 대한 '거부'와 '저항'이 있다. 청소도 아이도 제대로 돌보지 않았다는 남편의 불평은 완다가 애초부터 사회가 원하는 여성의 역할을 수행하지 않는 방식으로 저항했음을 나타낸다. 그렇기에 이혼 법정 장면은 완다가 사회에 길들여지기를 거부하는 선언으로 볼 수도 있다. 훌륭한 어머니도, 성실한 노동자도, 예속된 성적 희생물로의 역할도 마다하고 시스템으로부터 벗어나기를 결정한 순간이기 때문이다. 그녀는 시스템 속에서 길들여져서 '정상인'으로 살기보다 차라리 사회가 보호해 주지 않는 거리로 나서기를 선택한다.

관습을 벗어난 반영웅적 캐릭터와 결말

1960-70년대에 완다와 같은 캐릭터가 영화의 주인공으로 등

She's anti-heroic, and she doesn't give the audience any fantasies, courage, or lessons. She makes weaknesses and passivity hidden inside us to surface, making her a dystopian character we want to turn away from. We can't relate or feel sorry for Wanda who looks like she's dead although she's alive.

Wanda's partner Norman Dennis is also far from a typical gangster. He's just a cowardly petty thief who believes he can rob banks without a detailed plan. Perhaps the biggest challenge this film took was to tell a story with anti-heroic characters. From beginning to end, *Wanda* grasps the audience's hearts and tries to make them understand that there are such people in this world through the characters unprecedented in film history. Through them, the film is able to make people aware of a new type of people who are undefined by society and aren't normally seen.

In terms of narrative composition, this film is far from conventional as well. It does not present any hope or alternatives at the end. It is difficult to say that there is an ending at all. *Wanda* ends with Wanda disappearing through the crowd. Unlike

← *Wanda*
〈완다〉

Foundation For
Filmmakers
Copyright ©1970

장한다는 것은 사실상 불가능했다. 완다는 영화에서 주인공이라고 부를 법한 부류 어디에도 속하지 않는 인물이다. 영웅적 캐릭터와는 반대로 완다는 관객에게 환상도, 용기도, 교훈도 주지 않는다. 인간 내면에 자리하고 있지만 숨어 있는 연약함과 사회화된 수동성이 어떤 표피도 없이 드러나 오히려 외면하고 싶은 반이상향의 인물이다. 살아 있지만 마치 죽은 상태처럼 보이는 완다의 모습은 아무 공감도 연민도 불러일으키지 못한다.

완다의 파트너 드니스 또한 전형적인 갱과는 거리가 멀다. 치밀함이 없어도 은행을 털 수 있다고 믿는 겁 많은 좀도둑일 뿐이다. 어쩌면 이 영화의 가장 큰 도전은 반영웅적인 인물들로 이야기를 풀어 나가는 것이리라. 영화 역사에 있어 본 적이 없는 듯한 주인공을 통해 영화가 끝나는 순간까지 관객의 마음을 붙잡고 세상에 이런 종류의 사람도 있다는 것을 보여 주고 이해시키는 것, 그로써 우리의 시야에 보이지 않고 사회적으로 규정할 수 없는 새로운 종류의 타인을 인지하게 하는 것이다.

내러티브 구성 면에서도 이 영화는 관습을 멀찍이 벗어난다. 결말에 어떤 희망도, 대안도 제시하지 않는다. 결말이 있다고 말하기도 어렵다. 영화는 그녀를 군중 속에 넣고 끝이 난다. 다른 영화의 주인공들처럼 영화의 의미를 강화해 주고, 희망찬 미래를 암시하며 새로운 출발을 만들어 주는 것이 아니라 마치 관객이 영화가 시작하기 전에 외면했던 그녀의 존재를 영화가 진행되는 동안 잠시 보여 줬다 다시 눈에 띄지 않게 군중 속으로 사라지게 한다. 원래 세상은 그랬고, 원래 그녀는 그랬던 것마냥, 길에서 우연히 눈을 마주치고 사라져 버린 사람처럼.

other films that emphasize the meaning of the film or hint a hopeful future through a new beginning. It's just like how the audience neglected her existence prior to the film, until they were exposed to the character during the running time, and before she disappears again at the end. The world has always been this way and Wanda was always like that. She becomes just another person we might meet eyes with by chance on the streets before they disappear again.

Interestingly, this unique ending is the scene that makes people the most emotional. When we watch Wanda sitting on a bench and quietly eating her dry sandwich squashed between strangers sharing drinks and conversations, the feeling of overwhelming solitude hits us like waves. Like the French author Marguerite Duras said, this scene may be the point where Barbara Loden found a way to create holiness. After getting a taste of what corruption feels like within a violent society that doesn't protect her, she's facing the glory of being put back into the crowds. Even after the film ends, the scene lives on inside the hearts of the audience. Wanda's anxiety seeps out from the screen to the audience, and our emotions continue to thrash even after the film is finished. This is because Wanda, who wants to escape from her hateful existence and live freely, has no means of escaping this societal prison.

In court, Alma Malone said she's happy everything is over while heading to jail. What happened in reality seems to have a more cinematic ending than the movie. Loden must have imagined what life outside of the system would be like where one must beg for the basic human rights while barely hanging onto each day on the streets.

이 독특한 결말은 묘하게도 영화에서 가장 강력한 감정을 불러 일으키는 장면이다. 좁은 의자에 사람들과 붙어 앉아 타인의 술 병과 대화가 오고 가는 와중에 묵묵히 마른 샌드위치를 씹는 완 다를 지켜보자면 압도적 고독이 해일처럼 덮쳐 온다. 프랑스 작 가 마르그리트 뒤라스의 말처럼 이 장면은 바바라 로든이 거룩 함을 만드는 방법을 찾은 지점일 것이다. 인간의 기본적인 삶이 보장되지 않고 보살핌을 받을 수 없는 폭력적인 사회에서 일종 의 타락을 맛본 한 여인이 다시 사람들 속에서 마주하는 영광. 그래서일까, 영화가 끝이 나도 관객의 마음속에서는 영화는 지 속된다. 완다의 응축된 불안감이 스크린 너머로 전이되어 영화 가 끝나도 요동치는 마음은 쉽게 가라앉지 않는다. 추악한 실존 에서 벗어나 자유롭게 살고 싶은 완다에게는 이 바닥을 빠져나 갈 도구가 없기 때문이다.

알마 멀론이 감옥에 가면서 "모든 것이 끝나 기쁘다"고 한 현실 법정의 마지막 발언이 오히려 더 영화적인 결말로 보인다. 로든 은 길거리에서 하루하루 겨우 살아 나가며 의식주라는 인간의 기본 삶의 조건과 권리를 구걸해야 하는 시스템 밖의 삶이 무엇 인지 상상했을 것이다. 자유를 속박하더라도 최하위 수준의 보 호 체계를 가진 감옥이라는 사회 속으로 들어가고 싶던, 위험하 고 불안하게 살기보다 안전한 수형자로 사는 게 낫다고 생각한 멀론의 심정을 이해했을 것이다. 그렇기에 로든은 엔딩에서 시 스템 속은 아니지만 사람들 속으로 일말의 희망을 전하며 여전 히 지속되는 통제할 수 없는 삶 속으로 그녀를 놓아 버린다.

Even if she had to give up her freedom, Malone wanted to go to jail, a society where she'd get the lowest level of protection. Loden must have understood Malone who wanted to live as a prisoner in safety rather than living in danger and anxiety. This is why Loden puts Wanda in a crowd at the end. Although Wanda is not placed within a system, but she's free to continue living a life that's uncontrolled, giving the audience a tinge of hope.

"I would not call it a love story; it's more a story about 'lumpen,' the poor drifters-of the world who simply exist, leading to tally pointless lives."[5]

Wanda is a film about the subject that exists in the world but is regarded as non-existent. Since it's based on a true story, Loden could've made a crime film to strengthen its story by using the elements of a genre film. However, she focused on putting weight on telling the story of women just like her. Through a woman who cannot fulfil the qualities demanded by society, who is regarded as invaluable, who doesn't know what she's capable of, and who has nothing but her body, a human being who is being put outside by the society's system.

After being nameless for a long time, Barbara Loden first received public recognition for her performance as a sexy blonde character. But the fact that she was neglected once again through Wanda, a woman the society does not want, she clearly proves the position of women in society. In the film, Loden unfolds the society's expectations and betrayals towards women she experienced during her acting career. Dennis throws away the pants and the lipstick Wanda bought on the streets. He tells her to wear pretty skirts instead of the pants, and yells at her to wear high heels. The film speaks of

5
A. H. Weiler
(1970.8.16), "Polansk
Tynan And 'Macbeth'",
The New York Times,
p.89

"나는 로맨틱 영화를 만든 게 아니라, 어떤 삶의 방향
도 없이 그저 존재하기만 한 여성을 그린 거예요."[5]

〈완다〉는 세상에 존재하지만 존재하지 않는 것으로 치부되는
대상에 관한 영화다. 실화를 바탕으로 했기에 범죄 영화로서의
장르적 재미와 구조를 더 강화할 수도 있었겠지만 로든은 완다
를 통해 자신과 같은 여성들의 이야기를 하는 데 무게중심을 두
었다. 사회에서 요구하는 여성의 자질을 갖추지 못한 여자, 여
성으로서 가치가 없다고 치부되는 여자, 자신이 무엇을 할 수
있는지 모르는 여자, 가진 것이라고는 몸밖에 없는 여자를 통해
영화는 한 사회 시스템으로부터 내쳐지는 인간을 그린다.

바바라 로든이 오랜 무명 끝에 금발의 섹시스타 캐릭터를
연기하며 처음 사회에서 인정을 받았지만, 사회가 요구하지 않
는 여성상인 완다를 통해 다시 외면당했다는 사실은 너무도 자
명하게 사회 속 여성의 위치를 증명한다. 로든은 자신의 배우
생활 동안 여성에 대한 사회의 기대와 배신을 느꼈던 경험을 영
화 속에서 풀어놓는다. 드니스는 완다가 사 온 바지와 립스틱
을 길바닥에 버린다. 그는 바지를 입지 말라고, 어여쁜 치마를
입으라고, 하이힐을 신으라고 소리친다. 여성이라는 존재가 사
회가 규정한 틀 속에서만 인정받고 증명되는 구조를 영화는 말
한다.

로든은 스스로를 남부 출신 가난한 촌뜨기였다고 말하곤 했는
데, 토니상 이후 인지도가 생겼을 때에도 사람들의 기대에 맞춰
금발 가발을 쓰는 등 사랑받기 위해 애썼다. 어린 시절 학교에

the societal structure in which women can only be recognized within the framework defined by society.

Loden often said that she's from the Southern countryside, but once she gained recognition after her Tony Award, she struggled to remain popular and meet people's expectations by wearing a blonde wig. Ever since she was a child, she was a lonely girl who never received any attention at school. Whenever she returned home, she hid behind the stove and took the time to contemplate about her being. Her religious maternal grandmother is seen through the elderly character in the beginning of *Wanda*, who only holds onto her rosary even when a baby begs her to play. As soon as she became an adult, Loden moved to New York hoping to find a better life, but there wasn't much she could do. She modeled for a minor magazine and she found a simple job to glue envelopes at an office. When she received a letter from her superior suggesting he would pay her to be his girlfriend, she declined but also lost her job. She was rarely selected to appear on television shows, and even then, she'd be asked to switch to a supporting role where she'd get hit by a pie on her face because her face has no character. The more she tried to stand on her feet, the more the society tried to make deals with her. And when she didn't accept, she'd be kicked out. In order to relieve her depression, she took acting classes at Actors Studio with a friend whom she worked with at Copacabana Club. This method acting workshop run by Paul Mann had the participants read newspapers and books, and they were told to study their own backgrounds. Through this process, the students were encouraged to understand how their history shaped them. Loden says she didn't mean to become an actress from the beginning. But the

서 한 번도 주목받은 적 없는 외로운 아이였고 집에 오면 주방 오븐 뒤에 숨어서 자신이 누구인지 고민하며 시간을 보냈다고 술회하기도 했다. 애정 표현이 별로 없던 독실한 신자인 외조모는 〈완다〉 도입부에 아기가 놀아 달라고 애원해도 묵주만 손에 들고 있는 노인 캐릭터로 투영된다. 더 나은 삶을 꿈꾸며 성인이 되자마자 뉴욕에 왔지만 할 수 있는 일은 많지 않았다. 이류 잡지의 모델을 하거나 사무실에서 편지봉투붙이기 등 단순 업무를 구했는데 애인이 되면 돈을 주겠다는 상사의 편지를 받고 거절하면 일이 없어지곤 했다. TV쇼에 겨우 발탁이 됐다가도 특색이 없다며 얼굴에 파이를 맞는 보조역으로 바뀌기도 했다. 삶에 발을 붙이고 뭔가 하려고 할수록 사회는 거래를 제안했다. 조건을 받아들이지 않으면 쫓겨날 거라고. 그녀는 우울한 기분을 떨치기 위해 코파카바나 클럽에서 함께 일하던 친구를 따라 '액터스 스튜디오'에서 연기 수업을 듣는다. 폴 만이 주도한 메소드 워크숍은 참가자들에게 신문이나 책을 읽게 했고 자신의 배경을 탐구하게 했다. 그 과정에서 지난 역사가 어떻게 자신을 형성했는지 이해하도록 부추겼다. 로든은 처음부터 배우가 되기 위한 목적은 아니었다고 한다. 하지만 결과적으로 연기 수업은 로든에게 집단상담 같은 경험을 통해 배우가 되는 훈련을 선사했다. 이후 심리치료도 받았는데 일련의 과정에서 평생 자신이 피해자와 고아의 역할이었다는 걸 깨달았다.

> "나는 항상 침묵했어요. 이제 내게 뭐가 남았냐고? 내 모든 것이 사람들에게 들려야 합니다. 그래서 〈완다〉를 만들었어요. 내 존재를 확인하는 방법으로."[6]

acting classes acted like group counseling sessions for Loden, and it gave her training to become an actress. She received psychological therapy later on, and through a series of sessions, she realized that she only played victims or orphans throughout her life.

"Before I never said a word, I was always silent. And now, what's left for me to do? He told me you've got to be heard. Everything you do must be heard. That's why I made Wanda. As a way of confirming my own existence."[6]

Her husband, Elia Kazan, complains in his autobiography that the award *Wanda* received from the Venice International Film Festival Film Festival changed his wife. He said that he became uninterested in Loden's duty as a wife who no longer relied on her appearance and said, "I realized I was losing her. But I was also losing interest in her struggle."[7]

Kazan asked Nicholas T. Proferes, "Can you work with a woman?" while suggesting Proferes to film *Wanda* as a cinematographer. He didn't ask Proferes' consent to work on a low-budget film, or sugarcoat the film as an independent film in the New American Cinema movement. That one question alone shows how difficult it was for a female filmmaker to make a film in the industry at the time, and especially why it took Loden 11 years to make and show *Wanda* to the world.

After writing the screenplay, Loden asked many directors to direct the film, but they all declined. Their clear reasons weren't made public, but Kazan suggested her to direct it herself because of the situation. When the French New Wave came over to the US, Loden was interested in their films. Among them, she saw Jean-Luc

6
Nathalie Léger (2012) *Supplément à la vie de Barbara Loden* (*Suite for Barbara Loden*), Paris: P.O.L – quoting *FILM Magazine* (1971)

7
Reynaud, Bérénice (2004). "For Wanda." In Thomas Elsaesser, Alexander Horwath and Noel King, eds. *The Last Great American Picture Show. New Hollywood Cinema in the 1970s*. Amsterda University Press, p.223–248.

남편 엘리아 카잔은 〈완다〉의 베니스국제영화제 수상이 아내 로든을 변화시켰다고 자서전에 불평한다. 로든이 자신의 취향이 아닌 사람으로 변했다고. "더 이상 자신의 외모에 의존하지 않는 로든은 아내의 의무에 무관심하게 되었어요. 나는 그녀를 잃고 있다는 걸 깨달았지만 나 역시 그녀의 투쟁에 대해 관심을 잃어가고 있었습니다."[7]

"여자랑 일을 할 수 있겠나?" 엘리아 카잔이 촬영감독 니콜라스 프로페레스에게 〈완다〉의 촬영을 제의하며 건넨 말이었다. 저예산 영화에 참여할 수 있겠냐는 양해나 뉴아메리칸시네마의 정신을 이어 가는 독립영화라는 명분의 치장도 아니었다. 촬영감독 섭외를 위한 이 한 문장에서 당시 영화산업에서 여성감독이 영화를 만들기가 얼마나 어려웠을지, 특히 로든의 〈완다〉가 세상에 나오기까지 11년이나 걸린 이유를 유추해 볼 수 있다.

로든은 시나리오를 쓴 후 연출자를 고용하기 위해 많은 이에게 제의를 넣었지만 모두 거절했다. 명확한 사유가 공개된 적은 없지만, 이런 상황에서 카잔은 로든에게 직접 연출할 것을 권했다. 로든은 프랑스 누벨바그 열풍이 미국에 전달될 때 관심있게 작품들을 보았고, 그중에서 장뤼크 고다르의 〈네 멋대로 해라〉(1960)와 이른바 뉴아메리칸시네마의 발현 당시 현장에서 존 카사베츠, 앤디 워홀 등의 작품을 본 후 시스템 밖의 실험적인 서사와 촬영 방식이라면 스스로 연출을 해 볼 수 있겠다는 자신감을 갖게 됐다. 지인인 해리 슈스터가 투자한 십만 달러에 자비를 보태 예산이 마련되자 그녀는 최소의 스태프를 구성했다.

Godard's *À bout de souffle* (*Breathless*, 1960)
and she was also able to witness the works
of John Cassavetes and Andy Warhol at the
scene of the New American Cinema movement.
After watching such works, she became
confident she'd be able to direct if she breaks
away of the preexisting system and go with an
experimental narrative and shooting methods.
Harry Schuster who is an acquaintance of hers
invested 100,000 dollars in the project,
and she was able to put together the minimum
number of staff.

Proferes, who joined the project as the cinematographer and the editor, was a co-director of
Free at Last (1968), the winner of The Gold Lion
for Best Television Documentary at the 1969
Venice International Film Festival. The film, which
documented Martin Luther King's "Poor People's
Campaign" was shot in a *cinéma vérité style*
for PBS (Public Broadcasting Service). Proferes
played a part in creating the vividness in *Wanda*.
They were able to book an operating sewing
factor, and they shot during work hours with the
cooperation of the factory workers. They used real
places for the scenes where Wanda borrows
money fom the elderly who collects coal, where
she buys ice cream from an outdoor kiosk, where
she passes through an alley leading to a theater
where a Spanish film is showing, and where she
looks at clothes at a shopping mall. Whenever
they were shooting outside, they used natural light
and followed Wanda with a handheld camera.

But not all of these filming techniques came
from Proferes' experience. Ever since she was
young, Loden hated the perfect world created
in classic Hollywood films. She felt insignificant
because of them, and that world didn't feel
realistic. This attitude of hers was reflected in

촬영감독 겸 편집자로 합류한 프로페레스는 1969년 베니스국제영화제에서 최우수다큐멘터리상을 받은 〈마침내 자유〉(1968)의 공동 감독이었다. PBS(Public Broadcasting Service, 미국공영방송)의 지원으로 제작된 마틴 루터 킹의 '빈민 운동 캠페인'을 기록한 이 영화는 시네마베리테 형식으로 촬영됐다. 〈완다〉가 극영화임에도 다큐멘터리와 같은 생동감을 더한 데에는 프로페레스의 다큐멘터리 경력이 일조했다. 실제 운영 중인 봉제공장을 섭외했고, 공장 노동자들이 협조해 일하는 중간에 들어가 촬영했다. 완다가 석탄 줍는 노인에게 돈을 빌릴 때, 야외 매점에서 아이스크림을 살 때, 스페인 영화가 상영되는 극장으로 들어가는 골목을 지나칠 때, 쇼핑몰에서 옷을 구경할 때도 모두 실제 장소를 이용했고, 실외장면은 자연광 아래 핸드헬드로 완다를 따라가는 방식을 취했다.

이런 촬영 형식이 전적으로 프로페레스의 경력에서 온 것은 아니다. 로든은 어린 시절부터 클래식 할리우드 영화의 완벽한 세상을 싫어했다. 자신이 너무 하찮게 보이고 그 세계가 사실적으로 보이지 않기 때문이었는데 이러한 그녀의 태도는 〈완다〉의 연출 스타일에 반영되었다. 특히 할리우드 영화의 말끔한 사운드보다 앤디 워홀 영화처럼 나쁜 음질의 불완전성이 더 자연스럽다고 믿었다. 따라서 시네마베리테 스타일은 스크린 위의 균질화되고 완벽한 세계가 아닌 자신이 경험하고 바라보던 세상을 최대한 사실적으로 생동감 있게 구현하기 위해 찾은 방식이었다. 좁은 차 안에서 완다가 신문 기사를 읽는 것만으로도 긴장감을 고조시키는 장면은 달리는 차 안에서 핸드헬드로 클로즈업을 했는데 16mm 카메라가 아니었다면 불가능했다.

the way she directed *Wanda*. Instead of the clean sound you get in Hollywood films, she felt that the imperfect sounds you can find in films like Andy Warhol's felt more realistic. That is why she chose the cinéma vérité style which isn't homogenous or perfect. She had found a way to materialize the world she experienced and saw in the most realistic and vivid way. The scene where Wanda reads a newspaper article in a narrow car wouldn't have been so full of tension if they didn't use a 16mm camera to get a handheld close-up shot in a running car. Except for Michael Higgins, none of the cast were professionals, and at the time, both Loden and Higgins weren't seen as star performers either. The 16mm camera which was chosen for budget reasons was lightweight, so it was the best device to respond to and follow the protagonist's movements with. The rough film texture was also able to realistically convey the anxiousness of the protagonists who wandered the barren streets of a coal mining village in a stolen car.

"It is easy to be avant-garde but it is really difficult to tell a simple story well."[8]

After Loden's death, Kazan claimed that he had written the draft of *Wanda*'s screenplay. However, Kazan's films were made closer to the Hollywood style, and his overly gorgeous female characters are in contrast to *Wanda*. Without anyone having to recall this claim, in a 2003 conversation between Marguerite Duras and Kazan published in *Cahiers du Cinéma*, Kazan waters down his initial statement which we have no way of confirming. He mentions that Loden revised the screenplay countless times to a point it was nothing like the original draft, and that she made too many minor changes to the lines and the settings on site. Even if one

8
Nathalie Léger (201.
*Supplément à la
vie de Barbara Lode.
(Suite for Barbara
Loden)*, Paris: P.O.L

배우들도 마이클 히긴스를 제외하면 모두 비전문 배우였고, 당시 로든과 히긴스도 스타 반열의 배우는 아니었다. 예산 절약을 위해 선택한 16mm 카메라는 경량이었기에 주인공의 움직임에 반응하며 따라다니기에 최적의 기기였고 거친 화면 질감 역시 영화의 배경인 광산 지역의 척박함과 훔친 차로 길 위를 떠도는 주인공들의 불안함을 더 사실감 있게 전달했다.

> "아방가르드가 되는 건 쉬워요. 그렇지만 단순한 이야기를 잘 이야기하는 건 어려운 일이에요."[8]

로든이 사망한 후, 카잔은 〈완다〉의 시나리오 초고를 자신이 썼다고 주장했다. 카잔의 영화는 할리우드 고전의 형식을 취하고 있고 그가 그린 과도하게 화려한 여성 캐릭터들은 〈완다〉와 대척점에 있다. 그 사실을 상기하지 않더라도 2003년 '카이에뒤 시네마'에 실린 마르그리트 뒤라스와 카잔의 대담에 따르면 확인할 길이 없는 이 주장을 스스로 희석시키는 듯한 언급이 나온다. 로든이 시나리오를 수없이 고쳐 초고를 못 알아볼 정도였다는 것과 심지어 현장에서 즉흥적으로 대사나 세팅 등 사소한 것을 너무 많이 변경했다는 것이다. 설사 카잔의 주장을 믿는다 하더라도 초고 시나리오가 영화의 결과를 보증할 수 없을뿐더러 연출의 재능은 영화 전체의 분위기와 리듬을 총괄하는 것으로 이야기의 구조, 연기의 균형, 사소한 물건 하나까지 아우르며 지휘를 하는 것이다. 카잔은 이 영화에서 유일하게 로든의 재능으로 볼 수 있는 것은 연기임을 한정 지어 인정한다. 이때 마르그리트 뒤라스가 카잔에게 말한다. "〈완다〉는 '어떤 사람'

believes Kazan's claims to be true, a draft screenplay cannot determine the result of a film. In addition, the director's abilities determine how the overall mood and rhythm of the film will be led, while overseeing the composition of the story, the balance of the performances, and even the smallest props. But Kazan says that the only area he can see Loden's talent in this film is her acting. This is when Duras says this to Kazan. "*Wanda* is a movie about 'someone'. Have you ever directed a film about someone?"[9]

Duras questions Kazan if he has ever made a film about a person who was isolated and separated from society, someone who observes oneself, and someone who fails to overcome life when trying to avoid the society's system. She paid attention to the fact that there is an instant and permanent continuity between Loden and Wanda, and that Loden looks more like herself in the film. What Duras said "I think that there is a miracle in *Wanda*. Usually there is a distance between the visual representation and the text, as well as the subject and the action. Here this distance is completely nullified; there is an instant and permanent continuity between Barbara Loden and Wanda."

"I tried to be independent and to create my own way, otherwise, I would have become like Wanda, all my life just floating around."[10]

The experience of completing *Wanda* motivated Loden to live independently. She felt that she could be stronger, self-dependent, and go out into the world alone. There weren't many opportunities for *Wanda* to be shown in theaters, but there were several screening opportunities at various universities, and she had conversations with the audience after her screenings. Loden

9
Cahiers du Cinéma
(2003.7-8),
Conversation excerpt
selected by Serge
Daney, Jean Narboni
and Dominique Villair
Cahiers du Cinéma,
December 1980

10
Kate Taylor (2010.8.
"Driven by Fierce Visi
of Independence",
The New York Times

에 대한 영화입니다. 카잔, 당신은 어떤 사람에 대한 영화를 만들어 본 적이 있나요?"[9]

뒤라스는 사회에서 고립되고 분리된 사람, 스스로를 관찰하게 되는 사람, 사회 시스템이 손에 닿지 않고 삶을 극복하고 헤쳐 나갈 수 없는 존재에 대한 영화를 카잔이 만들어 본 적이 있는지 묻는다. 로든과 완다 사이에는 즉각적이고 영구적인 연속성이 존재하고 로든이 영화에서 실제 삶보다 더 자신처럼 보인다는 것에 주목했다. "일반적으로 시각적 재연과 텍스트, 즉 주체(캐릭터)와 연기 사이에는 간격이 있습니다. 이 영화에서는 그 간격이 무효화됩니다. 로든과 완다 사이에는 영구적인 연속성이 있습니다. 그 지점이 이 영화의 온전한 기적입니다."

> "나는 독립적인 인간이 되기 위해, 나만의 길을 만들기 위해 노력했습니다. 그렇지 않았다면 내 인생은 완다처럼 그저 떠다니는 인생이 되었을 겁니다."[10]

〈완다〉를 완성한 경험은 로든에게 주체적 삶을 위한 동기를 부여했다. 스스로 더 강하고 자립할 수 있으며 홀로 세상에 나아갈 수 있다고 느꼈다. 〈완다〉가 극장에 걸릴 기회는 많지 않으나 여러 대학에서 상영 기회가 있었고, 상영 후 관객과 대화를 나누곤 했다. 로든은 이런 경험을 자랑스러워했고, 가치 있는 일로 여겨 뿌듯해했다. 그즈음 카잔과의 이혼을 결정하며 진정한 홀로서기를 준비하고 있었다.

was proud of such experiences and found it worthwhile. Around that time, she decided to divorce Kazan and prepared to stand on his own.

It is said that the process of preparing for her next project was not easy. She completed the screenplay for the adaptation of *Lulu*, a tragic story about a woman's affection by German playwright, Benjamin Franklin Wedekind. She also finished a screenplay about a star actor called *A Movie Star of My Own*, but she couldn't find any investors. In addition, *Love Means Always Having to Say You're Sorry* was announced to soon be made by Loden, Proferes and Higgins, but it never came to fruition. The last film she was working on was a feature film based on American novelist Kate Chopin's *The Awakening* (1899). This novel describes the process of an American woman from the south in the late 19th century who becomes self-aware and struggles to find her identity. It was criticized because it showed a woman's sexual desires and a longing to deviate which were taboo at the time. The novel was controversial enough to almost be banned from publication, but 60 years after Chopin's death, the author was seen as a pioneer of feminist novels in the US. But even this project came to a halt when Loden was diagnosed with breast cancer.

Appear and disappear

When *Wanda* was released in the 1970s, this film was considered uncomfortable. The woman in it wasn't the kind of woman the society wanted to see, nor was it a genre film that gave viewers catharsis. Even some feminist groups who needed to build a progressive image of women for their movement unwelcomed the film. The general audience ignored the film that

차기작을 준비하는 과정은 결코 쉽지 않았던 것으로 전해진다. 독일의 희곡 작가 프랑크 베데킨트의 원작을 토대로, 한 여성의 비극적인 애정 행각을 그린 오페라 '룰루'를 영화화하기 위해 시나리오를 완성했고, 스타 영화배우에 대한 〈나만의 영화배우〉라는 시나리오를 썼으나 역시 투자 받지못했다. 그 외 〈사랑은 항상 당신이 미안하다고 말해야 함을 의미한다〉 역시 로든, 프로페레스, 히긴스의 조합으로 제작될 것이라고 발표됐지만 결실을 맺지 못했다. 마지막으로 준비하던 영화는 미국 소설가 케이트 쇼팽의 장편 『각성』(1899)이다. 19세기 후반 미국 남부 여성이 자아에 눈뜨며 독립된 존재로서 자신의 정체성을 찾기 위해 고군분투하는 과정을 담은 이 소설은 당시 금기시되던 여성의 성적 욕망과 일탈을 그려 비난을 받았다. 책은 출판이 금지될 정도로 논란을 일으켰지만 쇼팽 사후 60년이 지나 작가는 미국 페미니즘 소설의 선구자로 평가되며 재조명된 바 있다. 이마저 로든이 유방암 판정을 받자 작업은 중단되었다.

나타남과 사라짐을 반복하는 영화

〈완다〉가 나왔던 1970년대 이 영화는 '불편한' 영화였다. 사회가 보고 싶던 여성도 아니었고, 카타르시스를 선사하는 장르영화도 아니었다. 당시 여성운동의 흐름 속에서 진취적인 여성의 이미지가 필요했던 일부 페미니스트 그룹에게 환영받지도 못했다. 일반관객들에게도 내면의 뭔가를 건드리는 외면하고 싶은 영화였다. 소수 비평가와 팬에 의해 세상에 그 존재를 내보

made them feel something inside. Thanks to just a number of critics and fans, this film was able to show itself to the world, but just like Wanda's character, the film disappeared.

It was two female artists who took the initiative to bring *Wanda* back to life. With Marguerite Duras' help, French actor Isabelle Huppert was able to watch *Wanda*, and she pushed ahead to get the film restored digitally. With the support from Martin Scorsese's The Film Foundation and the fashion brand Gucci, UCLA Film & Television Archive's restoration team was able to restore the film. In 2010, *Wanda* had a special screening at the Venice International Film Festival where it first screened in 1970. Huppert made many plans to have *Wanda* screen at various cinematheque screenings and theaters, and even released the DVD in France.

"Wanda is not some romanticised positive role model, but a real person. As a character I find her very moving. I feel as if I identify with Wanda, in that she's both fragile and strong at the same time; she may be alone, but deep down there is a real resistance in her. I find that very touching. I can't imagine such a film ever having been made by a man. But Loden did make it, and she did everything." (Isabelle Huppert, speaking to Geoff Andrew)[11]

Wanda is based on a real event, but because it comes to a different conclusion, because it was dramatized, and because it includes autobiographical content, its genre is vague and unclear. Nevertheless, Loden created a very natural and realistic film style and was able to skillfully create tension that immerses the audiences in the film. In addition, *Wanda* does not take the easy way out and become a victim

11
Isabel Stevens, Bryony
Dixon and othrs
(2020.10.2), The fema
gaze: 100 overlooked
films directed by
women, *Sight & Sour*

이는 기회가 있었지만 마치 영화 속 완다의 운명처럼 이 영화는 영화 역사의 수면 아래로 가라앉았다.

〈완다〉를 다시 세상에 떠오르게 하는데 불을 지핀 이는 두 명의 여성예술가였다. 프랑스 배우 이자벨 위페르는 마르그리트 뒤라스의 도움으로 〈완다〉를 접한 후 영화의 디지털 복원을 추진한다. 마틴스콜세지영화재단과 패션 브랜드 구찌의 지원으로 UCLA영화텔레비전보관소에서 성사시킨 디지털 판본은 1970년 〈완다〉가 처음 공개되었던 베니스국제영화제에서 2010년 특별상영 되었다. 위페르는 시네마테크와 여러 극장에서 〈완다〉를 상영하는 기획을 마련했고, 프랑스에서 DVD를 출시하기도 했다.

"완다는 낭만적이고 긍정적인 역할 모델은 아니지만 실재하는 사람입니다. 나는 그녀의 캐릭터가 매우 감동적이라고 생각해요. 완다가 연약하면서도 동시에 강인하다는 점에서 나는 완다와 동일시되는 기분이 듭니다. 그녀는 혼자일 수는 있지만 마음 깊은 곳에서 진정한 저항이 자리하고 있고 그 지점이 내게 매우 감동적입니다. 남자가 만든 이런 영화는 상상할 수 없습니다. 로든은 이 영화를 만들었고, 그녀가 모든 것을 다 했습니다."(이자벨 위페르, 제프 앤드류와의 대화 중)[11]

〈완다〉는 실제 사건에서 시작했지만 전혀 다른 결론에 다다르는 극화된 이야기, 자전적 내용까지 얽혀 장르가 희미하고 불명확하다. 그럼에도 매우 자연스럽고 사실적인 영화형식으로 긴

of self-pity or display a sophisticated kind of sadness to provide comfort. In particular, it conveys conceptual and universal anxiety about social alienation in a story that seems to tell something far from ordinary daily life.

Even though Wanda is a fictional character, we interestingly feel that she conveys true emotions to the audience. Female artists in particular identify with Wanda, and they feel a sense of urge in wanting to contribute in doing something for the film. This must be an act of resistance

← Wanda
⟨완다⟩

장감과 몰입도를 솜씨 좋게 이끌고 간다. 또한 〈완다〉는 자기 연민의 희생양이 되거나 세련된 슬픔을 전시하며 위안을 주는 손쉬운 방식으로 흘러가지 않는다. 특히 평범한 일상과는 어떤 측면에서도 연결지점을 찾을 수 없는 듯한 이야기에서 사회적 소외에 대한 개념적이고 보편적인 불안감을 전달한다.

신기하게도 완다는 허구적 인물임에도 관객에게 진실한 감정을 전하는 느낌을 만들어 낸다. 유독 여성예술가들이 완다를 동일시하고 이 영화를 위해 뭔가 기여하고 싶은 충동을 일으키는 것은 여성에 대한 사회적 배척과 길들이기에 대한 저항일 것이다. 바바라 로든이 알마 멀론의 기사를 통해 느꼈던 감정 역시 같은 선상에 있다.

〈완다〉는 50년이 넘은 지금도 여전히 힘을 잃지 않는 신비로운 영화다. 이 영화는 사회가 개인에게 요구하는 것들, 삶의 조건과도 같은 억압을 벗어나 독립적인 하나의 존재가 되기 위해 우리가 마주해야 하는 실존적 불안을 농밀하게 응축시켜서 전달한다. 자립적인 여성으로 살고 있다고 믿지만, 여전히 스리슬쩍 부드러운 친구처럼 다가와 스스로를 검열하게 만들고 고정된 이미지의 여성으로 살도록 억압하는 사회의 시선으로부터 자유롭지 못한 내면의 현실을 느끼게 한다. 그리하여 우리는 이 영화가 너무도 불편하지만 동시에 〈완다〉는 우리의 영혼 어딘가 잠자고 있는 저항정신을 움직이게 한다. 그것은 사회에 소리치고 싶은 목소리다. 나를 길들이려 하지 말라고.

against societal ostracization and the taming of women. What Barbara Loden felt through the article on Alma Malone was something of the same nature.

Wanda is a mysterious film that still remains strong even after 50 years. This film condenses and conveys the existential anxiety we must face in order to escape the oppression the society demands from individuals, a basic condition of life, in order to become an independent being. Women believe they're independent, but society's gaze approaches gently and friendly towards them to make them self-inspect while pressuring them to live in the predetermined image of women. The film makes us realize the reality that women aren't free from the society's gaze. This is why *Wanda* feels uncomfortable, but at the same time, it awakens our resistant spirits that have been lying dormant. And that is the voice we want to make heard to society: Don't try to tame me.

Sung Moon
Started her career at JEONJU International Film Festival in 2004. She has been active in international film festivals and documentary forums, including Busan International Film Festival, KT&G Sangsangmadang Cinema, JEONJU Project Market, and Docs Port Incheon. Since 2013, she has served as a representative of Latin American territory for the Korean Film Council. Moon has been working as a programmer for JEONJU IFF since 2019.

1   바바라 로든 인터뷰 인용, 케이트 테일러(2010.8.27), 독립에 대한 날카로운
    시선에서 출발한, '뉴욕타임즈'
2   '잡지 필름'(1971.2.21) 인터뷰 기사 인용 − 출처: 나탈리 르거(2012), 『바바
    라 로든의 삶에 대한 보충서』, 파리:P.O.L
3   '포스티프' 168호(1975.4) 인터뷰 기사 − 마이클 클리멩, 바바라 로든과의 인
    터뷰
4   '선데이뉴스'(1960.3.27) 인터뷰 기사 인용 − 출처: 나탈리 르거(2012), 『바
    바라 로든의 삶에 대한 보충서』, 파리:P.O.L
5   A.H. 웨일러(1970.8.16), 폴란스키, 타이난과 맥베스, '뉴욕타임즈', p.89
6   '잡지 필름'(1971.7) 인터뷰 기사 인용 − 출처: 나탈리 르거(2012), 『바바라
    로든의 삶에 대한 보충서』, 파리:P.O.L
7   브르니스 레이너드(2004), 완다를 위하여, 『최후의 위대한 아메리칸 픽쳐
    쇼. 1970년대 뉴할리우드시네마』, 토마스 엘세서, 알렉산더 호워스, 노엘킹
    편집, 암스테르담대학교출판, p.223−248
8   나탈리 르거(2012), 『바바라 로든의 삶에 대한 보충서』, 파리: P.O.L
9   '카이에뒤시네마'(2003.7−8), 1980년 12월 카이에뒤시네마에서 세르주 다
    네, 장 나보니, 도미니크 빌랭에 의해 인용된 대화
10 케이트 테일러(2010.8.27), 독립에 대한 날카로운 시선에서 출발한, '뉴욕타
    임즈'
11 이자벨 스티븐스, 브리오니 딕슨 외(2020.10.2), 여성의 응시: 과소평가된 여
    성감독 작품 100편, '사이트 앤 사운드'

    문성경
2004년 전주국제영화제 프로그램 팀을 시작으로 부산국제영
화제, KT&G 상상마당시네마, 전주프로젝트마켓, 인천다큐
멘터리포트 등 국제영화제 및 다큐멘터리 산업행사에서 활동
했다. 2013년부터 영화진흥위원회의 중남미 주재원을 역임
했고 2019년부터 전주국제영화제에서 프로그래머로 재직 중
이다.

Barbara (Ann) Loden

1932 + Born in Asheville, North Carolina, USA as the child of
mother Ruth Senior Loden and father George Thomas
Loden. As a child, she moves to Marion, Virginia to
her maternal grandmother's due to the divorce of her
parents. She lives with her maternal grandmother who
was a devout religious person until her late teens.

1948 + Moves to New York. She makes a living with simple jobs
such as modeling for detective or romance magazines,
being a pin-up girl, and pasting office envelopes.
At Copacabana Nightclub, she gains recognition as a
chorus girl nicknamed "Candy". She takes acting lessons
from Actors Studio located on Ninth and Tenth Avenue
in Manhattan for five years. While taking Paul Mann's
method acting classes known to make the participants
read newspapers and books to give them intellectual
stimulation, Loden takes the opportunity to understand
her background and history.

1952 + With the help of Larry Joachim who imported and
distributed Hong Kong Kung Fu movies in the US at the
time, she appears as an assistant dressed lightly in
The Ernie Kovacs Show. She becomes a stunt assistant
who rolls on the carpet or gets hit by pies.

1954 + Marries Larry Joachim in New York. Their son
Marco is born (exact year is uncertain).

1957 + Takes on the role of Myra Seligman in the theatrical play
Compulsion and debuts as an actress in New York.
+ Meets Elia Kazan who is 23 years her senior at the
rerecording scene and afterparty of the film *A Face in
the Crowd* (1957) and begins a relationship.

1960 + Plays Betty Jackson, Montgomery Clift's secretary,
in Elia Kazan's film *Wild River*.
+ The case that becomes the beginning of *Wanda* (1970)
is reported on *Sunday Daily* newspaper on March 27.
The case is about Alma Malone (alias) who was caught
while trying to rob a bank with a man after leaving home.
In the article, it said that Malone thanked the

바바라 로든 연보

1932년 + 미국 남부 노스캐롤라이나 애슈빌에서 어머니 루스
        시니어 로든과 아버지 조지 토마스 로든의 자녀로 출생.
        어린 시절 부모의 이혼으로 외조모가 있는 버지니아주
        매리언 지역으로 이사. 십 대 후반까지 독실한
        종교인이었던 외조모와 생활.

1948년 + 뉴욕으로 이주. 탐정 잡지나 로맨스 잡지의 모델, 핀업 걸,
        사무실 편지봉투붙이기 등의 단순 업무로 생계를 이어감.
        코파카바나 나이트클럽에서 '캔디'라는 애칭의 코러스
        걸로 인지도를 쌓음. 맨해튼 9-10번가에 위치한 액터스
        스튜디오에서 5년간 연기과정 수강. 참가자들에게
        신문과 특정 책을 읽게 해 지적 자극을 주는 워크숍으로
        알려진 폴 맨의 메소드 수업을 듣고 자신의 배경과 역사를
        이해하는 계기가 됨.

1952년 + 당시 미국에 홍콩 쿵후 영화를 수입, 배급하던 래리
        조어킴의 도움으로 '어니 코박스 쇼'에 가벼운 차림의
        조수로 출연. 스턴트 보조 역, 카펫을 구르거나
        파이로 얼굴을 맞는 역이 주어짐.

1954년 + 래리 조어킴과 뉴욕에서 결혼. 둘 사이의 아들 마르코가
        태어남(연도 불확실).

1957년 + 연극 '충동'에서 마이라 셸리그먼 역을 맡아 뉴욕에서
        배우로 데뷔.
      + 영화 〈군중 속의 얼굴〉(1957)의 재녹음 현장과
        파티에서 로든보다 23살이 많은 엘리아 카잔을 만나
        둘의 관계가 시작됨.

1960년 + 엘리아 카잔의 영화 〈대하를 삼키는 여인〉에서 몽고메리
        클리프트의 비서 베티 잭슨 역으로 출연.
      + 3월 27일, 〈완다〉(1970)의 시초가 된 사건이
        '선데이데일리' 신문에 보도됨. 집을 떠나 만난 남자와 은행
        강도를 시도하다 현장에서 잡힌 알마 멀론(가명)에 대한

judge for giving her a 20-year-long sentence, and Loden has a hard time understanding this woman's behavior. Because of that, Loden researches about her and even requests to visit her at the penitentiary, but gets rejected.

1961 + Performs in *Splendor in the Grass* as Warren Beatty's sister, Ginny Stamper. At a time when women were divided into just good or bad women, she takes the role of a bad woman who is rebellious and sexually free.

1962 + Despite being married to Joachim, she gets pregnant with Kazan's child. Begins writing the screenplay of *Wanda*. Loden's second son Leo is born on January 2.

1963 + When Elia Kazan's wife Molly Day Kazan passes away, Loden gets a divorce from Joachim and starts living with Kazan.

1964 + After playing the role of Maggie in the play *After the Fall*, who represents Marilyn Monroe, Loden wins the Tony Award for Best Featured Actress in a Play, the grand prize at the Theatre World Awards, and the Other Awards from the Outer Critics Circle Award.
     + Selected as the cover model for the magazine, *Saturday Evening Post*.

1966 + While on a safari vacation with Kazan and Harry Schuster, Loden receives 100,000 dollars of investment funding from Schuster to produce her film.
     + Gets recruited to play Laura in *The Glass Menagerie*, a CBS production. While promoting the film, she is published on television guide magazines and is shown through the media.

1967 + Registers her marriage to Elia Kazan on June 5. Kazan frankly exposes personal information about his relationship with Loden in his autobiographical novel called *The Arrangement*, damaging Loden's public image.

1968 + She is given a key role in *The Swimmer*, a Hollywood production, but due to a conflict with director Frank Perry, they reshoot a part of the film and Loden's scenes are replaced with a different performer.

기사. 신문에는 물론이 20년 형을 선고받자 판사에게
감사함을 표했다는 지점을 언급했는데, 로든은
이 여성의 그러한 행동을 이해하지 못했고, 그녀를 더
알고 싶어 자세한 조사를 시작함. 교도소 면회까지
신청했으나 거절당함.

1961년 + 〈초원의 빛〉에서 워런 비티의 여동생 지니 스탬퍼 역으로
출연. 나쁜 여자 혹은 착한 여자로 여성을 이분법적으로
나누던 시대에 반항적이고 성적으로 자유로운 나쁜 여자
역을 맡음.

1962년 + 조어킴과 혼인 상태였으나, 카잔의 아이를 임신함.
〈완다〉 시나리오 작업에 착수함. 로든의 둘째 아이 레오가
1월 2일 출생.

1963년 + 엘리아 카잔이 몰리 카잔과 사별하자, 로든은 조어킴과
이혼하고 카잔과 동거.

1964년 + 연극 '추락 이후'에서 마릴린 먼로를 상징하는 매기
역으로 분해 1964년 토니상 시상식에서 연극 부문
여우주연상, 시어터월드 시상식에서 대상, 아우터비평가
시상식에서 특별상을 받음.
+ 잡지 '새터데이 이브닝 포스트' 표지 인물로 선정됨.

1966년 + 로든은 카잔, 해리 슈스터와 사파리 여행을 하던 중
슈스터로부터 영화제작 투자금 십만 달러를 제안받음.
+ CBS 제작 '유리동물원'에 로라 역으로 섭외됨. 작품
홍보를 하며 TV 가이드 잡지 화보 등 언론에 보도됨.

1967년 + 6월 5일, 엘리아 카잔과 결혼 신고. 카잔의 자전적 소설
『열망』이 출판되나 로든과의 사적인 관계를 적나라하게
묘사해 로든의 이미지에 타격을 입음.

1968년 + 할리우드 스튜디오 제작 영화 〈애증의 세월〉에서
주요 배역을 맡았지만, 후반 작업 중 프랭크 페리 감독과
제작사의 갈등이 발생, 일부 재촬영에 들어가며

1969 + Elia Kazan's autobiographical novel *The Arrangement*
becomes a film. Instead of Loden who is the actual
figure in the novel, Faye Dunaway is cast for the role,
damaging Loden's acting career.

1970 + For 10 weeks, Loden shoots *Wanda* in and around
Pennsylvania. Loden continuously puts in effort into
editing the screenplay and she changes many
elements on site throughout the shoot. Aside from
Michael Higgins, her casts are nonprofessionals,
and Loden finishes *Wanda* with a budget of
approximately 115,000 dollars.
  + *Wanda* is the only American film invited to the Venice
International Film Festival, and it wins the Pasinetti
Award. *The New York Times* and *The LA Times* among
many other media spotlight Loden.

1971 + *Wanda* releases at New York's Cinema II on
February 28.
  + *Wanda* gets invited to the Cannes Film Festival, and
Loden meets Ono Yoko and John Lennon by chance.

1972 + Loden appears on CBS's *The Mike Douglas Show* with
Ono Yoko and John Lennon on February 15.

1978 + Through invitations from universities, *Wanda* continues
to meet with audiences. While teaching acting,
Loden works on developing the cinematization of Kate
Chopin's novel, *The Awakening* (1899), but is
diagnosed with breast cancer and holds off the project.
Kazan and Loden agree on a divorce, but it gets
postponed after they find out about her cancer.
She continues teaching while trying not to show her
illness, and continues to live her everyday life.

1979 + *Wanda* is invited to the Edinburgh International Film
Festival's Women and Film section.

1980 + Loden spends five weeks at the hospital. On
September 5 at the age of 48, Loden passes away at the
Mount Sinai Hospital in New York from breast cancer.
  + *Wanda* is screened at Deauville American Film Festival.
According to an interview with Kazan in 1988, Loden

로든의 분량도 다른 배우로 대체됨.

1969년 + 엘리아 카잔의 자전적 소설『열망』이 영화화됨. 소설의
실제 주인공 로든이 아닌 페이 더너웨이가 캐스팅되며
로든의 배우 경력에 타격을 입음.

1970년 + 펜실베이니아를 중심으로 10주간 〈완다〉 촬영.
로든은 시나리오 수정에 지속적으로 공을 들였고
현장에서도 많은 요소를 바꾸며 촬영을 진행함.
마이클 히긴스를 제외하곤 모두 비전문 배우로 약
115,000달러의 예산으로 〈완다〉를 완성함.
+ 베니스국제영화제의 유일한 미국 영화로 초청받은
〈완다〉가 파지네티상을 받음. 뉴욕타임스, LA타임스 등
언론에서 로든을 조명함.

1971년 + 뉴욕의 극장 시네마 II에서 2월 28일 〈완다〉 개봉.
+ 칸영화제에 초청받은 〈완다〉, 그곳에서 로든은 오노
요코와 존 레논을 우연히 만남.

1972년 + 2월 15일, CBS '마이크 더글러스 쇼'에 오노 요코,
존 레논과 함께 출연함.

1978년 + 〈완다〉의 대학 초청 상영을 통해 관객들을 꾸준히
만남. 연기를 가르치며 차기작 개발에 힘쓰던 중
케이트 쇼팽의 '각성'(1899)을 영화화하려 했으나
유방암 판정을 받고 작업을 보류함. 카잔과 이혼에
동의했으나 암을 발견하고 이혼을 미룸. 가능한 한
아픈 표시를 내지 않고 수업을 하고, 사람들을
만나며 일상생활을 지속함.

1979년 + 에든버러영화제 '여성과 영화' 부문에 〈완다〉 초청.

1980년 + 5주간 병원에서 지냄. 9월 5일, 48세의 나이로 뉴욕
시나이산병원에서 유방암으로 사망.
+ 도빌영화제에서 〈완다〉가 상영됨. 카잔의 1988년
인터뷰에 따르면, 로든이 파리에서 도빌로의

passed away on the day her flight was scheduled from
Paris to Deauville, and her death is informed to the
audience at the Deauville American Film Festival during
the screening announcement.

항공편이 예약되어 있던 날 사망했으며,
그녀의 죽음은 도빌영화제에서 상영 공지를 통해
관객들에게 알려짐.

아이 엠 인디펜던트 ― 바바라 로든

طيران الأمن الشعبى

©한옥희

한옥희

©한옥희

Han Okhi
Director, Film critic

Han Okhi (1948–). Even during the "dark ages"
under political oppression, Han championed
women's involvement in filmmaking. She is a
pioneer in Korean experimental films, who made
experimental films with fellow women filmmakers.
Even in the highly conservative society, she
carried her camera like a machine gun and
filmed everywhere, including restricted areas
and the busiest streets of the country. She made
films as a cultural movement and a means for
resistance. She continuously challenged viewers
and their consciousness by her cinematic
experimentation. In the 70s, she led a women
filmmakers' collective, Kaidu Club. Together,
they made various experimental and independent
films and organized the country's first film
festival solely focusing on experimental films.
As such, she contributed to expand the intension
and extension of early Korean experimental films.

Han Okhee and
Han Okhi, both names
were used for the
director. JEONJU IFF
opts for Han Okhi with
the director's request.

한옥희
영화감독, 영화비평가

1948 –. 유신정권 시기에도 불구하고
여성영화인의 활동과 실험영화 제작에
앞장선 개척자이다. 한옥희 감독은
보수적인 한국 사회에서 16mm 카메라를
기관총처럼 매고 출입 금지 지역과 거리를
거침없이 헤치며 촬영했다. 관객들의
의식을 실험하고 도전하는 저항운동으로
영화를 만들며 끊임없이 새로운 것을
추구하는 영화적 실험을 감행했다. 70년대
한옥희 감독이 주축이 된 여성영화인 모임
카이두 클럽은 다양한 실험영화를 제작했고,
한국에서 최초로 실험영화만을 모아
상영회를 개최하며 국내 초기 실험영화의
내외연을 확장하는 데 기여한 중요한
인물이다.

Han Okhi

Experimental Cinema, Activism, and Amateurism: three keywords encompassing Kaidu Club and Han Okhi's films

By Jiha Kim (ACC – Asian Culture Center – Cinematheque Programmer)

South Korea's #MeToo movement ignited public interest in feminism. Its influences are not limited to the culture and art world. Rather, feminism became a major issue in South Korean society. Feminism did not emerge out of the blue. Since the 60s and 70s, feminism was often discussed in the culture and art sectors. In art history as well, it has been widely accepted (also well-established and considered to be reasonable) throughout the video epoch. In the history of cinema, cinefeminism has a long history and legacy. Park Nam-ok, the first documented South Korean film director made *The Widow* (1955). Other influential figures include Hong Eun-won, Choi Eun-hee, Hwang Hye-mi, and Lee Mi-rye, who started her career as a scripter assisting Yu Hyun-mok and made a commercial success. Cinefeminism in the 80s created a nourishing environment for cinefeminism to bear fruit during the recent 30 years. Despite the high number of feminist artists, their names are often left unmentioned or mentioned in passing. Given this, we can address a question as to whether they receive a proper recognition for their contribution. Many female filmmakers are often underappreciated or marginalized in the history. In this review, I would like to introduce "Kaidu Club",[1] a South Korean feminist artists' collective in the 70s, and discuss their contribution and legacy in the art and film history. In particular,

1
Asia Culture Center (ACC) Cinematheque has collected some films and data of Kaidu Club and introduced them to film festivals in the world. Since the films have been shown in the Archives section of the International Short Film Festival Oberhausen in 2018, they were featured at the National Gallery Singapore, Image Forum Festival in Japan, Toronto International Film Festival, and more

실험영화, 액티비스트, 아마추어리즘
— 카이두 클럽과 한옥희 작품에서의 세 가지 키워드

글: 김지하
(국립아시아문화전당(ACC) 시네마테크 프로그래머)

미투(metoo)운동으로 촉발된 페미니즘에 대한 관심은 문화예술 분야를 넘어 한국 사회 전반에 걸쳐 주요한 사회적 화두가 되었다. 사실 페미니즘은 한국 사회에 느닷없이 등장한 흐름이 아니라 1960–70년대 전후부터 지금까지 줄곧 문화예술계에서 제기되어 온 흐름이었고, 미술에서는 비디오 세대를 거치면서 이미 진부한(하지만 상식적인) 키워드로 존재한다. 영화에서도 시네페미니즘은 비교적 오랜 역사와 계보를 갖고 있다. 최초 여성영화감독인 박남옥의 1955년 작품 〈미망인〉을 비롯하여 박남옥, 홍은원, 최은희, 황혜미, 그리고 유현목 감독의 스크립터로 데뷔하여 상업영화로 성공을 거둔 이미례까지 1980년대 시네페미니즘은 1990년대와 이후 30년의 본격적인 시네페미니즘의 전환기를 이끄는 자양분이었다. 그러나 문학과 영화, 미

I will discuss the contribution and legacy of
Han Okhi, a female filmmaker, who was one of
the founding members of the group.

The Beginning

In 1974, a group of Ewha Womans University
students and graduates formed Kaidu Club.
It was an interdisciplinary group of female artists
including Korean (Han Okhi and Lee Jeong-hee),
audiovisual education (currently education
technology; Kim Jeom-sun, Han Soon-ae),
communication and media studies (Wang Kyu-
won), and dance majors (Jeong Myo-sook).
Note that none of them majored in film or
theater studies. They participated in the club's
projects by talking roles of directing, writing,
filming, creating art, choreographing,
according to their interest and specialties and
coproduced films. Cinefeminism in the 70s is
not particularly well studied or discussed.
This tendency is probably because Korean films

↓ Kaidu Club
카이두 클럽
ⓒ한옥희

술 등 예술 전반에 걸쳐 활동한 여성주의 예술가들이 적지 않음에도, 여전히 우리가 놓치고 있는 여성예술가들은 많으며 이들은 각자의 분야에서 과소평가되거나 역사의 주변부에 걸쳐 있는 것이 사실이다. 필자는 최근 들어 국제적으로 재조명되고 있는 '카이두 클럽'[1]이라는 70년대 여성영화그룹과 그룹의 주축이었던 한옥희 감독의 활동을 통해 한국영화사를 비롯한 국내의 예술사조에서 이들이 획득한 가치와 유산을 생각해 보고자한다.

카이두 클럽의 결성

1974년 결성된 카이두 클럽은 이화여대에서 국어국문학과(한옥희, 이정희), 시청각교육과(김점선, 한순애), 신문방송학과(왕규원), 무용과(정묘숙) 등을 졸업한 영화 비전공자들이었다. 이들은 각자의 전공과 특기에 맞게 연출, 각본, 촬영, 미술, 안무 등의 역할을 맡거나 공동 제작 작품을 만들기도 했다. 카이두 클럽이 결성된 1970년대는 시네페미니즘에서도 매우 제한적으로 다뤄지거나, 적어도 담론적으로는 주변화되어 있는 시기이다. 이는 1972년 유신체제로 상징되는 강력한 국가의 문화 개입과 검열, 통제로 인해 한국영화가 제도적인 침체기에 있었던 데 일차적인 원인이 있다. 국가적 통제와 산업적 위축이라는 이중 난관으로 인해 작은 영화들의 진입은 어려워지고 검열로 인한 내용적, 형식적 측면이 축소될 수밖에 없었고, 이는 영화예술인들의 제도권으로부터의 일탈을 가속화함으로써, 역설

were strictly censored by the government, which is probably best exemplified by 1972 Yushin constitution. Government control over films led to strict restrictions in the film industry. Thus, filmmakers had to face two challenges: passing the government control over their work and continuing film production in a rapidly shrinking industry. From this background, low-budget and small-scale filmmaking became even more difficult. Filmmakers could only speak about limited topics allowed by the government in highly restricted formats granted to them. Some filmmakers chose to deviate from such institutionalized filmmaking, which ironically, resulted in an increase in their involvement in low-budget projects outside of the home for mainstream commercial filmmakers, Chungmu-ro. As a result, during the 70s, many filmmaking experiments were carried out as a way to address questions regarding the foundations of filmmaking and cinematography as well as filmmakers' aesthetic view and self-awareness. Some filmmakers actively sought for freedom of expression and new aesthetic discoveries. They were exposed to international films such as New German Cinema, the French New Wave films, and New American Cinema through Goethe-Institut Korea and the French Culture Centre, among others. They formed film research groups, which contributed to the increase in cinephiles. Such cultural context might have contributed to the formation of Kaidu Club. Some of its members, Han Okhi and Kim Jeom-sun, interacted with other active cinephile groups of the time, such as Moving Image Research Group, whose founding members include Lee Hwang-lim, Kim Hyun-joo, and Park Sang-cheon, and Cinepoem Coterie led by Yu Hyun-mok.

"Kaidu" is the name of a great-grandson of

적으로 충무로 바깥에서 작은 영화 중심의 활동을 촉진시키고 영화적, 미학적 자각과 다양한 실험의 토양이 마련되는 결과를 가져왔다. 영화를 통한 표현의 자유와 미학적 가치를 발견하고자 하는 이들은 독일문화원, 프랑스문화원에서 당시 유럽과 북미에서 새로운 경향으로 등장한 뉴저먼시네마, 누벨바그, 뉴아메리칸시네마 등을 접하며 영화 소모임들을 만들고 씨네필 또한 늘어났다. 이황림, 김현주, 박상천 등이 결성한 '영상연구회' 및 한국소형영화동호회, 그리고 유현목을 주축으로 한 '씨네포엠'과 교류하던 한옥희, 김점선 등도 이러한 배경에서 카이두 클럽을 결성했다고도 볼 수 있다.

'카이두'는 징기스칸의 고손녀이자 몽골의 전설적인 여전사라 불리는 '쿠툴룬'의 아버지 이름이다.[2] 카이두 클럽은 호스티스 영화가 판치는 영화계와 가부장적 사회에 반기를 드는 딸들의 저항적 이름이자, 개인이 아닌 집단으로서의 행동을 내포한다. 대학 모임에서 나아가 사회운동으로서 활동하려는 이들의 결의는 영화 작업뿐만 아니라 퍼포먼스, 심포지엄, 영화제 등으로 다양하게 표출된다. 흥미로운 부분은 이들이 표현하고자 했던 장르가 '실험영화'였으며, 당시 북미, 유럽, 일본 등에서 다른 예술 장르와 결합하거나 파생된 형태의 영화를 실험영화라는 큰 범주 안에서 논의해 왔다는 것을 알고 전략적으로 차용했다는 것이다. 이렇게 카이두 클럽은 한국 최초로 실험영화라는 장르를 내걸고 활동한 단체이자, 최초 여성영화단체이며, 국내 첫 실험영화제를 주최한 단체가 된다. 이들은 3회에 걸쳐 자신들이 제작한 작품들을 대중과 매체에 소개하기 위해 실험영화 페스티벌을 개최했다. 한편, '카이두 실험영화연구회'라는

Genghis Khan, whose daughter is Khutulun. She was a great warrior of Old Mongolia.[2] Kaidu was a resistance name for daughters opposing the film industry, which then was predominated by hostess films and the patriarchal society. They acted as a group, not as an individual, as the name "club" implies. They started from a college club and determined to expand their scope to activism, as suggested by the wide range of activities they participated in: filmmaking projects, creating stage and street performances, organizing symposiums and film festivals, among others. One interesting aspect is that the genre they focused on as their means of expression was experimental cinema. They were well aware that the umbrella term "experimental cinema" could include interdisciplinary endeavors, probably because they were exposed to experimental cinema of North America, Europe, and Japan. They strategically adopted the filmmaking style of blending themes and elements from different genres of art. As such, Kaidu Club became one of the first groups of people, whose main purpose was to study and make experimental films. Also, it was the first South Korean female filmmaker group and the first group to host an experimental film festival in South Korea. They organized three experimental film festivals to screen and publicize their projects. They also hosted a symposium—for such events, they went by the name of "Kaidu Experimental Film Research Society." At their symposium entitled *Women and the Movie World*, they had talks by notable speakers including Byun In-shik (title roughly translated as: *Is it possible to increase women's participation in film art?*), Lee O-young (*Female images in literature and films: the dark and light*), Hong Eun-won and Park Nam-ok (*Women's situation in the Korean film industry*),

2
Media reports said th the club was named after a Mogul female warrior. However, he name is Khutulun; w her father's name is Kaidu.

↗ Newspaper mate reporting the Kaic Experimental Film Research Societ 1970s
1970년대 카이두 신문보도

이 實驗映畵페스티벌 10

한국영화 장래를 말겨라.

女優는 입고 女 監督은 누드

세계 最初, 한국實驗映畵클럽서 제2차 映畵

Song Suk-yeong (*Female filmmakers' social activities*), and Lee Jin-seop (*On screen representations of women*).[3] Given the themes of talks given at the symposium, we can infer that they had a discussion on gender issues surrounding the South Korean film industry, which then was almost exclusively led and operated by men, rather than discussion on the aesthetic value of experimental films and research thereon.

As a matter of fact, the Club's main focus was somewhat different from that of other cinefeminism groups. In addition, they do not seem to fit well into any single branch the genealogy of Korean cinefeminism as well. For these reasons, many do not discuss Korean cinefeminism the 70s in depth, or it is just mentioned in passing. It is contrary to the fact that the 70s was marked by diverse and significant feminisms' achievements in many sectors of Korean society. In the Western world, second-wave feminism emerged after the protests of 1968. In the 1970s, feminism received a lot of attention and became one major topics of academic research in the post-modern world. Radical and liberal feminist movement emerged under the agenda of women's liberation, covering a wide range of social issues pertaining to women's experience. During the 70s, a number of feminist theories were introduced to South Korea as a new academic discipline, women's studies. The Christian Academy, founded in 1965, organized regular programs for academic research and discussion sessions to support women's studies. In 1975, Lee Hyo-jae and fellow researchers published a series of books focusing on feminism. Note that feminism in the Western world stemmed from non-institutional interest and later landed in institutions and in the social

3
Kaidu Experimental F
Research Society
(1974), *Women and the Movie World*,
Symposium Material

명칭으로 심포지엄도 개최하는데, '여성과 영화세계'라는 제목으로 열린 이 심포지엄에는 '영화예술에 있어서의 여성 참여도의 확대는 가능한가?(변인식)', '문학과 영상 속의 여성 이마쥬, 그 명암(이어령)', '한국 영화계에서 여성이 처한 상황(홍은원, 박남옥)', '여성 영화인의 현실참여(송숙영)', '스크린에 비친 여성백태(이진섭)'[3]라는 주제들로, 실험영화의 미학적 가치나 연구라기보다는 여성을 배제한 한국영화계에 대한 보다 거시적 담론에 대해 논의하는 장을 마련했다.

사실, 카이두 클럽은 시네페미니즘 경향과는 다소 다른 문제의식을 갖고 있었고, 이는 한국영화의 시네페미니즘 계보에서도 다소 이질적이라고 할 수 있다. 이 때문에 1970년대는 시네페미니즘 논의에서 아예 부재하거나, 적어도 매우 제한적인 수준에서 다뤄지고 있다. 이는 페미니즘 운동이 가장 활발했고, 매우 혁신적인 제도적 성과를 올렸던 시기가 70년대였다는 점을 상기하면 다소 아이러니하다. 실제로 1970년대 페미니즘은 서구에서는 68혁명 이후 탈근대적 학술장으로의 구조적 개혁을 주도하는 제2물결의 핵심학문분과로 등장하였고, 급진적인 여성운동이 '여성해방'이라는 어젠다를 중심으로 폭발하던 시기이기도 하다. 한국 사회에서도 1970년대 '여성학'이라는 이름의 신생 학문으로 페미니즘 이론이 번역되어 들어오기 시작하였고, 1965년 설립된 한국크리스천아카데미는 정기적인 학술연구와 세미나를 통해 학술담론을 전개하였으며, 1975년에 이효재를 중심으로 이러한 결과물을 총서로 발간하였다. 그런데 한 가지 주목해 보아야 할 것은, 서구의 페미니즘이 비제도권의 투쟁으로 시작되어 제도권에 진입하였다면, 70년대 한국

system. In contrast, feminism in the 70s of South Korea entered social institutions by importing Western feminist discourse, which was in line with government policies focusing on human resources development for women, childcare, welfare, and education for women, etc. In this social context, academic research on feminism started and rapidly grew in South Korea during the 70s. Rather than turning into a radical political movement, feminism encouraged aesthetic and artistic exploration and experimentation of art at colleges.

Experimental Attempts

After the '68 protests, feminism of the 70s in the West started focusing on various issues including visuality and vision, women's desire and means of expression, and gender politics. Feminist artists worked on expressing the female gaze and female desire, thus it was necessary for them to destruct existing grammar of the film language. As a result, more artists started to experiment on new and alternative way to express themselves, probably best exemplified by postmodern art. Contrary to this tendency, in Korea, hostess films made commercial success, leading the domestic film industry. As a result, the Kaidu Club members wanted a medium of expression that can directly counter the mainstream film industry. They also had diverse areas of interest and specialties. Thus, they also needed a medium that is inclusive enough to cover their wide range of interests. To meet these requirements, they chose the genre of experimental film because it is non-institutional, unconventional, and very inclusive. Also, working on experimental films can represent a challenge to the existing social order. We can

페미니즘은 서구담론의 유입과 여성자원의 개발, 모자복지, 여성고등교육이라는 정책적 이슈와 맞물려 제도권 내에서 진입했다는 것이다. 이러한 시대적 배경으로 인해 70년대 학문제도에 진입한 페미니즘은 정치적 급진주의와 직결되기보다는 오히려 대학 내에서 페미니즘에 관한 미학적, 예술적 탐구와 실험을 자유롭게 하는 조건이 되었다.

실험적 시도들

68혁명 이후 1970년대 서구의 페미니즘에 제기된 어젠다는 시각성과 시선의 문제, 여성적 욕망과 여성적 표현양식, 성정치와 같은 것들이었다. 페미니즘 예술가들은 여성적 시선과 욕망을 표현하기 위해 기존의 영화적 문법을 파괴할 필요가 있었고, 그에 따라 포스트모던 표현양식으로 대변되는 대안적 표현양식에 대한 실험들이 활발하게 일어났다. 카이두 클럽이 결성된 당시의 한국영화계는 위와 같은 흐름과는 다르게 호스티스 영화가 흥행과 함께 주류 영화에 포진되어 있었고 문학, 미술 등 다양한 전공과 관심사를 가지고 있었던 카이두 클럽에게는 제도권 영화와 사회에 대한 반기를 들 수 있는 직접이고도 느슨한 표현매체가 필요했던 것이다. 이를 위해 비제도권, 반사회적 장르로 채택한 실험영화는 그들의 작업에서 다양한 방식으로 보여지고 있다.

감옥에 갇힌 죄수의 억압과 해방에 대한 욕망을 그린 〈구멍〉(1973), 인간의 삶과 죽음, 그 안에서의 고뇌와 해결 등을

see these aspects from many of their projects.

The Hole (1973) depicts a prisoner, restrained and suffocated, desiring for freedom. *The Middle Dogs Day* (1974) shows us various images of ropes, which symbolize life and death as well as agony and resolution therein. *Batjul* (1974) is a metaphorical piece showing restraint and yearning for liberation, reminding us of young people living in dark ages, yearning for freedom and liberation. Images of rope appear in all these three films. They form a direct motif for restriction and constraint. In terms of forms, audio and visual effects such as intentional exclusion of spoken lines, scattered plot with jump cuts, stop motion animation seem to follow cinematographic techniques frequently used in surrealist cinema. Meanwhile, their another work, *2minutes 40seconds* (1975) shows an assemblage of short and montage-like images of South Korea, such as buildings, streets, traditional architecture and artworks. Together, they symbolize a broader theme of longing for unification of North and South Korea. It does not have any characters or motifs. Rather, this experimental documentary is composed almost exclusively of images of Korea. It won a prize at the first Korea Youth Film Festival (Currently Seoul Independent Film Festival). In the following year, they produced *Colour Of Korea* (1976), which more comprehensively captures

↓ *The Hole*
〈구멍〉

다양한 밧줄의 이미지들로 형상화한 〈중복〉(1974), 현대인의 속박과 욕구를 은유적으로 담아낸 〈밧줄〉(1974)은 암울한 시대 속에서 자유를 갈망하는 젊은이들의 무의식을 보여 준다. 세 작품에서 모두 등장하는 밧줄은 속박에 대한 직접적인 모티브가 되면서도 형식적 측면에서는 의도적으로 대사를 배제하고 이음새 없는 전개와 점프 컷, 스톱모션 애니메이션 등의 효과를 통해 초현실주의 영화의 기법들을 답습하고 있다. 한편 〈2분 40초〉(1975)는 분단국가인 남한의 이미지들을 각종 건축물과 거리, 전통적인 조형물 등의 짧은 몽타주들로 나열하면서 통일에 대한 염원이라는 보다 거시적 주제들을 담아 낸다. 이 작품은 특정 등장인물이나 모티브 없이 당시 한국의 풍경들로만 이루어진 실험 다큐멘터리로 제1회 한국청소년영화제(현 서울독립영화제) 우수상을 받았다. 이듬해 제작된 〈색동〉(1976)은 보다 포괄적인 한국의 이미지들을 담아 내는데, 이전의 흑백 작품과는 다르게 갖가지 색들을 통해 한국의 전통과 현대의 문화들을 탐색한다. 이중인화 기법을 통한 여러 색들이 담긴 단편적 이미지들의 조합은 카이두 클럽의 저항적 제스처는 가려져 있으나 형식에 얽매이지 않는 표현들은 동일하게 찾아볼 수 있다. 카이두 클럽이 제작한 작품들은 당시의 몇몇 기사와 자료들을 통해 알 수 있지만 실제로 찾아볼 수 있는 작품은 많지 않다. 유일하게 볼 수 있는 작품들은 한옥희가 연출한(위의 언급된 작품 포함) 여섯 작품 정도이다. 이 작품들 안에서 유일하게 여성이 주인공으로 등장하는 〈무제 77-A〉(1977)는 한국의 사회상을 담아 낸 작품들과는 달리 감독 한옥희의 창작에 대한 고민과 남성중심사회에서 여성예술가로서 살아가야 하는 내적인 불안

diverse images of Korea. Contrary to their prior works that were typically black and white, this film explores Korean culture throughout the history with diverse colors. Fragmentary images were superimposed on top of each other, creating various colors. The message of resistance may be obscured in this piece, but the unconstrained and free-spirited techniques of expression is found across all of their films. It is not easy to watch Kaidu club's work now, although we can learn about their projects from newspaper and magazine articles. We have access to only about six films (including the aforementioned films), all of which were directed by Han Okhi . Among all of their films, *Untitled 77-A* (1977) is an exception in many ways. Unlike their previous films, images of the country and society are not highlighted. However, one female protagonist, probably the female artist's self-image, is at the very foreground of the film. It tells a story about the anxiety of creation, concerns about living as a female artist in a patriarchal society, and resistance toward the system and censorship that many artist had to face from the society. A complicated mixture of these feelings is revealed in the film. Images of the female protagonist

↗ *The Middle Dogs Day*
〈중복〉

↗ *Colour Of Korea*
〈색동〉

← *Untitled 77-A*
〈무제 77-A〉

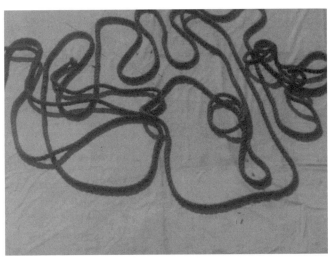

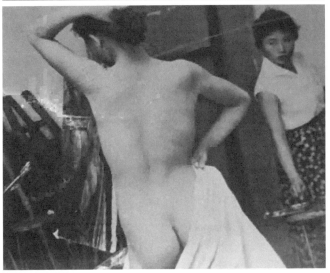

아이 엠 인디펜던트 ― 한옥희

shooting in the middle of a street with no
hesitation or worries are followed by images of
her cutting and editing films. At the end we
get to meet Han, the director, holding scissors,
smiling and shouting "the end!" This film looks
like a documentary, which is somewhat more
specific and realistic than other experimental films.
However, the director's appearance at the end
makes it a fake documentary, which is essentially
a self-reflexive art experiment.

Intermedia Activism

The club's activities were incredibly diverse,
especially considering its short five years of
history. They produced films, hosted symposiums
and organized film festivals. During the
processes of filmmaking, researching, and finally
releasing their projects, a few "accidents"
happened. Their street performance during which
a "shaman" practiced a ritual on busy streets of
Myeong-dong is one such instance. In fact, their
art world was not limited to experimental films.
It might be more appropriate to understand their
work as intermedia art practices, where different
genres come together. Their motto as suggested
by their club name—an uprising against the
patriarchal society—is clearly feminist. However,
the themes of their films and their filmmaking
practices suggest that the club's activities were
not solely dedicated to feminism. Instead, their
focus was broader and more similar to filmmaking
as social activism. It was around the time when
Korean visual artists formed collectives such
as the Fourth Group, the A. G. (Korea Avant-
Garde Association), and ST (Space & Time). They
introduced conceptual art, which was a trend in
art practice of the time. They moved on to
establish their own theories and practices, rather

감, 제도권에서 벗어난 영화들을 만들어 내면서 검열에 대한 두려움과 저항이 복합적으로 드러난다. 거리 한복판에서 카메라를 들고 거침없이 찍고 주저앉는 모습, 편집실의 필름들을 조각조각 잘라 내는 모습의 마지막에는 가위를 들고 "끝!"이라고 큰 소리로 외치며 회심의 미소를 짓는 감독 한옥희가 등장한다. 〈무제 77-A〉는 이전 작품들과 비교했을 때 다소 구체적이면서 사실적으로 진행되는 다큐멘터리로 보이지만 감독의 등장으로 끝나면서 페이크 다큐라는 자기반영적이면서도 실험적 시도들을 놓치지 않는다.

인터미디어 액티비즘

카이두 클럽의 활동은 약 5년 남짓한 기간이라고는 믿기 어려울 만큼 다양했다. 영화제작과 심포지엄 그리고 영화제 개최까지, 제작과 연구에서 발표로 완결되는 과정 사이사이에는 명동에서 굿거리 해프닝이나 퍼포먼스를 벌이기도 했다. 실제 카이두 클럽의 예술 세계는 실험영화라는 영화 범주에 국한시키기보다는 다양한 영역들을 넘나들고 조우하는 인터미디어로서 이해하는 것이 맞을 것이다. 또한 카이두 클럽의 그룹명이 가부장적 사회에 대한 봉기와 같은 타이틀을 달고 있으면서도 영화에서의 주제들과 작업의 실천 과정에서 보여 준 다양함은 70년대의 페미니즘을 강조하고 있다기보다는 더 광범위한 측면에서의 액티비즘으로 볼 수 있다. 당시 미술계에서도 새로운 미술실천을 보여 주고자 했던 단체들이 등장하는데, '제4집단',

than following and blindly emulating Western modernist art. Kaidu club's activities might be similar to the approaches that the aforementioned visual artist groups were taking. Kaidu club's filmmaking practices are distinct from those of more traditional experimental filmmakers, in that the club focused less on individual consciousness and exploration of the means of expression. However, their work is in line with traditional experimental films in that they clearly deviated from the mainstream commercial industry. Their work is also in line with Korean experimental art practices in that they explored a new means of expression such as experimental cinema and performances as a way to address themes such as collective unconsciousness.

We can find the club's legacy in the subsequent projects by individual members of the club. The members continued their experimentation by deliberately deviating from the conventions set by institutional cinema. They kept using the media of film as an intermedium to explore different genres of art. In the early 90s, the domestic video market rapidly grew. With this expansion of the market, unauthorized copies of movies were illegally distributed and circulated all over the country. During this time, Han continued the Kaidu-style experiments with metaphors, as shown in her project, *The Silence of Love* (1991). It is her film adaptation of Han Yong-un's poems. 15 poems are visually represented in 55 minutes of video, each of which takes about two or three minutes of running time. *The Silence of Love* can be an example of video poetry and/or educational film. In 1993, she was invited to make a commemorative film for Taejon Expo and produced *Running Koreans* (1993), a 70mm IMAX film. It was screened at the government

'AG(한국아방가르드협회)', 'ST(Space&Time)' 등이 전 세계 예술사조로 떠오른 개념미술을 도입하면서 서구 모더니즘 예술의 답습이 아닌 고유한 이론과 실천을 만들어 나가던 시기였다. 카이두 클럽의 작품들은 개인적인 사유와 매체의 탐색을 보여 주는 전통적 실험영화와는 다르면서도 충무로 극영화와는 확실하게 선을 긋고, 영화와 퍼포먼스 등의 다각적 시도를 통해 작품 속에서 공통적으로 찾아볼 수 있는 '집단무의식'이라는 대주제를 다룬다는 점에서 당시의 한국 실험미술 운동과도 궤를 같이하고 있다.

카이두 클럽이 제도권 영화에서 벗어나 인터미디어로서 영상의 경계를 횡단하려고 했던 시도는 단체 활동 이후 개인 작업에서도 드러난다. 90년대 초 비디오 시장이 커지고 영화의 무단복제와 불법유통이 범람하던 시기에 한옥희는 카이두 클럽에서 시도했었던 은유적 실험들을 한용운의 〈님의 침묵〉(1991)을 통해 재개한다. 한용운의 시집에 수록된 15편의 시를 2–3분 가량으로 쪼개어 총 55분의 영상으로 보여 준 이 작품은 일종의 교육비디오이자 영상시로 구현된다. 93년에 개최된 대전 엑스포에서는 정부관에 상영될 기념영화를 의뢰받아 70mm 아이맥스영화 〈달리는 한국인〉(1993)을 제작한다. 〈달리는 한국인〉은 선전영화의 성격을 띠지만 1970년 오사카 만국박람회에서 마츠모토 토시오, 이이무라 다카히코 등 실험영화와 비디오 아트라는 두 영역을 넘나들던 작가들이 상업주의와 손잡았다는 비난을 받으면서도 이를 통해 장르의 경계를 확장시킨 계기를 만들었던 행보와도 유사하다. 대학 졸업 후 홍대 대학원에 들어가 본격적인 미술 활동을 펼쳤던 김점선의 실험적인 작품

building during the Expo. She produced a propaganda film chimes with Matsumoto Toshio and Iimura Takahiko's projects for Expo '70 held in Osaka, Japan. In their work, the artists crossed the boundaries between film and video art in an attempt to expand the horizon of artistic expression. However, at the time when their Osaka Expo project was released, some criticized that they merely pursued commercial interests. The spirit of experimentation can also be found from another member of the club, Kim Jeom-sun's art world. After her Kaidu days, Kim pursued a degree in fine arts at the graduate school of Hong-ik University and later became a full-time artist. In the work by Kaidu Club members, a canvas becomes a film. Unexpected events are reenacted in films. A film can turn into a poem, and vice versa. Taken together, the club's artistic activities were at the vanguard of contemporary visual arts by converging and merging different genres of art and media. The club's view of genre and experimental films also reminds us of Kim Kulim's work. He is one of the first experimental filmmakers in South Korea, who greatly influenced establishing the framework of early Korean experimental films by his film, *The Meaning of 1/24 second* (1969) and his activities in the Fourth Group. Kim Kulim's modern art practice is considered to made an important landmark in art history as well as in film history of South Korea.

The Legacy: Kaidu Club as a Mediator

The activities of Kaidu Club and Han Okhi's works have continuously been discussed by film researchers. However, in the history of Korean cinema, their contribution has not been

에서도 마찬가지인 것처럼, 이들의 작업은 캔버스가 필름이 되기도 하고, 해프닝이 필름으로 재연되기도 하며, 필름이 하나의 시가 되기도 한다. 즉 '제4집단'에서 활동한 김구림의 〈24분의 1초의 의미〉(1969)가 초창기 한국 실험영화의 뼈대가 되고 현재 미술과 영화의 역사를 아우르는 현대예술의 주요 작품이 되었듯이, 카이두 클럽의 작품 역시 현대 시각예술에서 나타나는 융복합적 시도들의 선구적 역할을 한 것이라 볼 수 있다.

매개자로서의 유산

카이두 클럽의 활동과 그 안에서 보여 준 한옥희의 작품들은 영화연구자들에 의해 지속적으로 회자되긴 하였으나 한국영화사에서는 그들이 주요하게 언급한 만큼 비중 있게 거론되지는 않았다. 적어도 집중적으로 다뤄질 수 있었던 여성영화나 독립영화에서도 마찬가지다. 이는 짧았던 그룹 활동과 산발적으로 흩어진 이후의 개인 활동들에서 비롯된 것도 있겠지만, 80년대 민주화운동을 거치면서 정치적 이념과 주제를 직접적으로 드러냈던 문화운동으로서의 영화들이 실험보다는 독립이라는 용어에 강조를 두면서 주변화되어 버린 것도 원인으로 생각해 볼 수 있다. 또한 카이두 클럽의 미학적 토대를 이어갈 수 있었던 90년대의 '뉴이미지그룹(이후 한국실험영화연구소)'이 대표 권중운의 지병으로 인해 해산되고 이후의 활동을 확장시키지 못한 이유도 있을 것이다. 무엇보다 가장 큰 요인은 실험성, 다양성이라는 장르적 담론이 영화 내부에 형성되기 이전에 너무나

focused on. The contribution and legacy of the
club could have been discussed in depth, at least
in the fields of woman's film or independent
film. However, in these fields as well, Kaidu Club
tends not to be discussed frequently. This might
be due to the fact that the club was active only for
a very brief period of time (five years) and its
members' activities after the club were distributed
(or rather scattered) across diverse genres of art.
Their apparently missing legacy could also be
due to their main focus being marginalized, in part
because many filmmaking endeavors concentrated
on political activism in the 80s as South Korea
was struggling for democracy. As a result,
filmmakers who regarded their work as cultural
activism focused more on independence, rather
than experimentation. The aesthetic legacy
of the club could have continued by the New
Image Group (Later Korean Experimental Cinema
Research Society) of the 90s. Unfortunately,
the group could not continue its endeavor in part
due to the loss of the leader, Kwon Joong-un.
After his passing, it became even more
challenging to expand the horizon of experimental
films in South Korea. In addition to these reasons,
the time greatly mattered. The club's activities
could have been too ahead of time. This might be
the most compelling reason for the apparent
loss of their legacy. They focused on experimental
films even before discourse on cinematic
experimentation and diversification naturally
emerged in the domestic industry. Maybe
because of this reason, many researchers today
find their innovative works as something to
truly enjoy, appreciate, and exhilarate. Their films
are non-cliché, because they rejected mannerism
and conventions of the mainstream. Also, they
never worked to emulate existing commercial
films. Their inherent amateurism allowed them to
directly face against the mainstream. Instead, they

앞서갔던 것이다. 그리고 지금에서야 이들의 진취적인 활동들이 새롭고도 통쾌한 희열로 다가온다. 카이두 클럽의 작품들이 현재도 진부하지 않은 것은 기성영화를 흉내 내려는 매너리즘이나 관습이 없기 때문이다. 그들에게 내재적으로 담겨 있는 아마추어리즘은 시대와 조류에 편승하지 않고 사회와 예술, 제도권과 개인, 전통과 실험 사이에 침범할 수 없는 간극과 질서를 무너뜨리는 매개자로서의 자세를 보여 줬다. 역사는 기록들이 파장하면서 만들어진다. 비록 카이두 클럽이 지금까지의 영화사에서는 흐릿하게 존재하지만, 현재 영화관과 미술관을 넘나들며 새로운 예술지형을 만들어 나가는 작가들에게는 단단하고도 귀중한 유산이 될 것이다.

김지하

영화와 미술을 매개하는 프로그램과 전시 등을 기획해 왔으며, 현재는 국립아시아문화전당(ACC) 시네마테크 프로그래머로 활동하고 있다. 저서로는 『차학경 예술론』(2013, 기획/공저), 『한국 나쁜영화 100년』(2019, 기획/공저), 『아다치 마사오의 은하계』(근간)가 있다.

worked to deconstruct barriers between the society and the art, those between the system and an individual, and those between the tradition and experiment. These apparently indestructible orders were challenged by the Kaidu Club, who worked as a mediator to an art trend. History is written by records resonating with each other. Although their presence might not strongly stand out, for those who are working to create new terrain of art by crossing the boundaries between movie theaters and art museums, Kaidu Club's legacy remains cherished and venerated.

Jiha Kim

Jiha Kim is a programmer at Asia Culture Center (ACC) Cinematheque. She has curated programs and exhibitions mediating film and visual art. Her work includes book projects *On Theresa Hak Kyung Cha* (2013, Producer and Co-author), *The History of Marginalized Films in Korea* (2019, Producer and Co-author), and *Gingakei (Galaxy) by Adachi Masao* (Forthcoming).

↗ Han Okhi
한옥희
ⓒ한옥희

1   국립아시아문화전당(ACC) 시네마테크는 2017년 카이두 클럽의 작품과 자료 일부를 수집하고 해외 영화제 등에 소개해 오고 있다. 2018년 오버하우젠 국제단편영화제 아카이브 부문에 첫 공개한 이후 싱가폴내셔널갤러리, 일본 이미지포럼페스티벌, 토론토국제영화제 등에서 상영되었다.

2   카이두 클럽의 '카이두'는 몽골의 여전사 이름을 딴 것으로 기존의 기사 자료들을 통해 알려져 왔으나, 본래는 '쿠툴룬'이라는 이름이며, 카이두는 그녀의 아버지 이름이다.

3   카이두 실험영화연구회(1974), 〈여성과 영화세계〉, 심포지엄 자료집

아이 엠 인디펜던트 — 한옥희

Han Okhi

1948–Early Life + Born on July 24, 1948.
Her childhood is poor. She dreams of being a ballerina.
She wants to freely roam around a stage, which is the
little universe. She grows up in a very conservative family
and she is not allowed to take ballet lessons. Still, she
wants to be an artist, who can create a world of her own.
She has been pursuing this dream ever since.

1971 + Earns a B.A. in Korean Language and Literature from
Ewha Womans University.
She publishes poems in Ewha Munhak and the Ewha
Weekly. She recalls that her aspiration around 1971 was
to write poems by capturing an instantaneous and unique
imagery. She thinks that literature, which is essentially
a part of language arts, is abstract and speculative.
On the contrary, that cinematic art comprises visual and
auditory images attracted her. In particular, she wants to
show a cinematic representation of unique images that
occur in her own creative world.

1973 + Earns an M.A. in Korean Language and Literature from
Ewha Womans University.
M.A. Thesis: An Aesthetic Analysis of Korean Modern
Poetry
Joins Moving Image Research Group, a group of
amateur filmmakers.
+ Directs The Hole. It is screened at the 4th meeting of
Moving Image Research Group, which took place in
November 1973 at the Press Building. Film 73 (directed
by Kim Jeom-sun) is screened at the same venue.

1974 + Founds a women's creative collective with Kim Jeom-sun,
Lee Jeong-hee, Han Soon-ae and other Ewha alumnae.
They names their group 'Kaidu Club'. She is a president
for the group.
At that time, the mainstream film industry, Chungmu-ro,
enjoyed a commercial success with hostess movies and
erotic films. Kaidu Club films the things that they are
eager to shoot. They aims to make films that can only
be made by them. They holds a 16mm camera like warriors
carrying machine guns. They do not mind running around

한옥희 연보

1948년 + 7월 24일 출생.
가난한 어린 시절을 보냄. 어린 시절의 꿈은 작은 우주인
무대 위를 마음껏 뛰어노는 발레리나였으나, 보수적인 집안
분위기로 발레 수업을 들을 수 없었음. 그러나 자신의 세계를
자유자재로 창조할 수 있는 예술가가 되고 싶어 했고, 이는
그가 추구한 삶의 지표였음.

1971년 + 이화여대 국문학과 졸업.
이화문학, 이대학보에 시를 발표. 이 세상의 단 하나밖에
없는 시의 이미지를 순간적으로 포착해서 보여 주고 싶은
강렬한 욕망이 타오르기 시작하던 시기였음. 문학은
언어예술이기 때문에 추상적이고 사유적인 데 비해서,
영화는 시각적 청각적 이미지들로 이뤄진 예술이라는 점에
매료됨. 특히 보편적 이미지가 아닌 자신의 창작 세계 속
유일한 이미지를 영화로 재현해 보여 주려는 시도를 하게 됨.

1973년 + 이화여대 대학원 국문과 졸업.
석사논문 '한국 현대시의 미학적 분석'
순수 아마추어 영화인들의 모임 '영상연구회' 가입.
+ 〈구멍〉 연출.
+ 11월 신문회관, 제4회 영상연구회 발표회
〈구멍〉, 〈필름73〉(김점선 연출) 등을 상영.

1974년 + '영상연구회'에서 여성들만의 창작동인을 결성. 이화여대
출신의 김점선, 이정희, 한순애 등과 함께 실험영화집단
'카이두 클럽'을 결성, 대표로 활동. 당시 충무로 영화계가
소위 호스티스 영화와 애로 영화로 전성기를 누릴 때,
카이두 클럽은 가장 진실하고 자신만이 할 수 있는 영화의
대상을 찾아다님. 16mm 카메라를 기관총처럼 등에 메고
뜨거운 아스팔트 위를, 명동 거리를 뛰어다니며 거리의
군상들을 찍기도 했고, 맨홀이나 동굴 속을 헤매기도 하였고,
출입금지 지역을 촬영하다 안기부에 불려 다니기도 함.
+ 〈밧줄〉, 〈중복〉 연출.
+ 7월 27일-31일, 신세계백화점 옥상에서 '제1회 실험영화

on hot asphalt paving. They do not mind filming on busy streets of Myeong-dong to shoot the crowd. They even dives into a manhole and a cave, wandering around and looking for things to shoot. They films around restricted areas and were summoned by agents from Agency for National Security Planning (currently National Intelligence Service, South Korea).

+ Directs *Batjul* and *The Middle Dogs Day*.
+ She, along with the Kaidu Club members, organizes the first experimental film festival on the roof of Shinsegae department store, Seoul. Although there are screenings and film projects related to experimental films, it is the first South Korean film festival solely focusing on experimental films, where only experimental films are screened.
The films that are screened at the venue are as follows: *Batjul, The Middle Dogs Day, Film 74-A* (directed by Kim Jeom-sun), *Film 74-B* (directed by Kim Jeom-sun), *XXOX* (directed by Lee Jeong-hee), *OVER* (directed by Han Soon-ae), *Song of Genocide* (co-directed by four members of Kaidu Club), and *Elevator* (co-directed by four members of Kaidu Club).

1975 + Directs *The Three Mirrors* and *2minutes 40seconds*.
+ *2minutes 40seconds* wins the Excellent Picture Award at the first Seoul Independent Film Festival (formerly Korea Youth Film Festival, then Korean Independent Short Film Festival).
+ On May 23 and 27, she and the club members organizes the second experimental film festival, which is held at the Goethe-Institut. At the venue, three films were screened: *The Three Mirrors*, *75-13* (directed by Kim Jeom-sun), and *Still, We Get to Set and Go* (directed by Lee Jeong-hee).

1976 + *Colour Of Korea* wins the Excellent Picture Award at the first Seoul Independent Film Festival (formerly Korea Youth Film Festival, then Korean Independent Short Film Festival).

1977 + Directs *Untitled 77-A*.
Performs at the opening art festival of "Space". Her films are screened as well.

1980–1988 + Studies theater and film at the Free University of Berlin, West Germany, supported by the DAAD artist program.

페스티벌' 개최. 한국에서 개별적인 실험영화 작업과
움직임은 있었지만 실험영화만을 위한 상영회는 최초였음.
〈밧줄〉, 〈중복〉, 〈필름 74-A〉 (김점선 연출),
〈필름 74-B〉 (김점선 연출), 〈XXOX〉 (이정희 연출),
〈OVER〉 (한순애 연출), 〈몰살의 노래〉 (카이두 클럽
4인 공동연출), 〈엘리베이터〉 (카이두 클럽 4인
공동연출) 상영.

1975년 + 〈세 개의 거울〉, 〈2분 40초〉 연출.

+ 제1회 서울독립영화제 (구 한국청소년영화제,
한국독립단편영화제)에서 〈2분 40초〉가 우수상을 받음.

+ 5월 23일, 27일 독일문화원, '제2회 실험영화 페스티벌' 개최
〈세 개의 거울〉, 〈75-13〉 (김점선 연출), 〈그러나 우리는
다시 출발해야 한다〉 (이정희 연출) 상영.

1976년 + 제2회 서울독립영화제 (구 한국청소년영화제)에서
〈색동〉이 우수상을 받음.

1977년 + 〈무제 77-A〉 연출, '공간' 개관예술제에서 행위예술과
공동 상연.

1980년-1988년 + 독일 예술가교류프로그램 (DAAD) 지원으로 서독 체류.
베를린자유대학에서 연극영화를 전공함. 당시 유학 경험은
영화를 보는 안목을 키우는 기회를 제공함. 독일생활과
교육을 통해 세상에 대한 객관적이고 합리주의적인 시선,
특히 인생을 조감할 수 있는 눈이 비로소 열렸다는 것을
깨닫는 기회가 됨. 한국에서 엘리트 의식을 가지고서
살았던 잘난 척했던 자존심, 치기만만함 등이 배타적이고
냉소적인 독일인들과 살면서 깨어져 버리고, "이 세상에
나보다 못한 사람 (여자)은 없다."는 것을 깨닫게 됨.

1981년-1988년 + 영화진흥위원회 베를린 통신원, 공연예술지 '객석' 특파원.

+ 베를린자유대학 연극영화과 박사 수료.

1988년 + 제작사 '카이두 프로덕션' 설립 후 기록영화와
홍보영화 작업.

The study abroad experience helps her to develop an eye
for films. She later recalls that living and studying in
Germany helped her to think again about life and have a
more unprejudiced and reasonable attitude towards the
world. She mentions that she has to learn how to live with
Germans, who first look exclusive and cynical to her.
She adds that later, her vain pride stemmed from elitism
was shattered thanks to her time in Germany. From this
experience, she comes to realize "There is no single hu(wo)
man who is not as good as me in the world."

1981–1988 + Serves as an overseas (Berlin) correspondent for Korean
Film Council overseas and for *Auditorium*, a South Korean
monthly magazine on music and performing arts.
+ Becomes a PhD candidate at the Free University of Berlin.

1988 + Founds a production company called Kaidu Production.
She directs and produces documentary films as well as
promotional films.

1990 + She makes a multi-cube video, which is screened as
part of a special performance entitled *Sounds, sounds for
a thousand years* for Inter-Korean high-level talks on
December 11th.

1991 + Directs *The Silence of Love*, her film adaptation of
Han Yong-un's poems.
Wins a golden video award for director at Golden Disc
Awards (formerly the Korea Visual and Records Grand
Prize Award).

1991–1998 + She teaches at Cheongju University, Division of Theater
and Film.

1992 + Directs a documentary film, *Hope Today is the Day*.
It is an educational film where a song and dance come
together. The song is written to revive Korean people's
spirit and enthusiasm and urge people to be brave,
courageous and never lose hope. The film combines the
song and dance, aimed at introduce the performance
as an instruction for those who want to sing the song and
dance to the song at various events.

1990년	+	12월 11일 남북고위급회담 특별공연 '소리여, 천 년의 소리여' 프로그램의 멀티큐브 영상물 제작.
1991년	+	만해 한용운의 시를 영화화한 〈님의 침묵〉 연출. 대한민국 영상음반대상 골든비디오상 감독상 수상.
1991년 – 1998년	+	청주대학교 연극영화과 출강.
1992년	+	다큐멘터리 〈오늘이 오늘이소서〉 연출. 잃어버린 우리 민족의 신명과 흥을 되살려, 진취적이고 희망적인 삶을 살아가자는 취지로 만들어진 "오늘이 오늘이소서"에 춤을 붙여 각종 행사놀이의 교재용으로 활용하고 보급하는 데 목적.
1993년	+	대전엑스포 정부관 영상물 〈달리는 한국인〉 제작, 연출.
1995년	+	한솔제지 30주년 기념영화 〈종이의 꿈〉 연출.
1996년	+	〈작은 도서실의 꿈〉 연출.(금성출판사, 독서출판문화협회 제작)
1996년 – 1999년	+	방송위원회(구 종합유선방송위원회) 제3심의(영화심의)위원회 위원.
1998년	+	자전적 에세이 『영화에 미친 사람은 아름답다』(이웃사람) 출간.
	+	서울국제가족영화제 심사위원장.
1999년	+	『여성문화/예술이론』(도서출판 동인) 출간. 하남국제환경엑스포 주제관 영상물 〈어린 왕자의 지구별 여행〉 연출.
1999년 – 2009년	+	충청남도 백제문화 개발자문위원회 위원.
2000년	+	다큐채널 CTN 제작본부장.

아이 엠 인디펜던트 ― 한옥희

1993 + Produces and directs *Running Koreans*, a promotional
film for Taejon Expo '93, Government Hall.

1995 + Directs *The Dream of Paper*, a commemoration film
for the 30th anniversary of Hansol Paper.

1996 + Directs *The Dream of a Little Library*, produced by
Kumsung Publishing and Korean Publishers Association.

1996–1999 + Serves as a member of film division, Korea Broadcasting
Commission (formerly Korea Communications
Commission).

1998 + She publishes an autobiographical essay entitled *People
who Go Crazy about Films are Beautiful* (Iutsaram).
+ Serves as the jury president for Seoul International
Family Film Festival.

1999 + Publishes *Feminist Culture / Art Theory* (Donginbook).
Directs *Little Prince's Trip to Planet Earth*,
a promotional video film for Hanam Expo, International
Environment Hall.

1999–2009 + Serves as a member of Baekje Culture Promotion
Committee, Chungcheongnam-do.

2000 + Works as a general manager for the production
department of CTN, a documentary channel.

2000–2009 + She teaches at Sungshin Women's University.

2001 + Joins Green Post Korea as an executive, in charge of
production and broadcast programming.

2003–2007 + Serves as the jury president for UNICA KOREA
International Film Festival.

2003–Present + She has been working as CEO of Green Communication.

2004 + On December 10, *Colour Of Korea* is screened at
the 30th Seoul Independent Film Festival. It is one of the
opening films.

2000년-2009년 + 성신여자대학교 출강.

2001년 + 환경TV 제작, 편성이사.

2003년-2007년 + 유니카세계단편영화제 심사위원장.

2003년-현재 + 그린커뮤니케이션 대표.

2004년 + 12월 10일 제30회 서울독립영화제 개막작 중 한 편으로
〈색동〉 상영.

2005년 + 한국관광공사 해외 홍보영화 〈5000 Years of Mystery〉
제작 및 연출.

2005년 + 〈격동의 시대를 뛰어넘은 반란의 기록들〉 연출.

2008년-2012년 + 영상물 등급위원회 심의위원.

2010년-2018년 + 제1회-제9회 국제청소년평화·휴머니즘 영상공모제
심사위원장.

2011년 + 국제영화비평가연맹(FIPRESCI) 제7대 한국본부 회장.

2012년 + 제5회 서울세계단편영화제 심사위원장.
올해의 여성영화인 공로상 수상.

2013년 + 제50회 대종상영화제 심사위원장.

2015-2019년 + 유니카코리아(UNICA KOREA) 국제영화제 심사위원장.

2018년 + 독일 오버하우젠국제단편영화제 〈구멍〉 초청.

2019년 + 제44회 토론토국제영화제 파장 부문 〈2분 40초〉 초청.

2005 + She produces and directs a promotional film,
5000 Years of Mystery, for international audience.
The project is supported by Korea Tourism
Organization.

2005 + Directs *Records of Resistance Transcending the
Era of Turmoil*.

2008 – 2012 + Serves as a committee member, Korea Media
Rating Board.

2010 – 2018 + Serves as the jury president for the first nine editions
of the Institute for Future and Religionship Youth
Video Contest For Peace and Humanism.

2011 + Serves as the 7th president of FIPKO,
Korean chapter of FIPRESCI (International Federation
of Film Critics).

2012 + Serves as the jury president for Seoul World Short
Film Festival.
She wins an Honorary Award from the annual
meeting of Women in Film Korea.

2013 + Serves as the jury president for the 50th Grand Bell
Award.

2015 – 2019 + Serves as the jury president for UNICA KOREA
International Film Festival.

2018 + *The Hole* is invited to the International Short Film
Festival Oberhausen.

2019 + *2minutes 40seconds* is invited to the Wavelength
section at the 44th Toronto International Film Festival.

Filmography

1973 + The Hole (16mm)
1974 + Batjul (16mm)
1974 + The Middle Dogs Day (16mm)

필모그래피

1973 + 구멍(16mm)
1974 + 밧줄(16mm)
1974 + 중복(16mm)
1974 + 몰살의 노래(카이두 클럽 공동연출)
1974 + 엘리베이터(카이두 클럽 공동연출)
1975 + 세 개의 거울(16mm)
1975 + 2분 40초(16mm)
1976 + 색동(16mm)
1977 + 무제 77-A(16mm)
1991 + 님의 침묵(VHS)
1992 + 오늘이 오늘이소서
1993 + 달리는 한국인 (70mm, 대전엑스포 정부관 영상물)
1995 + 종이의 꿈(한솔제지 30주년 기념영화)
1996 + 작은 도서실의 꿈(금성출판사, 독서출판문화협회 제작)
1999 + 어린 왕자의 지구별 여행(하남국제환경엑스포
          주제관 영상물)
2005 + 5000 Years of Mystery(한국관광공사 해외 홍보영화)
2005 + 격동의 시대를 뛰어넘은 반란의 기록들

수상경력

1975 + 서울독립영화제(구 한국청소년영화제)
          우수상, 〈2분 40초〉
1976 + 서울독립영화제(구 한국청소년영화제)
          우수상, 〈색동〉
1991 + 대한민국 영상음반대상 골든비디오상 감독상
          수상, 〈님의 침묵〉
2012 + 올해의 여성영화인 공로상 수상

1974 + Song of Genocide (co-directed with Kaidu Club members)
1974 + Elevator (co-directed with Kaidu Club members)
1975 + The Three Mirrors (16mm)
1975 + 2minutes 40seconds (16mm)
1976 + Colour Of Korea (16mm)
1977 + Untitled 77-A (16mm)
1991 + The Silence of Love (VHS, Cinepoem)
1992 + Hope Today is the Day
1993 + Running Koreans (70mm, promotional film for Taejon Expo '93, Government Hall)
1995 + The Dream of Paper (commemoration film for the 30th anniversary of Hansol Paper)
1996 + The Dream of a Little Library (produced by Kumsung Publishing and Korean Publishers Association)
1999 + Little Prince's Trip to Planet Earth (promotional video for Hanam Expo, International Environment Hall)
2005 + 5000 Years of Mystery
2005 + Records of Resistance Transcending the Era of Turmoil

Honors and Awards

1975 + Excellent Picture Award, the first Seoul Independent Film Festival (formerly Korea Youth Film Festival) – *2minutes 40seconds*
1976 + Excellent Picture Award, the Seoul Independent Film Festival (formerly Korea Youth Film Festival) – *Colour Of Korea*
1991 + Golden Video Award for director, Golden Disc Awards (formerly the Korea Visual and Records Grand Prize Award) – *The Silence of Love*
2012 + Honorary Award, Women in Film Korea

↗ Newspaper mater
reporting the Kaid
Experimental Film
Research Society
1970s
1970년대 카이두
신문보도

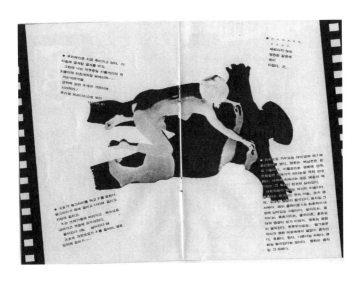

아이 엠 인디펜던트 ― 한옥희

안나 카리나

Anna Karina
Model, Actor, Director, Writer

Anna Karina (1940 – 2019). A highly famous actor known as the French New Wave (Nouvelle Vauge) icon, Anna Karina directed two feature films. Her directorial debut *Vivre Ensemble* (*Living Together*, 1973) depicts a young woman who leads a new life as an independent woman after a life-changing and turbulent love affair. In was screened at the Cannes Film Festival in 1973 only to face "lots of resistance." Her work was not seriously considered, with some people claiming that directing is not her job and she should stay being an actress. There was also resistance from the industry side, resulting in difficulties in financing her films. She was not given enough opportunities to pursue her career as a filmmaker and showcase her talent during her lifetime. She was an early case of a star actor turning into an auteur.

안나 카리나
모델, 배우, 영화감독, 작가

1940-2019. 프랑스 누벨바그의 대표
얼굴로 알려진 배우이자, 두 편의 장편
극영화를 연출한 감독이다. 감독 데뷔작
〈비브르 앙상블〉은 운명적 사랑 후에
독립적으로 자신의 삶을 살아가는 여성을
그렸다. 이 작품은 1973년 칸영화제에
초청되었지만 작품성에 대한 논의보다
정상급 배우로 남는 게 낫다는 언론의
종용과 배우로는 인정하지만 감독으로는
지원을 하지 않겠다는 영화산업의
반응으로 결국 감독으로서의 재능을 표출할
충분한 기회를 갖지 못한 채 세상을 떠났다.
카리나는 스타 배우가 상업영화가 아닌
작가로서 예술영화의 감독이 된 초기 사례로
기록되었다.

©GRAGNON Francois/ Getty Images

Anna
Karina

Thoughts carved on a film

By Lee Ji-hyun (Film Critic)

The film is set in Paris in the early 70s. Alain
(Michel Lancelot), a high school history teacher,
is walking down the street with a friend. There,
he randomly meets Julie (Anna Karina) and
immediately falls in love with her. As soon as he
sees her sitting at a café, a spell is cast on
him. Some may call it a huge crush. He cannot
even move a bit. And not long after this first
encounter, he abandons his partner for a long
time, Sylvie, and moves in with Julie. That is how
their "vivre ensemble (living together)" begins.
They are just a bit better than broke, but they
are all happy and merry. Alain even gives up his
teaching job to spend more time with Julie.
One day, Julie hands to Alain two tickets to New
York, suggesting they spend a good time with
buddies. Not long after they get to New York,
Alain realizes that an unplanned and wild dream
is not at all different from being on a sinking ship,
reckless and dangerous. But nobody knows
how to stop it. He tries to avoid the reality by
boozing and getting high.

Anna Karina's *Vivre Ensemble* (*Living Together*,
1973) can possibly fit into the category of a
romance film. Set in Paris and New York in 1972,
the film tells us a turbulent love story. Some say
that this film is just "so Anna Karina," the French
New Wave icon. Indeed, she starred in the
movie. It was her directorial debut, which can be
a surprise to some. The plot has a few interesting
turnovers. The light-hearted love affair turns
out to be grave like destiny. It quickly ends in
tragedy. In the process of breakdown, nothing

하나의 필름에 새겨진 생각
안나 카리나의 〈비브르 앙상블〉

글: 이지현
(영화평론가)

1970년대 초의 파리, 고등학교에서 역사를 가르치는 '알랭(미셸 랑슬로)'은 친구와 함께 길을 걷던 중 우연히 마주친 '줄리(안나 카리나)'와 사랑에 빠진다. 카페에 앉은 그녀를 보자마자, 그는 마법처럼 움직일 수 없게 된다. 그리고 얼마 지나지 않아, 오랜 연인 실비를 떠나서 그는 줄리의 집으로 이사한다. 그렇게 두 사람의 '함께 살기(vivre ensemble)'가 시작된다. 풍족하지 않지만 둘은 마냥 행복하다. 심지어 학교 일을 그만두면서까지, 알랭은 줄리의 곁에만 머물려 한다. 그러던 어느 날 그녀가 알랭에게 비행기표 두 장을 내밀면서 특별한 목적이 없는 둘만의 휴가가 시작된다. 그저 편히 친구들과 함께 어울려 놀자고 줄리는 제안한다. 하지만 뉴욕에 도착하고 얼마 지나지 않아, 알랭은 깨닫는다. 대안 없는 꿈은 흡사 난파선을 타고 있는

can stop Julie and Alain. It is rather surprising that a successful actress of the time came up with such a despairing love story. The storylines turn dark and hopeless. It is interesting that we can find bits of Anna Karina's life from various moments in the movie. Anna Karina was a 17 year old Danish girl when she first arrived in Paris. She was doing a shoot for a magazine and met Coco Chanel, who said to her "You should call yourself Anna Karina." A couple of years later, she was discovered by Jean-Luc Godard and became the New Wave icon. Ironically, *Vivre Ensemble* is a complete opposite of her life story in some senses. Alain's life is full of misfortune. He keeps making the worst decisions, rendering his life miserable. Julie's case is not at all different. She was an out-of-work actress. She gives up finally her dream to work as a salesgirl. All these happened to be so, simply because Alain and Julie fell for each other. They were meant to be together. They were trapped in a downward spiral of a destined love. Julie finds Alain irresponsible. She confirms that Alain is not at all capable of taking responsibilities, especially after the baby is born. The man Julie loved so much is not there anymore. Such details in the scenario remind us of Karina's own miscarriage in May 1961. She was a star, which made many people comment

← *Living Together*
〈비브르 앙상블〉
©Malavida

것과 마찬가지로 위험하다는 걸 알게 된다. 하지만 멈출 방법이 없다. 오직 술과 담배에 의존하면서, 그는 현실을 탈출하려고 한다.

안나 카리나의 〈비브르 앙상블〉(1973)은 한마디로 '로맨스 영화'다. 1972년의 파리와 뉴욕을 배경으로 영화는 어느 커플의 격동적인 관계를 그린다. 하지만 사람들은 이 영화를 '누벨바그의 여신, 안나 카리나의 영화'라고 부른다. 실제로 그녀가 출연하기 때문이기도 하지만, 놀랍게도 직접 연출한 작품이기 때문이다. 영화의 줄거리에는 몇 가지 흥미로운 반전 포인트가 있다. 가벼운 리듬의 운명적 사랑은 가파른 파국을 맞이한다. 그 과정에서 인물들을 통제할 만한 힘 있는 브레이크는 발견되지 못한다. 성공한 여배우가 직접 쓴 시나리오라 믿기 힘들 정도로, 플롯이 어둡고 비극적이다. 극의 전개 과정에서 배우의 실제 모습이 연상된다는 점도 특별하다. 덴마크 출신의 안나 카리나가 프랑스에 도착했던 때는 고작 17살 무렵이었다. 그녀는 우연찮게 사진 촬영장에서 만난 코코 샤넬에게 '카리나'란 예명을 얻었다. 이후 장뤼크 고다르의 눈에 띄어서 단번에 '시대의 아이콘'이 됐다. 아이러니하게도 영화는 이와 같은 실제의 에피소드를 정반대로 반영한다. 이를테면 주인공 알랭은 매우 운이 없는 인물로 그려진다. 매번 스스로 택한 현명하지 못한 선택으로 그는 점점 더 나락에 빠진다. 배우를 꿈꾸는 줄리의 상황도 마찬가지다. 그녀는 결국 자신의 꿈을 버리고 상점의 판매원이 되는 결말을 맞는다. 영화 속 모든 사건이 우연히 시작된 '운명적 사랑'에서 비롯된다는 점은 아이러니하다. 아이가 태어나

on that incident. Maybe Karina, as a director, wanted to tell her own life story. Now we see how *Vivre Ensemble* comes across as an interesting blend of memories from the New Wave days and Anna Karina's own life stories.

Anna Karina was a star. She was famous, which unfortunately made her filmmaking even more of a challenge. Her directorial work was not smooth sailing. Her application for French CNC (the National Centre for Cinema and the Moving Image) was under the name of Michel Wally, probably because she believed that her work would be taken more seriously under that pseudonym. This may also be a piece of evidence suggesting that she wanted to become a director, who is somewhat detached from her own identity. Note that she chose a name that she believed to sound masculine and foreign. She later recalled that she was one unconventional actress who directed a film around that time. There were exceptions such as Agnès Varda, but still, it seemed almost impossible for women to direct films then. Female directors were extremely hard to find and they struggled. As a director, Karina was very proactive. She was actively involved in production. She wrote scenarios. She started a production company. She starred in her directorial work. Even after establishing her own production company, Raska, she reached out to René Pignères of SNC Production and suggested a collaboration. Although she was an established name in the arena of cinema, it was still a challenge for her to direct and make films. French cinema was largely dominated by men, adding extra burden on her challenges. After its completion, *Vivre Ensemble* was invited to Semaine de la Critique (Critics' Week), Cannes Film Festival in 1973.

는 과정에서 알랭의 책임감 없는 태도를 보면서, 이 사실을 다시금 확인한다. 줄리가 한때 사랑했던 남자는 이곳에 없다. 시나리오의 이러한 설정은 1961년 5월에 카리나가 직접 겪은 유산의 경험을 떠올리게 만든다. 그녀는 잘 알려진 스타였고, 너무 많은 사람들이 이 사실을 언급했다. 어쩌면 연출자로서 카리나는 1960년대에 자신이 겪었던 일들을 영화에 담으려 했던 것 같다. 그 속에는 누벨바그의 추억이, 그리고 개인적인 경험담이 자연스레 녹아 있다.

유명 스타이긴 했지만 영화제작의 과정이 순조롭진 않았다. 1972년 프랑스국립영화센터(CNC)에 보낼 제작지원 신청서를 작성할 때, 그녀가 가명을 사용한 것은 단적인 증거가 된다. 그편이 업계 관계자들에게 객관적이고 진지하게 이 프로젝트를 소개하는 방식이라 그녀는 믿었다. 당시 카리나가 사용했던 '미셸 월리'라는 이름은 남성적으로 들리는 이국적인 호칭이었다. "당시에 영화를 연출했던 배우는 나뿐이었던 것 같다." 훗날 그녀는 스스로 말한다. 사실 당대에는 여성감독 자체가 드물었다. 아녜스 바르다와 같은 일부 예외가 존재했지만, 여성감독으로 일하는 것은 불가능해 보였다. 게다가 카리나는 다른 어떤 감독들보다 적극적으로 제작에 관여했다. 시나리오를 작성하고 제작사를 세웠으며, 연출과 연기를 직접 맡았다. 영화제작사 라스카를 설립한 뒤에도, 그녀는 SNC 프로덕션의 르네 피녜르에게 연락해 공동제작을 제안했다. 그녀 스스로 유명한 영화계의 인사였지만, 시스템 바깥에서의 도전은 마찬가지로 험난했다. 프랑스 사회가 남성 위주 분위기였단 점도 이유였다. 하지만 완성 이후 이 영화는 1973년 칸영화제의 비평가주간에

It must have been a huge reward for her effort. In 2017, a restored version of *Vivre Ensemble* (4K digital) was officially released on DVD. The running time of the restored version is shortened to 93 minutes compared to 110 minutes of the original version.

To an artist who lived in the era of New Wave, "making your own film" never seemed like a mission impossible. Rather, filmmaking was more like something that can naturally follow from having a career related to films. The New Wave movement made it possible for everybody to make films. Filmmaking became more accessible and inviting. New Wave filmmakers did not make films following strict filmmaking conventions or formalisms. Rather, filmmaking was almost a social phenomenon. From 1957 to 1962, 150 directors made more than 250 films. Interestingly, it is quite impossible to find a common thread among the films of that time. That time, television platform was gaining popularity. As a consequence, the new genre of film, namely TV film, was emerging. Production companies tried to produce more films with lower budget, and as a natural consequence, more opportunities were given to novice directors. They made their directorial debut through references from a director who just made a successful film. But among the numerous directors who started their career during the New Wave days, only about twenty survived and are still remembered as influential names of the era. All of them were never afraid to reject conventions and explore new ways of filmmaking. And that is probably the single thing that binds them together. Other than that, it is extremely difficult to find some elements that they all share. For this reason, for a

초청되어 그간의 노력을 보상받는다. 그리고 〈비브르 앙상블〉은 2017년 9월에 4K 디지털로 복원되어 DVD로 정식 출시되었다. 그 과정에서 기존의 110분 러닝타임은 93분으로 줄어들게 된다.

어쩌면 누벨바그 시대를 거쳐 온 아티스트가 '스스로 영화를 제작한다'는 사실은 그다지 놀랍지 않은, 예정된 보상처럼 여겨지기도 한다. 누벨바그야말로 "누구든지 영화를 만들 수 있다"라는 모토로 움직이는 영화운동이었기 때문이다. 요컨대 누벨바그 시기의 영화제작자들은 형식주의를 따르는 영화를 만들지 않았다. 그보다는 영화제작 자체가 일종의 '사회현상'에 더 가까웠다. 이를테면 1957년에서 1962년 사이에만 무려 150여 명의 감독들이 250편 이상의 영화를 창작했다. 그리고 이들 작품의 공통점을 찾기는 불가능했다. 당시는 '텔레비전 플랫폼'이 유행하며 이른바 'TV 영화'라는 새로운 장르가 생겨나던 시기

아이 엠 인디펜던트 ― 안나 카리나

comprehensive and exhaustive explanation for the New Wave cinema, one might need to regard the New Wave filmmakers as a "circle" of people who shared common interests rather than those who shared cinematographic techniques or aesthetic viewpoints.

One major group of influential names of the New Wave is the directors associated with *Cahiers du cinéma*. They are probably the best known New Wave directors, including Jean-Luc Godard, Claude Chabrol, François Truffaut, Éric Rohmer, and Jacques Rivette. Their works are considered to show the very gist of the New Wave auteurism. Also well-established are Rive Gauche directors including Alain Resnais, Chris Marker, Pierre Kast, and Agnès Varda. Some of them collaborated with nouveau roman writers. Overall, their works tended to touch on political and cultural issues. A third group of directors are often called *aventuriers de la caméra* (*camera adventurers*), who were deeply interested in documentaries. Such directors include Jean Rouch and Pierre Schoendoerffer. They preferred to take their camera to shoot raw material, showing a strong preference to the methods of direct cinema. A lot of wild-looking, rough scenes of the French New Wave films come from this group of directors' works. A fourth group of New Wave directors would include Jacques Demy or Jacques Rozier. They are rather difficult to group under a certain category. They directed masterpieces that has major significant in the history of cinema, however, some of their works do not seem to directly fit in with the New Wave movement. The fifth group of directors, who some French academics consider the last generation of the New Wave, includes Louis Malle, Claude Sautet, and Roger Vadim, among others. They belonged to the studio system and made

였다. 제작사들은 적은 비용으로 더 많은 작품들을 생산하려 애썼고, 따라서 자연스럽게 신인 감독들에게 기회가 주어졌다. 한 명의 연출자가 성공하면, 그가 제작사에 또 다른 감독을 추천하는 식으로 많은 기회의 문이 열려 있었다. 하지만 수많은 신진 감독들 중 살아남은 연출자는 고작 20여 명 정도였다. 이들 감독들 대부분이 후대에 누벨바그의 대표 주자로 언급되고 있다. 고전주의적 시스템을 뛰어넘는다는 것을 제외하면, 여전히 그들 전부를 아우르는 공통적인 미학을 찾기는 어렵다. 따라서 누벨바그 영화를 설명하기 위해서는, 기법이나 성향보다는 '동일한 이해관계'를 통한 일종의 클럽(circle)으로 분류하는 편이 수월하다.

첫째, 가장 유명한 누벨바그 주자들은 영화잡지 '카이에뒤시네마' 출신의 필진들이다. 고다르를 비롯해 클로드 샤브롤, 프랑수아 트뤼포, 에리크 로메르, 자크 리베트 등이 여기 속한다. 이들이야말로 '누벨바그 작가주의'의 진정한 핵심이라 말할 수 있다. 둘째로 '좌익 작가들'도 잘 알려져 있다. 대표적으로 알랭 레네, 크리스 마커, 피에르 카스트, 아녜스 바르다 등이 이 부류에 해당한다. 이 두 번째 감독들은 간혹 누보로망 소설가들과 함께 일했고, 대체로 정치적이고 문화적인 성향의 작품을 만들었다. 세 번째로 '카메라의 모험가'라 불리는 다큐멘터리 학파가 존재한다. 장 루슈와 피에르 쇤도르페르 등이 여기 해당된다. 이들은 '날것'의 촬영 대상을 선호했다. 그리고 다이렉트 시네마의 방식으로 제작하려 노력했다. 다소 거친 누벨바그 화면이 이 세 번째 부류의 대표적 경향이었다. 넷째로 자크 드미 혹은 자

their debut after gaining experiences in making feature films during the 50s. They later made commercially successful films with some nuance of the New Wave. Some say that they jumped on the bandwagon, while others say that their works naturally resulted from what people of the time were most excited about.

Given this context, we can ask ourselves a question: where does Anna Karina belong? I think it is be fair to introduce her as a director who made non-mainstream films and who was largely influenced by Jean-Luc Godard. Godard did not only grant her an honor. He passed on to her a number of very useful tips for filmmaking and producing. What made it possible to shoot in the US with no permission or whatsoever? Probably her experience of working with Godard. Together, they made seven feature films. These include all of Godard's early works except for *À bout de souffle* (*Breathless*, 1960). For these reasons, one can summarize *Vivre Ensemble* as a film based on the Godard-style French New Wave techniques. At the same time, it is a film made with production methods originally designed and crafted by Anna Karina. As a matter of fact, many New Wave directors dreamt of some economic revolution. Karina was not an exception to this. Most directors of that time had little, if no, prior experiences with filmmaking. Then, *Vivre Ensemble* being a directorial debut would not be problematic. However, something other than the director's prior experience mattered. She was a woman. A famous woman. Ironically, her being a woman who was probably way too famous made things challenging. Her name would probably have put a significant psychological pressure on herself.

When *Vivre Ensemble* was made, the European society was moving towards social reforms

크 로지에 등과 같이 분류하기 어려운 거장들도 누벨바그 영역에서 언급된다. 이들은 각자 당대의 역사에 기록될 만한 대표작을 남겼지만, 지속적으로 누벨바그의 맥락에서 작업하지는 않았다. 그리고 마지막 다섯 번째로, 프랑스 학계에서 누벨바그의 최종 부류라고 간주되는 감독들이 있다. 이를테면 루이 말, 클로드 소테, 로제 바댕과 같이 스튜디오 시스템에 속했던 연출자들이 그렇다. 이들은 1950년대에 장편영화 현장에서 경험을 쌓아서 데뷔했고, 상업영화의 방식으로 누벨바그 느낌의 영화들을 만들었다. 정확히 말해 그들이 만든 영화는, 당대 유행한 조류에 자연스럽게 편승한 결과라 볼 수 있다.

안나 카리나의 경우, 그녀는 고다르에게 강한 영향을 받은 비주류 연출자라고 소개해야 한다. 고다르가 그녀에게 남긴 것은 단순한 명예만이 아니었다. 그는 제작 방식의 측면에서 유용한 팁을 여럿 전수하였다. 예를 들어 미국에서의 게릴라 촬영은 이전에 고다르와 함께 일한 덕분에 가능한 일이었다. 실제로 카리나와 고다르 커플이 함께 만든 장편영화는 무려 7편에 달한다. 〈네 멋대로 해라〉(1960)를 제외한 고다르의 초기작 전부가 이에 해당된다. 따라서 〈비브르 앙상블〉은 고다르식의 누벨바그 기법을 기초로, 카리나가 자율적으로 디자인한 제작 방식으로 완성된 영화라고 말할 수 있다. 사실 누벨바그 감독들은 대부분 '경제적인 혁명'을 꿈꿨다. 카리나도 별반 다르지 않았다. 당대 대부분의 신진 감독들이 경험이 전무했거나 아주 적었기 때문에, 데뷔작이란 것은 큰 문제가 아니었다. 하지만 그녀가 여성이었고, 지나치게 유명했다. 이 사실은 심리적 부담을 줬다.

happened after the Vietnamese war. Contrary to Godardian *La Chinoise* (*The Chinese*, 1967) and *Le Gai Savoir* (*Joy of Learning*, 1969), which touched on social issues surrounding '68 protests at a metaphysical level, Karina's film took an indirect way of addressing some issues of post-protest world. Unlike *Pierrot le Fou* (1965), which openly had a political theme, *Vivre Ensemble*, at least apparently, is a romance film. But it was never completely detached from social issues. The era was all about talking about peace. And she probably followed the crowd. But the purpose of her doing so was not to pursue romantic ideals. Instead, she took the indirect route to talk about social issues. All those who are in the film show us where they desire to belong. But they are not determined to change the world. What did she want us to find from the young people at Central Park and Greenwich Village? Probably not their proactive attitude and outgoing personality. I believe that she wanted us to find futile purposefulness. Mottos shouted out by those who merely needed people to hang out with or something to admire will end up being dismantled. Quick and cheap solidarity and passion roamed everywhere, but the mottos were going nowhere but just hovering in the air. Who made Karina's films political? Probably Godard. He must be the culprit.

With regards to cinematographic techniques, we can say that the New Wave dominated the New Wave icon. *Vivre Ensemble* was shot using a portable 16mm camera, often times handheld. Nagra recorder was used for a simultaneous recording. They had the minimum number of staff required. They took advantage of natural light. All these helped the filmmaking to be budget-friendly. Most of the scenes, except for those shot in New York, were shot inside and

〈비브르 앙상블〉이 제작되던 당시, 1970년대 유럽의 분위기는 베트남전 이후의 사회변혁을 향해 나아가던 중이었다. 비견컨대 〈중국 여인〉(1967)이나 〈즐거운 지식〉(1969) 같은 고다르의 영화들이 형이상학적으로 68혁명 당시를 묘사했다면, 카리나의 영화는 우회적 방식으로 '혁명 이후'를 그리려 했다. 그리고 〈미치광이 피에로〉(1965)가 대놓고 정치영화였던 것과 달리, 〈비브르 앙상블〉은 로맨틱 드라마의 외향을 뒤집어쓴 사회적인 영화였다. 시대가 평화를 말했기에, 그녀는 이를 표방했다. 하지만 에둘러 현실을 노래할 뿐 낭만성 자체가 목적은 아니었다. 실제로 이 영화의 등장인물은 이상향을 드러낼 뿐, 어느 누구도 세계를 움직이려 들지 않는다. 영화 속 센트럴파크와 그리니치 빌리지의 젊은이들에게서 우리가 진정 발견해야 하는 것은, 그들의 외향적인 모습이 아니다. 그보다는 허무한 목적성 자체를 살펴야 한다. 단지 구호에 그치는 동경이나 동질성의 개념은 결국 해체될 것이기 때문이다. 매우 빠르게 연대하고 열정적으로 소리치지만, 당대의 슬로건은 허공을 맴돈다. 어쩌면 카리나의 영화가 정치적인 것은 모두 고다르의 탓이다.

기술적으로도 누벨바그의 방식이 그녀를 지배했다. 〈비브르 앙상블〉의 촬영은 16mm 카메라와 핸드헬드 기법을 이용해서 가볍게 이뤄졌다. 그리고 나그라 녹음기를 사용해 동시녹음이 진행되었다. 최소한의 인원들이 모여 자연광을 이용해 촬영장의 경제성을 높였다. 뉴욕을 제외한 촬영 대부분을 실제 카리나가 거주하던 아파트의 내부와 외부에서 진행했다. 줄리의 '5층 다락방' 세트는 아파트 내부에 설치되었고, 길거리 촬영은 생 제

outside of an apartment that Karina lived in. Julie's 5th floor attic set was built inside of Karina's apartment. Most street scenes were shot just around Quartier Saint-Germain-des-Prés, not far from the apartment. She later explained that it took her about a month to write the scenario and four weeks to shoot and produce the film. She only had less than a week to shoot in New York. The shooting was never approved, so basically she had to sneak into places and shoot. She did not have a lot of time for shooting and things were under the covers, the outcomes are however quite satisfying. Also interesting is the background of Michel Lancelot, who played Alain. He was a presenter at a radio station called Europe 1. *Vivre Ensemble* was his debut as an actor. The New Wave movement also recruited a lot of new actors and actresses. This tendency contributed to the fresh look of many New Wave films.

It is commonly thought that films are less serious than performing arts such as theater and dance. However, I cannot agree with this preconception. Typically, films are made by carefully worked out plans ahead of time. Improvisation rarely occurs during filmmaking. Most basic filmmaking techniques are never open-ended and thus quite "heavy." This aspect of filmmaking has influenced the development of filmmaking techniques. Actors' active involvement in the filmmaking process emerged from the late 1950s. Before then, actors have typically been treated as some elements in mise-en-scène. One exception to this tendency might be Jean Renoir, who took advantage of improvisation in *La Règle du jeu* (*The Rules of the Game*, 1939). However, it was a rather unconventional case, especially during the time when it was made. Renoir let only a few of the

르맹 데 프레 근방에서 해결했다. 훗날 그녀의 설명에 따르면 시나리오 작성에 한 달이 걸렸고, 이후 제작 과정에는 총 4주가 소요되었다고 한다. 그중 뉴욕 촬영 일정은 일주일 이내로, 허가 없이 몰래 찍어야 했다. 짧은 촬영 기간 내내 비밀스럽게 움직였지만, 미국 분량의 결과물은 만족스럽다. 그 밖에 알랭을 연기하는 '미셸 랑슬로'의 등장도 재미있는 부분이다. 그는 1968년부터 1972년까지 '유럽 1'이라는 라디오채널에서 진행을 맡았는데, 이 작품은 그의 첫 번째 연기 도전이었다. 새로운 배우를 출연시키는 누벨바그의 연출 방식은 영화의 분위기를 신선하게 만들었다.

대부분의 관객들이 연극이나 무용 같은 무대예술보다 영화가 더 가벼운 매체라고 믿는다. 하지만 이 말은 사실이 아니다. 극영화에 즉흥성의 요소가 도입된 것 자체가 평범한 일이 아니기 때문이다. 기본적으로 영화의 테크닉은 폐쇄적이고 무거운 편에 속한다. 이 사실은 영화 제작 양식의 발달에 영향을 줬다. 본격적으로 '배우'가 영화에 능동적으로 개입하기 시작한 것은 1950년대 후반부터로, 이전까지 배우들은 마치 미장센의 요소처럼 소모되는 측면이 있었다. 일찍이 장 르누아르가 〈게임의 규칙〉(1939)에서 즉흥연기를 활용한 적이 있지만, 그는 예외적이고 특별한 경우였다. 르누아르는 특정 배우에게 비밀스럽게 연출 방향을 일러 주고, 나머지 배역들이 현장에서 즉각 반응하길 원했다. 〈게임의 규칙〉에서는 옥타브 캐릭터가 그 역할을 맡았다. 동일한 연출 방식이 후대에 모리스 피알라를 통해 재연된다. 피알라는 스스로 자신의 영화에 출연해서 배우들의

actors know about the directions and had others react to it. In *La Règle du jeu*, Octave took charge of a special role. Later, the same directorial technique was revived by Maurice Pialat. Pialat starred in his directorial work and led other actors' responses and acting. Some suggested that Sandrine Bonnaire's outstanding acting benefited from Pialat's implicit directions. However, allowing actors to improvise was not received as a mainstream filmmaking method. Until the 1940s, such methods were considered as extreme or even eccentric. So-called documentary acting became more prevalent only after the New Wave era. For instance, Jacques Rivette is well known for his adoption of improvised acting. He intended dissonance between unnatural emotion and actual movements. He did not release the pre-planned

← *Living Together*
〈비브르 앙상블〉
©Malavida

연기를 이끌었다. 실제로 상드린 보네르의 자연스런 연기는 피알라 덕분이란 말이 있다. 하지만 1940년대까지 이러한 급진적인 방법론은 일반화되지 못한다. 이른바 다큐멘터리 방식의 연기가 공식적으로 사용된 것은 누벨바그 시대 이후부터이다. 대표적으로 자크 리베트를 통해 즉흥연기가 사용되었다. 그는 인공적인 감정과 실제의 움직임이 만드는 불협화음을 의도했다. 대본을 미리 배우들에게 주지 않았고, 몇 장의 시놉시스로 현장을 통솔했다. 때로는 촬영 전날이나 당일에 스크립트를 넘기기도 했다.

이렇게 말한다면 어떨까. 만일 누군가 내게 〈비브르 앙상블〉을 좋아하지 않는다고 고백한다면, 나는 그가 전반부만 보았기 때문이라고 답할 것 같다. 그 정도로 이 영화의 매력은 중반 이후로 몰려 있다. 특히 미국에서의 에피소드부터 드라마틱한 에너지는 증대된다. 심지어 이 영화를 개봉한 뒤, 곧바로 카리나가 한 편을 더 만들었다면 어땠을까 상상하게 될 정도로 매력적이다. 그녀 스스로 주도하는 즉흥연기도 훌륭하지만 솔직히 말해 〈비브르 앙상블〉은 여배우 안나 카리나의 가장 훌륭한 연기를 담은 필름이 아니기에 다른 가치가 보인다. 당대의 그녀 모습이 매우 솔직하게 기록되어 있다는 면이 흥미롭다. 이토록 아름다운 슬픔의 뉘앙스, 이국적 억양과 자유의 몸짓을 그녀보다 더잘 표현할 배우가 있겠는가. 일부의 시네필들에겐 그것만으로도 작품의 가치는 충분하다.

고다르의 영화에서 발견했던 카리나 얼굴의 장엄한 이미지가

scripts to the actors. Instead, he sometimes directed with a few pages of synopsis. From time to time, he let the actors have the script only a few days before shooting or even on the shooting day.

If someone tells me that they are not a huge fan of *Vivre Ensemble*, I suspect one thing: they might have watched only the first half of the film. To that extent, I love the latter half of the film. I find it irresistibly attractive. More precisely, the dramatic energy builds up and gets amplified from the episodes in the US. The latter half of the film is so mesmerizing that it made me often wonder what if Karina made a sequel right after *Vivre Ensemble* came out. It is wonderful to watch Anna Karina improvising under her own directorial lead. Her acting was great, but I personally do not think *Vivre Ensemble* shows the best of her acting. However, that very aspect allows to find some extremely interesting things about the film. Why not we explore the most natural appearance of Anna Karina from *Vivre Ensemble*? Think about who would be ever able to portray a person who has a nuanced tone of beautiful sorrow like her. Who would be ever able to speak with such an interesting accent like her? Would anyone other than Anna Karina be ever able to embody such free-spirited movements? The film would be more than a joy for many cinephiles to find such special aspects of Anna Karina.

Karina's face from Godardian films had some solemnity on it. It turns into the mark of a vampire and gets engraved onto the scenes of *Vivre Ensemble*. That might explain why Alain could not move even a bit at the first scene of the film. Anna Karina was right there, leading him to Wonderland. She dominates his soul. In the US,

뱀파이어의 표식이 되어서 〈비브르 앙상블〉에 새겨지는 것 같다. 영화의 첫 부분에서 주인공이 움직일 수 없었던 것은 그 때문인지 모른다. 그녀는 다름 아닌 안나 카리나이고, '이상한 나라의 앨리스'로 인도하는 영혼의 지배자이다. 미국에서 그녀는 '흰 토끼'를 안고 등장한다. 토끼를 들고 거리를 걸어가는 줄리를 보고 있자면, 사실 알랭이 과거에 마주쳤던 모습은 다름 아닌 '토끼굴'의 입구였단 생각이 든다. 보헤미안 차림의 서른 살 여성은 전쟁이 아니라 '사랑'을, 소비가 아니라 '평등'을 꿈꾼다. 그렇지만 그녀가 제시하는 환영의 대가는 가혹하다. 만일 계속 꿈을 꾸려면 굶주림을 얻게 될 것이라고 영화는 이른다. 결국 그들이 소중히 안고 다닌 하얀 토끼는 고작 '5달러'의 값어치로 교환된다. 그러고 보니 영화 속의 모든 조연들이 동화의 캐릭터와 닮았다. 담배 피는 애벌레, 가발 쓴 두꺼비, 체셔 고양이의 역할처럼 독특한 인물도 보인다.

다시 첫 장면을 떠올린다. 학교를 퇴근하고 집에서 나와, 줄리와 마주치며 알랭의 모든 것은 바뀌었다. 지금 돌아보니 환상의 입구는 사라졌지만, 술에 취한 그는 그 사실조차 인지하지 못한다. 심지어 자신이 돌봐야 할 어린아이가 방 안에서 울고 있지만, 그에겐 중요하지 않다. 줄리는 그의 행동에 상처 받는다. 하지만 그녀 역시 택할 수 있는 방법은 많지 않다. 알랭 스스로 현실로 되돌아오길 기다릴 뿐이다. 그렇게 꿈을 잊고 그녀는 새 삶을 살아간다. 결국 영화가 변형해 드러내는 루이스 캐럴의 동화는 어른들을 위한 '잔혹우화'로 바뀐다. 이윽고 마지막 장면, 계단을 오르는 줄리의 발걸음을 관객들이 바라본다. '옛날 옛적

she shows up holding a white rabbit. As I watch Julie holding a rabbit and walking down the street, it comes to my realization that Alain randomly met an entrance to the rabbit hole, not just a woman. The free-spirited Bohemian 30-year old woman dreams of love, not war. She does not dream of consumption and exploitation. She dreams of equality. However, what she has to pay for her dream or illusion is quite pricey. If she chooses to dream on, she will need to pay for that. Finally, the precious white bunny she was cuddling and adoring gets exchanged to five bucks. Now I see some characters of the film are quite similar to those from fairy tales. We can find the film version of the hookah smoking caterpillar, frog footman, and the Cheshire cat.

Let me go back to the first scene. After work, Alain goes home. Then he leaves home again. An encounter with Julie changed everything about him. He looks back on his good old days. His entrance to Wonderland is no longer there. He is drunk. He is drunk and stoned. He is not even aware of what had happened to him. The baby is crying in the other room. He needs to take care of the baby. Well, it does not matter to him. He does not care. His behavior hurts Julie. However, Julie does not have a lot of options, either. She can only wait for Alain to come back to reality. This leads her to forget about her dreams. Her new life awaits her. At last, the Lewis Carroll tale turns into a cruel fairy tale for grown-ups. At that moment, we get to watch the last scene. We follow Julie's footsteps. She is running up the stairs. In the last tableau entitled "il était une fois… (Once upon a time…)," Julie is searching for a man who left. At that moment, he wakes up and looks into the mirror. The scene is followed by an image of women's legs in red pantyhose.

에'라고 이름 붙인 마지막 챕터에서, 줄리는 사라진 남자를 찾아 헤매고 있다. 그리고 그 순간에 그는 잠에서 깨어난다. 그리고 거울을 본다. 이어지는 여자의 두 다리는 붉은 스타킹을 신고 있다. 클로드 엥겔이 작곡한 주제곡이 아픈 사랑의 결말을 대신 일러 준다. 알랭이 과연 치유받을 수 있을 것인가. 영화는 직접 그 답을 보여 주지 않는다. 어쩐지 불길한 예감이 들지만 낙담하긴 이르다. 영원히 자유로운 얼터너티브의 대안이 그 길의 끝에 놓여 있을 수도 있다.

고다르의 영화를 보면서 낭만주의 비평가들은 "진정한 시는 다른 목표가 없다"고 말했다. 그들의 말처럼 '예술을 위한 예술'이야말로 진짜 예술가들을 위로하는 유일한 방법이란 생각이 든다. 동일한 평가를 나는 그녀의 영화에 덧씌우려 한다. 〈비브르 앙상블〉은 영화의 가능성을 재발견하게 만드는, 어느 위대한 여배우의 영화이다. 하나의 필름에 새겨진 생각은 결코 육체로부터 분리되지 않는다. 가상과 현실을 가로지르는 온갖 '카리나'들이 그곳에 박제되어 있다. 바로 이 지점에서 우리는 내러티브보다 강한 작가의 주관성을 발견하게 된다. 남자의 집 현관을 향해 뛰어가는 발걸음을 보며 관객들은 또다시 꿈을 꾼다. 흔들리는 카메라와 인물들을 쫓는 트래킹쇼트, 안나 카리나가 제시하는 스타일리시한 형상을 멍하니 바라본다. 그리고 스스로 빛을 내는 무질서의 자발성을 생각한다. 어쩌면 시네마야말로, 사라져 가는 모든 희망을 구원할 유일한 방법론일 것이다.

Claude Engel's theme music sings us the ending of this sad and turbulent romance. Can Alain heal himself? The film does not give us the answer to this question. For some reasons, we might have a bad feeling about that. But we should not let it discourage us too quickly. There may be an end – an open-ended, free-spirted forever, and utterly alternative end, at the end of the road.

After all, eloquent things give birth to ideas. True poetry has no other goal. Romantic critics mentioned, art for art's sake may be the only way real artists seek consolation. I would like to say the same for Anna Karina's *Vivre Ensemble*. It is one masterpiece directed and played by a great actress, which helps us rediscover the possibilities of cinema. Thoughts carved on a film are never separated from the body. We find so many Karinas crossing and blurring the boundary between fiction and reality. Right at the spot, we find the auteur's subjective self, which is much more robust and powerful than a narrative. Watching her footsteps running towards the man's doorstep, viewers fall into a dream again. The camera is swinging. Tracking shots follow. Anna Karina presents us her stylish images, which my empty gaze follows. They make me think again about the autonomy of disorder giving light of itself. Perhaps, every fading hope will find it way only through cinema.

Lee Ji-hyun
Lee Ji-hyun is a film critic and university lecturer. She is the winner of the 13th *CINE21* Film Review Contest (2008). She received her PhD from Department of Theater and Film at Hanyang University. She writes about films and makes independent films from time to time. She directed *Winter Garden* (2014) and produced *Chasing Wires* (2021).

↗ *Living Together*
〈비브르 앙상블〉
©Malavida

이지현

이지현은 영화평론가이며, 대학에서 강사로 일하고 있다. 2008년 제13회 '씨네21' 영화평론상을 통해 등단했고, 2016년 한양대학교 대학원에서 영화학 박사과정을 졸업했다. 현재 여러 지면에 영화 관련 글을 기고하는 중이다. 아주 드문 간격으로 독립영화 만드는 일도 한다. 2014년에 다큐멘터리 〈프랑스인 김명실〉을 만들었고, 2021년에는 〈전선을 따라서〉라는 영화를 제작했다.

Anna Karina

1940 – Early Life + On September 22, Anna Karina is born Hanne Karin
Blarke Bayer in Solbjerg, Frederiksberg, a town located
on the eastern coast of Denmark.

+ Karina's mother runs a dress shop. Her father leaves
the family a year after she was born. She lives with her
maternal grandparents for three years. After then, she
lives in foster care for four years before moving back with
her remarried mother. She has a rough childhood.
Her mother is in debt and her step-father is abusive.

1954 + She drops out of at the age of 14 and begins her
career. She works as an assistant to an illustrator and
plays small roles in commercials to make money.

+ She appears in Ib Schmedes's short film *Pigen og
skoene* (*The Girl and the Shoes*, 1959), awarded in
Cannes Film Festival 1959.

1957 + Her parents divorce. She runs away from home,
hitchhiking to Paris. She watches the same films five
times at movie theaters, looking for a cheap way to
pass time and to become familiar with French culture.
She is spotted by Catherine Harlé, a legendary
modeling agent, at a cafe called Les Deux Magots.
Not long after, she met Pierre Cardin and Coco Chanel,
who give her the stage name Anna Karina. She
appears on the cover of fashion magazines including
Elle and in commercials for Coca-Cola, Pepsodent,
and Palmolive soap, among others.

1958 + Jean-Luc Godard, then a film critic, sees Karina in
the soap commercial during a movie preview event at a
Monsavon pub. He offers her a small role in his first
feature film, *À bout de souffle* (*Breathless*, 1960).
She rejects the offer because the role requires nudity.
Three or four months later, she gets a telegram from
Godard and the production company, offering her a
leading role in *Le Petit Soldat* (*The Little Soldier*, 1963).
Then, she is under 21 so can not sign a contract. She
has to ask her estranged mother in Denmark to come to
Paris to sign a contract for her. She comes the next
day to Paris to sign the contract. Karina believes that

안나 카리나 연보

1940년부터 + 9월 22일, 덴마크 동쪽 바닷가 프레데릭스베르
어린 시절 솔비에르 출생. 본명 하네 카린 블라르케 바위에르.
+ 어머니는 옷 가게를 운영했고, 아버지는 카리나가
태어난 후 1년 만에 집을 나감. 외가 쪽 조부모와 3년간
살고, 위탁소에서 4년을 산 후 어머니와 합가. 그러나
재혼한 어머니와의 생활은 그리 행복하지 않았음.
어머니는 빚에 시달렸고, 양아버지는 폭력적이었음.

1954년 + 14세에 학업을 중단하고 아르바이트를 시작함.
일러스트레이터, 상업광고 엑스트라 모델을 하며
생활비를 마련함.
+ 이브 슈메데스 감독의 단편영화 〈신발을 신은
소녀〉(1959)에 배우로 참여함. 이 작품은 1959년
칸영화제에서 수상함.

1957년 + 부모님이 이혼하자 집을 나와 히치하이크를 해서
파리에 도착함. 저렴한 가격에 시간을 때울 수 있는
극장에서 같은 영화를 하루에 5편씩 보며 프랑스 문화에
적응함. 카페 레두마고에서 광고대행사 '퍼블리스트'
직원 카트린 아를레게 스카우트됨. 모델 일을 시작하고
얼마 후에 피에르 카르댕을 만나고 코코 샤넬은 안나
카리나라는 예명을 지어줌. '엘르'를 포함한 잡지 표지에
등장하는 인물이 되었고 코카콜라, 펩소던트 치약,
팜올리브 비누 등 광고도 촬영하며 인지도를 높여 감.

1958년 + 당시 영화평론가이던 장뤼크 고다르가 영화 시사회를
목적으로 방문한 몽사봉 펍에서 팜올리브 광고 속
카리나를 발견함. 자신의 장편 데뷔작 〈네 멋대로
해라〉(1960)에 조연으로 섭외 의뢰를 하지만 카리나는
누드 신이 있어 거절함. 서너 달 뒤 고다르는 제작사
전보를 통해 카리나에게 〈작은 병정〉(1963)의
주연을 제안함. 당시 21세 이하는 부모 동의가 있어야
했기에 카리나는 사이가 소원하던 덴마크의 어머니에게
전화해 영화 계약을 위해 파리에 올 것을 요청함.

her mother has never taken an airplane in her life before then.

1961 + Karina makes her lead role debut in *Le Petit Soldat*, which touches on a controversial topic of French actions during the Algerian War. The film is banned by censorship.

+ Michel Deville watches Karina playing in *Le Petit Soldat* at a private screening event and offers her to play Valérie, a leading role, in *Ce soir ou jamais* (*Tonight or Never*). It is her first appearance on screen. She becomes known to public thanks to this film.

+ She wins Silver Bear for Best Actress for her playing the lead role, Angela, in Godard's *Une Femme Est Une Femme* (*A Woman Is a Woman*).

+ On March 3, she marrys Jean-Luc Godard, who is ten years older than her. She has a rough time. She becomes pregnant. When she is six-and-a-half months pregnant, she has a miscarriage and attempts suicide. As she is still underage by law then, Godard becomes her guardian. Until 1967, women are not allowed to write a check. Godard has checks and manages her income. Later, she looks back on those time and says as follows: "The women had no rights to do anything at the time— just to shut up."[1]

1962 + Agnès Varda cast Karina and Godard in the silent movie extract in her *Cléo de 5 à 7* (*Cleo from 5 to 7*). They play a young couple in Varda's short film entitled *Les fiancés du pont Mac Donald* (*The Fiancés of the Bridge Mac Donald*, 1961).

+ Godard's *Vivre Sa Vie* (*My Life to live*) is screened. Karina plays the leading role of Nana.

1963 + On January 25, after a three-year delay, her first feature film *Le Petit Soldat* is finally screened.

+ Before she is cast for *Bande à part* (*Band of Outsiders*, 1964), Karina suffers from drug abuse. She has another suicide attempt and has an extremely difficult time. She later recalls *Bande à part* "probably saved my life."

1
Patricia Garcia (2016.5.10), Anna Karina on Loving and Working With Jean-Luc Godard, *Vogue*

평생 단 한 번도 비행기를 탄 적 없던 어머니는 다음 날
파리에 와서 계약서에 서명함.

1961년 + 카리나가 처음 주연배우로 참여한 〈작은 병정〉은
알제리 전쟁이라는 정치적 주제를 양가적인 입장에서
다루고 있어 정부의 상영금지 조치가 내려짐.

+ 〈작은 병정〉의 내부시사에 왔던 미셸 드빌 감독이 카리나의
연기를 보고 〈오늘 밤 아니면〉에 발레리 역으로 캐스팅함.
이 작품을 통해 카리나는 대중에게 처음 배우로 소개됨.

+ 장뤼크 고다르 감독의 〈여자는 여자다〉에서 주연
안젤라 역으로 베를린국제영화제 여우주연상을 받음.

+ 3월 3일, 10살 연상의 장뤼크 고다르와 결혼.
6개월 반 만에 유산을 하며 자살 시도를 하는 등 힘든
시기를 보냄. 당시 기준으로 여전히 미성년이었기에
고다르가 카리나의 법적 대리인이 됨. 프랑스에서 여성은
1967년까지 수표를 스스로 발행할 수 없었기에 그녀의
모든 수익을 고다르가 관리함. 카리나는 다음과 같이
당시를 회고함. "당시 여성은 어떤 것을 할 어떤 권리도
없었다. 단지 닥치고 있는 것 외에는."[1]

1962년 + 아녜스 바르다 감독의 〈5시부터 7시까지의 클레오〉 내
무성 단편 〈맥도날드의 약혼자〉(1961)에 고다르와 함께
젊은 연인으로 출연.

+ 장뤼크 고다르 감독의 〈비브르 사 비〉 개봉. 주인공 나나 역.

1963년 + 1월 25일, 60년부터 연기되었던 카리나의 첫 영화
〈작은 병정〉이 마침내 개봉.

+ 〈국외자들〉(1964)에 섭외되기 전 카리나는 약물 과다
복용에 두 번째 자살 시도까지 하며 힘든 시기를 보냄.
영화 촬영을 하며 다시 삶의 동기를 발견함.

1964년 + 장뤼크 고다르 감독의 〈국외자들〉
개봉. 주연 오딜 역. 영화에서
사미 프레이, 클로드 브라쇠르와
카리나가 카페에서 즉흥적으로 춤추는
장면이 특히 주목을 받았다.

1
패트리샤 가르시아
(2016.5.10),
장뤼크 고다르의
동료이자 연인이었던
안나 카리나, '보그'

1964 + Godard's *Bande à part* is released. Karina plays the
leading role of Odile. Her dance scene with Sami Frey and
Claude Brasseur has received a lot of attention.

+ Later, in an interview with *Vogue*, Karina talks about young
Korean students skipping school to watch *Bande à part* as
follows: "I went to South Korea once and I saw young
people, about 15, they had skipped school to come see
Bande à part. Kids!"

+ She plays a supporting role of Rose in Roger Vadim's
La Ronde (*Circle of Love*).

+ On December 21, Karina divorces Godard. She mentions
that her relationship with Godard is not at all easy, but
later adds that she feels grateful of his legacy.

1965 + She plays the leading role of Maria in Maurice Ronet's
Le voleur de Tibidabo (*The Thief of Tibidabo*).

+ She plays the leading role of Natacha von Braun in
Godard's *Alphaville*.

+ She plays the leading role of Marianne Renoir in Godard's
Pierrot le Fou.

1966 + She plays the leading role of Suzanne in Jacques
Rivette's *La Religieuse* (*The Nun*).

+ She plays the leading role of Paula Neilson in Godard's
Made in USA.

1967 + She plays the leading role of Elena in Michel Deville's
Zärtliche Haie.

+ She plays the role of Hostess 703 in *Le Plus Vieux Métier
du Monde* (*The Oldest Profession*) co-directed by
Claude Autant-Lara, Mauro Bolognini, Philippe de Broca,
Jean-Luc Godard, Franco Indovina, and Michael Pfleghar.

+ She plays the leading role of Lamiel in Jean Aurel's *Lamiel*.

+ She plays the leading role of Marie Cardona in Luchino
Visconti's Italian film *Lo straniero* (*The Stranger*),
which is based on Albert Camus's novel *L'Étranger*
(*The Stranger*, 1942).

+ She plays Anna in Pierre Koralnik's television musical
comedy film *Anna*. She contributes to the original
sound track of the same name. She sings songs written
by Serge Gainsbourg, including *Sous le Soleil
Exactement*, *Un jour comme un autre*, *Roller Girl*, and
Pistolet Jo. She also sings in duet.

+ 카리나는 이후 '보그'와의 인터뷰에서 한국에 방문했을
당시 15세 학생들이 〈국외자들〉을 보기 위해 학교를 빠지고
극장에 온 열정에 놀라움을 표함.
+ 로제 바댕 감독의 〈라 롱드〉 조연 로즈 역.
+ 12월 21일, 장뤼크 고다르와 이혼. 고다르와의 관계에서
힘듦을 고백했지만 훗날 그녀는 고다르를 만난 건
행운이었다고 소회를 밝힘.

1965년 + 모리스 로네 감독의 〈티비다보의 도둑〉 주연 마리아 역.
+ 장뤼크 고다르 감독의 〈알파빌〉 주연 나타샤 폰 브라운 역.
+ 장뤼크 고다르 감독의 〈미치광이 피에로〉에서 주연 마리안
르누아르 역으로 베니스영화제에 초청됨.

1966년 + 자크 리베트 감독의 〈수녀〉 주연 수잔 역.
+ 〈아메리카의 퇴조〉에서 주연 폴라 넬슨 역.

1967년 + 미셸 드빌 감독의 〈다정한 상어〉 주연 엘레나 역.
+ 클로드 오탕라라, 마우로 볼로니니, 필리프 드브로카,
프랑코 인도비나, 미하엘 플레가, 장뤼크 고다르가 공동
연출한 〈세상에서 가장 오래된 직업〉 호스티스 703 역.
+ 장 오렐 감독의 〈라미엘〉 주연 라미엘 역.
+ 알베르 카뮈의 동명 소설을 원작으로 한 루키노 비스콘티
감독의 이탈리아 영화 〈이방인〉에서 주연 마리 카르도나 역.
+ 피에르 코랄니크 감독의 TV 뮤지컬 코미디 〈안나〉의
안나 역. 동명의 사운드트랙에 참여해 노래를 부름.
세르주 갱스부르가 작곡한 '태양의 바로 아래서', '여느
때와 같은 하루', '롤러 걸', '피스톨렛 조' 등 솔로곡과 그 외
듀엣에 참여함.

1968년 + 2월 13일, 피에르 파브르와 결혼.

1969년 + 5월 11일, 블라디미르 나보코프의 소설을 토니 리처드슨이
각색한 〈비정〉 개봉. 주연 마고 역.
+ 5월 칸영화제에 초청받은 폴커 슐뢴도르프 감독의 〈미하엘
콜하스-반역자〉 조연 엘리자베스 콜하스 역.
+ 조지 쿠커 감독과 (크레디트에 이름을 올리지 못한) 조셉
스트릭 감독의 〈저스틴〉 조연 멜리사 역.

1968 + On February 13, she marrys Pierre Fabre.

1969 + On May 11, Tony Richardson's *La Chambre obscure*
        (*Laughter in the Dark*) is released. It is based on the
        novel of the same name by Vladimir Nabokov.
        Karina plays the leading role of Margot.
     + She plays a supporting role of Elisabeth Kohlhaas in
        Volker Schlöndorff's *Michael Kohlhaas – der Rebell* (*Man
        on Horseback*). It is entered into Cannes Film Festival.
     + She plays a supporting role of Melissa in George Cukor
        and (uncredited) Joseph Strick's *Justine*.

1971 + She plays a supporting role of Clara in Hans W.
        Geissendörfer's TV movie *Carlos*.

1972 + She plays the leading role of Anna Bryant in Lee H.
        Katzin's *The Salzburg Connection*.
     + She writes, directs, and stars in *Vivre Ensemble* (*Living
        Together*, 1973). It takes four weeks to shoot the film
        and one of the four weeks is spent in New York, USA.
        She shoots most of the scenes in and around her own
        apartment in Paris. She even makes food for staff to
        minimize budget. She learns how to plan the budget from
        François Truffaut's production manager. She finds her
        own production company to finance the film. Still, she
        do not have sufficient fund to make the film. She has to
        finance the film by herself and makes it with a low budget.
        She later mentions, at 2008 Busan International Film
        Festival that it had been extremely difficult for her to beg
        for money to make her film. She recalls that she had
        even felt ashamed.[2] In the early 70s, she observes that
        since the invention of the movies, 160 women has
        worked as directors as compared with 5,000 men. She is
        an early example of a star actress paving her way to
        become an auteur for an independent film in the early 70s.

1973 + Her directorial debut, *Vivre Ensemble* is invited to
        Semaine de la Critique (Critics' Week) at
        the Cannes Film Festival. She makes one
        of the first very few cases of a star actress
        writing, directing, and producing a film.
        However, her attempts are not particularly
        welcome. Skepticism surrounds her,

2
Lee Juhyun
(2008.10.9),
A woman who was
in a page of cinema
history, *CINE21*

1971년 + 한스 가이센되르퍼 감독의 TV 드라마 〈카를로스〉 조연 클라라 역.

1972년 + 리 H. 카친 감독의 〈짤즈버그 커넥션〉에서 주연 안나 브라이언트 역.

        + 〈비브르 앙상블〉(1973) 시나리오 작업과 촬영. 총 촬영 기간 4주 중 미국 뉴욕에서 일주일간 촬영. 파리 로케이션은 대부분은 카리나가 살던 아파트에서 촬영했고 스태프들을 위해 직접 요리도 함. 카리나는 프랑수아 트뤼포의 제작팀장에게 예산계획법을 배우고, 투자를 받기 위해 자신의 제작사를 차림. 그러나 투자가 되지 않아 모든 경비를 자비로 해결했으며 저예산으로 제작함. 당시의 어려움을 2008년 부산국제영화제에서 언급함. "사람들한테 제 영화에 투자해 달라고 돈을 구걸하는 일이 너무 힘들었어요. 때론 수치심도 느꼈어요."[2] 영화가 발명된 이래 남성 감독이 5,000명이었고 여성은 160명으로 집계된 1970년대 초기, 스타 여배우가 상업적인 이유가 아닌 작가로서 감독이 된 초기 사례였음.

1973년 + 감독 데뷔작 〈비브르 앙상블〉이 칸영화제 비평가주간에 초청됨. 여성감독의 존재 자체를 크게 반기지 않는 분위기에 배우 출신이 직접 시나리오를 쓰고 감독과 제작을 동시에 한 거의 첫 사례였음. 언론은 카리나가 연출에 도전하는 이유에 대해 회의적으로 접근하며 "배우로 남아야 한다"는 의견이 분분했음. 카리나는 "내가 연출을 할 수 있는지 알고 싶었고 내 방식으로 이야기를 하고 싶었다."[3]고 담담히 응대함.

        + 영화와 동명의 소설 『비브르 앙상블』 출판.

1974년 + 피에르 파브르와 이혼(이혼 날짜는 모호하며 1973년과 1974년 사이로 보임).

2
이주현(2008.10.9), 영화사의 한 페이지 속에 있었던 여인, '씨네21'

3
잔 브룩스 (2016.1.12), 사랑과 영화의 관점에서의, 그리고 장뤼크 고다르의 뮤즈로서 안나 카리나: 나는 더 이상 살아있고 싶지 않았어요, '가디언즈'

questioning reasons why she tries to direct and make a film. In an interview with the Guardian, she says, "Lots of resistance. People really didn't like it. 'What is she doing here? This is not her job, she should stay being an actress.' But I just wanted to see if I could do it, that's all."[3] She also mentions that she wanted to "tell a story my way."

+ She publishes a novel of the same name, *Vivre Ensemble*.

1974 + She divorces Pierre Fabre. The precise date of their divorce is unclear, but it is said that they divorces sometime between 1973 and 1974.

+ She plays a supporting role of Elena in Franco Brusati's *Pane e cioccolata* (*Bread and Chocolate*).

1976 + She plays the leading role of Irene Cartis in Rainer Werner Fassbinder's *Roulette chinoise* (*Chinese Roulette*).

1978 + On July 1, she marrys French actor Daniel Duval in La Garde-Freinet, Southeastern France.

1981 + She divorces Daniel Duval.

1982 + On December 27, she marrys American actor and director Dennis Berry.

1983 + She publishes a novel, *Golden City*, "a novel with an ambience reminiscent of the gangsters in *Bande à part*. She has been fond of writing short stories since she was a little girl.

1988 + She publishes a novel *On n'achète pas le soleil* (*One does not buy the sun*).

1994 + She divorces Dennis Berry.

1998 + On January 1, she publishes her novel *Jusqu'au bout du hasard* (*To the edge of chance*).

2003 + She plays a supporting role of Gloria in Richard Berry's *Moi César, 10 ans et demi, 1m39* (*I, Cesar*).

+ She receives Honorary Mikeldi from

3
Xan Brooks
(2016.1.12),
Anna Karina on love,
cinema and being
Jean-Luc Godard's
muse: 'I didn't want
to be alive any more',
The Guardian

+ 프랑코 브루사티 감독의 〈빵과 초콜릿〉 조연 엘레나 역.

1976년 + 라이너 베르너 파스빈더 감독의 〈중국식 룰렛〉 주연
아이린 카티스 역.

1978년 + 7월 1일, 프랑스 남서부 라가르드프레네에서 배우
다니엘 뒤발과 결혼.

1981년 + 다니엘 뒤발과 이혼.

1982년 + 12월 27일, 미국 배우이자 감독인 데니스 베리와 결혼.

1983년 + 어린 시절부터 종종 짧은 이야기를 창작하기를 좋아하던
카리나는 〈국외자들〉의 갱스터를 연상시키는 소설
『골든 시티: 로마』 출간.

1988년 + 소설 『우리는 태양을 사지 않는다』 출간.

1994년 + 데니스 베리와 이혼.

1998년 + 1월 1일, 소설 『기회가 끝날 때까지』 출간.

2003년 + 리샤르 베리 감독의 〈나 세자르, 10살 반, 1미터 39〉
조연 글로리아 역.
+ 빌바오국제다큐멘터리단편영화제에서 공로상을 받음.

2005년 + 영화에서 부른 노래를 모은 '영화의 샹송' 앨범을
발매함.

2008년 + 10월 4일, 제13회 부산국제영화제 뉴커런츠 부문 사상
첫 여성 심사위원장으로 위촉됨. 두 번째 연출작
〈빅토리아〉의 월드 프리미어 상영을 위해 부산을 찾음.

2009년 + 프랑스-캐나다 로드무비 〈빅토리아〉 프랑스 개봉.
근본적으로 외로운 사람들이 세상에서 자신이 속한 곳을
찾으려는 노력을 보여 주는 드라마. '롤리타들'이라는

ZINEBI – Bilbao International Festival of Documentary and Short Films.

2005 + She releases an album entitled *Chansons de films*, a compilation album of songs she sang in the films.

2008 + On October 4, she is appointed as a president of jury for New Currents section, Busan International Film Festival. She is the first woman to serve that role. She visits Busan to attend the world-premiered of her second directorial work, *Victoria*.

2009 + *Victoria* (2008), a French-Canadian road movie, is released in France. It is a drama about "fundamentally lonely people trying to find a place they belong." It tells us a story about two men who sing as a duo named 'Les Lolitas' and their encounter with Victoria, who becomes a sponsor for their Canada tour.

2010 + She participates in a fairy tale album project entitled *The Ugly Duckling*.

2013 + She releases an album entitled *The Little Mermaid*. She has special a stage where she met her fans.

2016 + Karina receives the 69th Bodil Honorary Award given by Danish Film Critics Association.

2019 + She dies on December 14 in a hospital. The official cause of death is cancer. She passes away in the presence of Dennis Barry. Her death is announced by French culture minister, Franck Riester, and her agent, Laurent Balandras. She is buried in the Père Lachaise Cemetery, Paris.

    * Madison Mainwaring wrote as follows in 2020: In the catalogue of the National Library of France, there are 152 critical studies taking on Jean-Luc Godard's work, and seem to be none devoted to Karina.[4]

4
Madison Mainwaring (2020.2.25), Finding Anna Karina, *The PARIS REVIEW*

이름으로 활동 중인 두 남자가 퀘백에서 빅토리아라는
후원자를 만나 캐나다 투어 공연을 하며 벌어지는
이야기를 다룸.

2010년 + '미운 오리 새끼'의 동화 CD에 참여함.

2013년 + '인어공주' CD를 발매했으며, 후에 팬들과 만나는
무대를 만듦.

2016년 + 덴마크 영화비평가협회에서 수여하는 보딜상에서
제69회 공로상 수상자로 선정됨.

2019년 + 12월 14일, 암으로 인해 투병하던 중 병원에서
편안하게 영면함. 데니스 베리가 임종을 지켰고,
그녀의 죽음은 프랑스 문화부장관 프랑크 리스테르와
소속사 로랑 발란드라스에 의해 전해짐. 페르라셰즈
묘지에 묻힘.

*2020년 기준. 프랑스 국립도서관에 장뤼크 고다르에
대한 152건의 비평연구가 있지만 안나 카리나에 대한
연구는 0건임.[4]

4
매디슨 마인워링
(2020.2.25), 안나
카리나를 찾아서,
'파리 리뷰'

아이 엠 인디펜던트 ― 안나 카리나

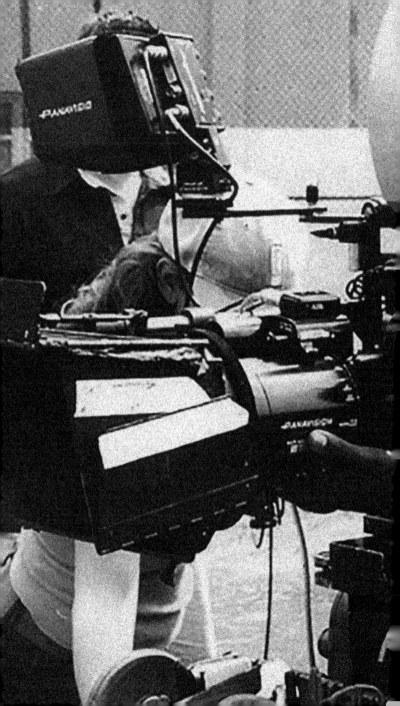

PANAVISION
PANAFLEX

셰럴 두녜이

Cheryl Dunye
Director, Actor, Producer

Cheryl Dunye (1966–) created a completely
novel and unique style of film referred to as
"Dunyementary," which is a brilliant mix of
narrative structures of fiction and elements of
autobiographical documentaries. Her groundbreaking work *The Watermelon Woman
(1996)* is a story about an African American
lesbian who makes a film about a black actress
credited as "The Watermelon Woman" in a
silent film. It is the first feature film directed by
an African American lesbian and a landmark
of New Queer Cinema, which emerged in
the 1990s. She won the Teddy Award at the
46th Berlinale.

셰럴 두녜이
영화감독, 배우, 프로듀서

1966 –. 극영화 내러티브 구조와 사적
다큐멘터리를 혼합한 자신만의 스타일을
"두녜멘터리"라 칭할 정도로 독특한
형식을 발견했다. 〈워터멜론 우먼〉(1996)은
섹슈얼 정체성과 영화의 역사를
유머러스하게 연결하여 무성영화 속
배우에 관한 영화를 만드는 흑인 여성감독에
대한 이야기를 그린다. 이 작품은 1990년대
뉴퀴어시네마라는 용어가 등장한 후
아프리카계 미국 레즈비언이 감독한 첫 번째
장편 극영화로 이름을 올렸다. 〈워터멜론
우먼〉은 1996년 베를린영화제에서
테디상을 받았다.

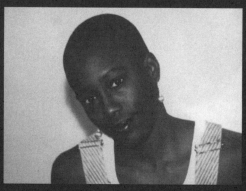

©Jingletown Films

Cheryl
Dunye

Dreams of History

By Devika Girish(Writer, Editor, and
Programmer of New York Film Festival)

"Sometimes you have to create your own
history. *The Watermelon Woman* is fiction."
– Cheryl Dunye, *The Watermelon Woman*

In her landmark film *The Watermelon Woman*
(1996), the Liberian-American filmmaker Cheryl
Dunye confronts a problem frequently faced
by historians and researchers of marginalized and
colonized communities: the lack of a historical
record. These gaps in the archive – which reflect
the biases and priorities of the institutions in
charge of making and preserving the records of
our times – have both social and personal
consequences. They often feed the misconception
that certain identities or lives didn't exist in the
past, and are modern inventions – hence the
common conservative refrain, for instance, that
queerness and transness are trendy and
newfangled phenomena. The elisions of the
record also deny the communities in question an
aspect crucial to identity formation: a sense of
continuity and ancestry; the knowledge that
you're a part of a larger narrative of history that
precedes and outlasts you.

In 1993, Dunye, who had by then made several
experimental films exploring Black lesbian life,
started researching Black actresses in early
Hollywood cinema for a graduate school class.
She found that they mostly appeared as
"mammies" in these films: pro-slavery caricatures,
epitomized by Hattie McDaniel in *Gone With the
Wind* (1939), of cheery, maternal maidservants

역사를 꿈꾸다
셰럴 두녜이의 〈워터멜론 우먼〉

글: 데비카 기리시
(작가, 에디터, 뉴욕영화제 프로그래머)

"우리는 때로 자신의 역사를 만들어 내야 한다.
〈워터멜론 우먼〉은 픽션이다."
— 셰럴 두녜이, 〈워터멜론 우먼〉 감독

라이베리아계 미국인 영화감독 셰럴 두녜이는 자신의 기념비적 작품 〈워터멜론 우먼〉(1996)에서 주변화되고 식민화된 공동체에 속해 있는 역사가와 연구자들이 빈번히 맞닥뜨리는 것, 바로 역사적 기록이 빈약하다는 문제를 정면에서 다룬다. 아카이브에서 발견되는 격차는 — 우리 시대에 관한 기록을 작성하고 보존하는 기관들의 우선순위와 편견을 반영한 것이겠다 — 사회적으로나 개인에게 갖은 폐단을 초래한다. 그것은 특정 정체성이나 삶이 과거에 존재하지 않았으며 현대에 와서야 발명

defined solely by their loyal devotion to their white families. Dunye found that there were barely any archival records of the lives of these actresses; often, they were credited in the films with racist monikers or not at all. So, in *The Watermelon Woman*, Dunye made a choice both playful and deeply political: she made up some history.

The film — a remarkable work of intersectional autofiction and by many accounts the first feature film directed by an African-American lesbian — features Dunye as a version of herself named Cheryl. Cheryl works at a video store in Philadelphia with her friend Tamara (Valerie Walker), with whom she also runs a videotaping business. Cheryl is an aspiring filmmaker, and she knows that her first film has to be about Black women — "because our stories have never been told," she says. Soon, she settles on her subject: the life story of a beautiful Black actress whom Cheryl spots in a mammy role in an old Civil War-era movie called *Plantation Memories*, which simply credits her as "the Watermelon Woman." As Cheryl tries to piece together the Watermelon Woman's life through research, interviews, and field trips, her personal life takes its own twists and turns. She begins a relationship with Diana (Guinevere Turner, the writer of the landmark lesbian film *Go Fish* (1994)), a white woman she meets at the video store, while her friendship with Tamara starts to fray. Interestingly, the stories of the Watermelon Woman and Cheryl start to intertwine: Cheryl eventually learns that the actress, whose real name was Fae Richards, was a lesbian, too, and she was involved in a fraught relationship with a white woman director named Martha Page.

Dunye depicts Richards's life through the

된 것이라는 오해를 불러일으키며, 바로 이런 이유로 보통의 보수주의자들이 퀴어와 트랜스가 트렌디하고 최근에 유행하는 현상이라는 식으로 흔히 말하는 것이다. 기록의 누락은 또한 정체성 형성의 결정적 요소인 계보성과 계속성의 감각(자신이 자신의 유한성을 능가하는 장대한 역사적 서사의 일부라는 인식)을 불확실의 영역으로 몰아넣으며 이들 공동체를 부정한다.

1993년, 이미 흑인 레즈비언의 삶을 탐구하며 여러 편의 실험 영화를 제작한 후였던 두녜이는 대학원 수업과 관련해 초기 할리우드 영화에 출연한 흑인 여배우들을 조사하기 시작하고, 그들이 대부분 '유모(mammies)' 역으로 나왔다는 것을 알게 된다. 노예제에 기꺼이 동조하는 희화화된 인물, 오로지 백인 가정에 대한 충성스러운 헌신으로 특징지어지는 쾌활한 유모 말이다. 〈바람과 함께 사라지다〉(1939)에서 해티 맥대니얼이 맡은 역할이 완벽한 본보기다. 두녜이는 이 여배우들의 삶에 관한 공식적 기록이 거의 없다는 점을 발견했다. 이들은 영화 크레디트에 인종 차별적 이름으로 오르거나 아예 이름을 올리지 못했다. 〈워터멜론 우먼〉에서 두녜이는 익살스러운 동시에 대단히 정치적인 선택을 했다. 바로, 역사를 지어낸 것이다.

〈워터멜론 우먼〉은 영화 역사상 명실공히 아프리카계 미국인 레즈비언 감독이 제작한 첫 번째 장편이자 오토픽션을 혼합한 놀라운 작품으로, 두녜이 감독 자신이 셰릴이라는 이름의 주인공으로 등장한다. 셰릴은 친구 태머라(밸라리 워커)와 필라델피아의 비디오 가게에서 점원으로 일하는데, 그녀와 함께 홈 비

various artifacts that Cheryl finds: faded,
archival photographs and fliers; clips from black-
and-white movies from the 1930s and '40s.
But here's the catch — all of that material is fake.
"Fae Richards" is an invented figure, played by
the actress Lisa Marie Bronson in *The
Watermelon Woman*, and the pictures and
movie clips were created for the film by the
photographer Zoe Leonard. In the credits of the
film, Dunye describes *The Watermelon Woman*
as a fiction. A scholar like Saidiya Hartmann
might today describe Dunye's approach as
"critical fabulation." "Is it possible to exceed or
negotiate the constitutive limits of the archive?"
Hartmann writes of this approach in her classic
text, *Venus in Two Acts*. "In fashioning a
narrative, which is based upon archival research,
and by that, I mean a critical reading of the
archive that mimes the figurative dimensions of
history, I intended both to tell an impossible

↓ *The Watermelon
Woman*
〈워터멜론 우먼〉

디오를 찍어 주는 작은 사업도 하고 있다. 셰럴은 영화감독 지망생으로, 흑인 여성에 관한 영화를 만들고 싶어 한다. "우리 이야기는 다뤄진 적이 없으니까." 셰럴은 말한다. 그러고는 곧 주제를 찾아내는데, 미국 남북 전쟁을 배경으로 펼쳐지는 '플랜테이션 메모리즈'라는 오래된 영화에서 유모 역할로 분한 아름다운 흑인 여배우의 삶을 좇기로 한 것이다. 크레디트에 표기된 그녀의 이름은 워터멜론 우먼이었다. 그런데 이 여인의 삶의 조각들을 모으기 위해 각처를 방문하고 인터뷰를 진행하고 자료를 수집해 나가는 동안 셰럴 자신의 삶도 우여곡절로 접어든다. 자신이 일하는 비디오 가게에서 만난 백인 여성 다이애나(귀너비어 터너, 선구적인 레즈비언 영화 〈고 피쉬〉(1994)의 작가)와 사귀게 되는 한편, 태머라와의 우정은 삐걱거리기 시작한다. 그러면서 흥미롭게도, 워터멜론 우먼과 셰럴의 이야기가 서로 얽혀 들어간다. 워터멜론 우먼의 진짜 이름은 페이 리처드로 레즈비언 배우이며, 마사 페이지라는 백인 여성감독과 긴장된 관계를 맺고 있었다는 정황이 드러난다.

두녜이는 셰럴이 찾아내는 갖가지 물품, 즉 빛바랜 기록 사진과 전단, 1930–40년대 흑백영화들의 클립 영상을 통해 리처드의 삶을 그린다. 그런데 여기에 묘수가 감춰져 있다. 바로 이 자료들이 모두 가짜라는 것이다. 리사 마리 브론슨이 연기한 '페이 리처드'는 가공의 인물로, 중간에 나오는 사진과 흑백영화 영상도 전부 사진작가 조 레너드가 〈워터멜론 우먼〉을 위해 만들어낸 것이다. 엔딩 크레디트에서 두녜이는 〈워터멜론 우먼〉이 픽션이라고 밝힌다. 사이디야 하트만 같은 작금의 학자가 본다면

story and to amplify the impossibility of its telling."
Both the modalities outlined by Hartmann as
central to critical fabulation – fashioning a
speculative history, and also, in the process,
critiquing the very methods of historiography that
create omissions and make speculation
necessary – are deployed by Dunye in *The
Watermelon Woman*.

The film's clever opening sets the scene. A video
camera scans the pixelated, multicultural faces
at a wedding party: Black, white, and kippah-
wearing Jewish attendees mingle in a garden in
their Sunday best. We only realize that we're
watching a film-within-a-film when, a few minutes
in, Cheryl moves from behind the camera to the
front to yell at a pair of male videographers
who've set up their cameras directly in her line of
sight to take pictures of the wedding guests.
"Don't you even see the video equipment?"
Cheryl asks them. "Why don't you just, like, wait
your turn?" That sly, lighthearted opening
immediately articulates the refusal that animates
The Watermelon Woman: the refusal of a Black
and queer woman to be on the sidelines of
filmmaking and history-making.

As Cheryl embarks on her project to discover
the life of the Watermelon Woman, Dunye details
the complications of researching and tracing
subcultural histories with both humor and
incisive insight. Cheryl employs every resource
at her disposal, mining both material and living
archives: she takes advantage of her job to
surreptitiously order in rare VHS tapes of movies
featuring Richards; she digs through various
personal libraries, including her hoarder mother's
disorganized basement and Tamara's uncle's
obsessive collection of Black film memorabilia;
and she records oral histories, interviewing

두녜이의 접근법은 '비평적 우화(critical fabulation)'에 해당할 것이다. "아카이브의 구조적 한계를 빠져나가거나 뛰어넘는 것은 가능한가?" 하트만은 자신의 탁월한 저술 『비너스 인 투 액츠』(2008)에서 말한다. "축적된 자료인 아카이브를 토대로 내러티브를 만들고자 할 때는 누락과 추정으로 얼룩진 아카이브 자료를 비판적으로 읽어내고 풍자적으로 활용함으로써 불가능한(가공의) 이야기를 창조하고 그 이야기의 상징적 의미를 더 키울 수 있다." 하트만이 '비평적 우화'의 핵심으로 제시한 두 속성 — 추정적 역사를 만들어 내는 동시에 그 과정에서 필요에 따라 누락과 추정을 자행한 주류 역사 서술 체계를 비판하는 것 — 이 바로 두녜이의 〈워터멜론 우먼〉에 잘 나타나 있다.

〈워터멜론 우먼〉은 재치 있는 오프닝 장면으로 앞으로 펼쳐질 이야기를 암시한다. 비디오카메라가 결혼식 피로연에서 다양한 문화권 사람들의 면면을 크게 크게 잡으며 훑는다. 잘 차려입은 흑인, 백인, 키파를 쓴 유대인 참석자들이 정원 여기저기에 삼삼오오 모여 있다. 얼마 안 가 그 화면을 찍고 있던 셰럴이 카메라 앞으로 등장하고, 우리는 우리가 보던 화면이 영화 속의 영화였다는 사실을 깨닫게 된다. 셰럴은 몇몇 남자들이 하객 사진을 찍겠다고 개인 카메라를 설치하는 통에 자신의 카메라 시야가 방해받자 화를 터뜨린다. "여기 촬영하고 있는 거 안 보여요?" 셰럴이 따진다. "자기 차례 좀 기다리면 어디 덧나나!" 이렇듯 능청스럽고 유쾌한 오프닝 장면은 〈워터멜론 우먼〉 전체를 관통하며 활기를 불어넣고 있는 거부의 메시지를 영화가 시작되자마자 확실하게 보여 준다. 영화를 만드는 데 있어서도 역

people like her mother's friend, also a Black lesbian, who frequented the nightclubs where Fae Richards used to sing. All these sources help Cheryl piece together the story of a Black actress who dreamed of being a movie star. After a start in Hollywood with mammy roles, Fae transitioned to lead parts in Black-cast movies. But her rise coincided with the decline in popularity of Black-cast films, and she eventually became a performer at clubs.

Cheryl also tries the local library but runs into issues that illuminate the limitations of institutional canons. The library only has references on "Black women in film;" finding references to specific Black women proves challenging. When Cheryl goes to the help desk, the white librarian offers a hilariously unhelpful and patronizing response: "Check the Black section in the reference library." When he looks up the Watermelon Woman and Martha Page on his computer, he can't find any mention of the former, though he does find some references to Page in the "women in film" section. The labyrinth of categories invoked in this brief scene gives us a sense of the inclusions and exclusions that invisibly structure broad labels like "women" and "film"; and the cracks in archiving and historiography that women of color frequently slip through.

From this highly regulated and organized space, Cheryl goes to the opposite: CLIT, or the "Center for Lesbian Information Technology" in New York, an independent women's library that is as ragtag as it is a goldmine. Based on the Lesbian Herstory Archives in New York, CLIT emerges in the film as a gentle parody of the labor of love that keeps these alt-institutions running. Writer and ACT UP activist Sarah Schulman plays

사를 만드는 데 있어서도 옆으로 물러서지 않겠다는 흑인이자 퀴어인 여성의 분명한 거부 메시지다.

셰럴이 워터멜론 우먼의 삶을 세상으로 건져 올리기 위한 프로젝트에 착수함에 따라, 두네이는 유머와 예리한 통찰을 곁들여 하위문화의 역사를 조사하고 추적하는 작업이 얼마나 복잡하고 까다로운 일인지를 구체적으로 묘사한다. 셰럴은 자신이 가용할 수 있는 자원을 총동원하며, 물질적 아카이브와 살아 있는 아카이브 모두 샅샅이 뒤진다. 자신의 직업적 특성을 이용해 리처드가 출연한 영화의 희귀 VHS 비디오테이프를 몇 가지나 사장 몰래 주문한다. 또 저장 강박증이라고 해도 과언이 아닌 자기 어머니의 엉망진창 지하실, 흑인영화 관련 물품을 광적으로 수집해 놓은 태머라네 삼촌 댁을 방문하며 여러 개인 수집실도 조사한다. 그런가 하면 마찬가지로 흑인 레즈비언이며 리처드가 노래를 불렀던 나이트클럽에 자주 드나들었다는 어머니 친구 같은 사람들을 인터뷰하며 구전 역사도 촬영한다. 이 모든 자료의 도움으로 셰럴은 무비 스타를 꿈꿨던 한 흑인 여배우의 이야기를 하나로 엮어 간다. 리처드는 유모 역으로 할리우드에 발을 들인 뒤, 흑인영화의 주역으로 변신한다. 그러나 그녀가 부상하기 시작하던 무렵 흑인영화의 인기가 시들었고, 리처드는 결국 나이트클럽 가수로 전향한다.

셰럴은 지역 도서관에도 가지만, 제도적 규범의 한계를 조명하는 문제에 부딪힌다. 그 도서관에는 '영화와 흑인 여성'에 관한 참고 문헌만 있고, '특정' 흑인 여성에 관한 자료를 찾는 것은 대

the nervous, distracted archivist, who keeps repeating that things are a "little disorganized because we're a volunteer-run collective, and these things take time." She is comically careless with the materials, emptying entire boxes onto the tables, while also being a stickler for rules and reprimanding Cheryl for documenting "strictly confidential" materials. Despite these slapstick shenanigans, Cheryl almost instantly finds more than what she's looking for: a box full of pictures of Fae Richards, with hand-scribbled dedications to one June Walker.

When Cheryl follows the trail of this clue, however, she ends up with more questions. After contacting June on the phone, Cheryl goes to her house, but before they can meet, June has a heart attack and is taken to the hospital. She leaves a package for Cheryl with pictures of her and Fae, and includes a note that says that the mention of Martha Page's name had brought up unpleasant memories for her. "Why do you even

↓ *The Watermelon
Woman*
〈워터멜론 우먼〉

단히 어려운 일로 판명이 난다. 셰럴이 안내 데스크에 문의하자, 백인 사서는 깔보는 태도로 입이 떡 벌어질 만큼 전혀 도움이 되지 않는 답변을 내놓는다. '레퍼런스 도서관(비대출 열람 전용 도서관) 흑인 섹션에 가 보세요.' 이어서 그가 직원용 컴퓨터로 워터멜론 우먼과 마사 페이지를 검색하자, 워터멜론 우먼에 관해서는 아무것도 안 나오지만 마사 페이지는 '영화와 여성' 섹션에 관련 자료가 몇 건 있다고 뜬다. 이 짧은 장면이 환기하는 범주의 미로는 우리에게 '여성' 또는 '영화'와 같은 광범위한 분류를 눈에 보이지 않게 구조화하고 있는 포함과 배제의 원리를 깨닫게 한다. 역사 서술과 기록 보관 체제의 깨진 틈으로 유색 인종 여성은 예사로 흘러 버리는 것이다.

셰럴은 상당한 규율로 조직화된 이 공간에서 나와서 정반대 편에 위치한 뉴욕 CLIT, 즉 레즈비언정보기술센터로 간다. 독립 여성 도서관으로, 분명히 금광은 금광이지만 척 봐도 오합지졸이다. 이곳은 실제로 뉴욕에 있는 레즈비언허스토리아카이브를 모델로 만든 허구적 장소로, 자원 봉사자들 덕분에 이러한 대안 기관들이 돌아가고 있다는 실정을 가볍게 패러디한다. 작가이자 ACT UP 활동가인 세라 슐먼이 다소 산만하고 성마른 성격의 기록연구사 역으로 나와, "자원봉사자들이 꾸려 나가는 단체이다 보니, 체계는 좀 없어요, 정리하려면 아무래도 시간이 걸리니까."라고 계속해서 말한다. 세라는 아카이브 물품들을 부주의하게 다루는데, 그 모습이 코믹하다. 자신은 테이블 위로 자료가 담긴 박스를 통째로 뒤집어 쏟으면서도 어찌나 규칙에 엄격한지, 셰럴에게 '극비' 자료는 찍으면 안 된다고 핀잔을

want to include a white woman in a movie on Fae's life?" She asks. "Don't you know she had nothing to do with how people should remember Fae?" Fae had regretted appearing in those mammy roles, June reveals. Urging Cheryl to tell her generation's stories, she insists that "our family will always only have each other." The film thus leaves us with an acknowledgement of both the inescapable contingency of the archive and its ultimate unknowability. Cheryl's research may have pointed to Fae's association with Martha, but the nature of their relationship, and Martha's lived experiences of being a lesbian and an aspiring Black actress in 1930s America, remain mysterious – known only to those who will take the memories with them when they pass.

The Watermelon Woman's focus on cinematic archives was particularly trenchant in the 1990s, as digital and video formats gained popularity, transforming film culture in two profound ways. One, they democratized filmmaking, introducing cheaper and more mobile equipment that removed a crucial barrier for Black, female, queer, and other marginalized filmmakers who had historically lacked institutional support. Though The Watermelon Woman is mostly filmed on 16mm stock, Cheryl's "documentary" segments are shot on videotape – her video camera allows her to document her process freely wherever she goes, requiring just a one- or two-woman crew. The capital-intensive nature of even video-based filmmaking is foregrounded early in the film, when Tamara and Cheryl bicker over sharing their camera, which they still have to pay deposits on.

The second consequence of video that The Watermelon Woman creatively incorporates into its form is the indexical crisis provoked by

준다. 슬랩스틱이 가미된 세라의 군소리가 계속되는가 싶더니, 그 즉시 셰럴이 찾던 것 이상이 모습을 드러낸다. 그곳에 페이 리처드의 사진이 가득 든 박스가 있었던 것이다. 사진 뒷면에는 준 워커에게 전하는 리처드의 친필 메시지까지 쓰여 있다.

그런데 셰럴은 이 단서의 흔적을 따라가며, 오히려 더 많은 의문을 품게 된다. 셰럴은 준과 통화를 나눈 뒤 그녀의 집으로 찾아가지만, 그 직전에 준이 심장마비를 일으켜 병원에 실려 가는 바람에 두 사람의 만남은 성사되지 못한다. 하지만 준은 셰럴 앞으로 자신과 리처드의 사진이 담긴 꾸러미를 남겨 두었다. 그 꾸러미에는 마사 페이지의 이름은 듣는 것만으로도 불쾌한 기억들이 떠오른다는 내용의 메모가 동봉돼 있다. "리처드의 삶을 다루는 영화라면서 왜 백인 여성을 집어넣으려고 하는 거죠?" 준이 묻는다. "대중에게 기억돼야 하는 리처드의 모습에 그 사람은 하등의 관련이 없어요." 그러면서 리처드가 유모 역들을 맡은 것에 대해 후회했다고 알린다. 또 자기 세대의 이야기를 만들어 달라고 격려하면서, "우리에게는 언제나 서로밖에 없다."라고 단언한다. 이렇게 〈워터멜론 우먼〉은 언제 어떤 식으로 필요한 자료를 얻게 될 지도 모르고, 또 사실을 알게 된다 하더라도 궁극적인 진실에는 도달할 수 없음을 인정한다. 셰럴의 조사는 리처드가 마사와 연인 관계에 있었다고 지시했지만, 그 교제의 본질과 리처드가 레즈비언이자 스타를 꿈꾸는 흑인 여배우로서 정말로 어떠한 경험들을 하며 1930년대 미국을 살아갔는지는 미스터리로 남는다. 그 기억들을 지닌 채 눈을 감을 사람들이 아니고서야, 아무도 알 길이 없는 것이다.

cinema's shift from analog to digital media. In one sense, digital formats expand our capacity for preservation: uninhibited by the cost and physical limits of film stock, Cheryl can take her camera everywhere, capture everything. But the intangible nature of video also poses a threat to the archive. Many of the crucial clues that Cheryl finds in her search for Fae are things that, even if no one sought to preserve or organize them, persisted simply by virtue of their existence as objects. *The Watermelon Woman* poses a troubling question for our present moment, when everything is "saved" in internet spaces owned and controlled by corporations: what if history had no way of enduring in material traces, outside and even in spite of human neglect?

These changes in technology also gave rise to a wave of reflexive cinema in the 1990s, which responded to the advent of digital media and computer-generated effects by playing with the codes of reality and the viewer's ability to distinguish between the authentic and the make-believe. Dunye's early work featured similar experimentations with mixed media and metafictional modes but from a pointedly Black lesbian perspective. *The Watermelon Woman* does something similar: it plays with the codes of familiar film and television genres, reimagining them within a thoroughly Black and queer cinematic universe. The scenes of Cheryl and Tamara going about their jobs and lives resemble a sitcom, with frontal shots, fade ins and outs, and wonderfully wry performances by the actors. Cheryl's documentary scenes are mostly shot with a deliberate shakiness and graininess, evoking the aesthetic of vérité nonfiction, while she also intersperses talking-head interviews and video diaries that are styled to mimic more conventional documentaries. As with the faux

〈워터멜론 우먼〉이 시네마 아카이브에 초점을 맞춘 것은, 디지털과 비디오 포맷이 대중화됨에 따라 영화 문화의 두 측면이 본질적으로 변화하기 시작한 1990년대가 배경인 점을 고려하면 특히 더 적확한 발상이 아닐 수 없다. 먼저, 당시 값싸고 이동성이 향상된 장비들이 출시됨에 따라 영화제작 여건이 민주화되었다. 역사상 제도적 지원 부족에 시달려 온 흑인, 여성, 퀴어를 비롯한 모든 주변화된 정체성을 지닌 영화제작자들의 업계 진입을 막았던 핵심 장애물이 제거된 것이다. 〈워터멜론 우먼〉 자체는 대체로 16mm 필름으로 촬영됐지만, 셰릴의 '다큐멘터리' 조각은 비디오테이프로 찍은 것들이다. 비디오카메라 덕분에 셰릴은 어디를 가든 자유롭게 자신의 조사 과정을 기록하고, 도와주는 사람도 한두 명의 여성이면 충분하다. 아무리 비디오카메라로 찍는대도 영화제작의 자본 집약적 특성을 피해 갈 수는 없다는 실정도 영화 초반에 나타나 있다. 태머라와 셰릴이 카메라를 함께 쓰는 문제로 말다툼을 할 때, 두 사람이 아직 카메라 보증금을 덜 냈다는 속사정이 비친다.

비디오카메라 보급의 두 번째 결과는, 〈워터멜론 우먼〉의 형식에 독창적으로 담겨 있듯, 영화의 기술적 환경이 아날로그에서 디지털로 전환됨에 따라 촉발된 지표적 위기다. 어떤 의미에서 보면 디지털 포맷은 우리의 보존 능력을 확장시킨다. 셰릴도 필름 스톡의 비용이나 물리적 제약에 구애받을 필요 없이 어디로든 카메라를 가지고 다니며, 모든 것을 포착한다. 그러나 비디오카메라 기록의 무형적 특성은 아카이브 구축에 위협이 되는 것 또한 사실이다. 셰릴이 리처드를 조사하는 과정에서 얻게 되

footage of Fae, it's not always clear which parts of the film are staged and which are "real." In the case of the images of Fae, this ambiguity draws on something deeper than just the quality of Leonard's creations – on the fact that we don't know what we don't know. How can we discern the authenticity of something that has never existed, for which there are no coordinates? The rest of the film has a similar unmooring quality. Most viewers will recognize the basic formal tropes of each segment in the film but will likely have never seen them deployed from a Black and lesbian gaze. (The film's cinematographer, Michelle Crenshaw, was also a Black lesbian).

Notably, Cheryl's gaze – and her sense of herself as a filmmaker and a person – develops in the film through the negotiation with a white woman's gaze. Her journey has strange echoes with what she discovers about Fae's life as a "sapphic sister." Fae's sexuality and her relationship with Martha are shrouded in mystery, murkiness, and taboo – a relative of Martha's kicks Cheryl out of her house when she brings up their affair. Cheryl's own relationship with Diana, which starts when the latter makes a pass at Cheryl at the video store, also faces suspicions and reservations. Tamara takes a dislike to Diana, accusing her of wanting to be Black and Cheryl of wanting to be white. Their interracial dynamic is complicated by class differences that emerge subtly in the background: Diana lives in a giant loft by herself, having moved recently to Philly from Chicago simply because she wanted a change. Cheryl also seems to be troubled by the anxiety of being fetishized, a reality that Dunye emphasizes through an interview with Camille Paglia, who – playing a parodic version of herself – tries to appropriate African-American tropes like the mammy and the watermelon by

는 결정적 단서 대부분이 사라지지 않고 있었던 까닭은, 비록 누가 일부러 정리하고 보존한 결과물이었던 것은 아니지만, 단순하게도, 그것들이 물건으로서 존재하고 있었다는 이점에 기인한 것이기 때문이다. 바야흐로 모든 것이 기업들의 소유와 통제하의 인터넷 공간에 '저장'되는 시대인 지금, 〈워터멜론 우먼〉은 우리에게 난처한 의문을 제기한다. 사람들의 방치 외에는, 나아가 사람들의 방치에도 '불구하고' 역사가 물질적 자취를 남길 방법이 없다면 어떻게 되는 것일까?

이러한 기술적 변화는 1990년대에 자기 반영적 영화의 물결을 일으키기도 했는데, 이는 현실 논리 및 진짜와 환상을 구별할 수 있는 시청자의 능력을 활용해 컴퓨터로 만들어 낸 이미지와 디지털 미디어의 출현에 대응하려는 움직임이었다. 두녜이의 초기작도 혼합 매체와 메타픽션 방식을 끌어들이며 이와 같은 실험을 한 것으로, 다만 흑인 레즈비언으로서의 예리한 시각이 반영돼 있다는 점이 달랐다. 〈워터멜론 우먼〉에서도 비슷한 시도가 엿보인다. 두녜이는 대중에게 친숙한 영화와 텔레비전 드라마의 장르적 코드를 쓰는데, 철저하게 창조된 흑인과 퀴어인의 영화적 세계관 속에서 이 코드들을 재구성했다. 정면 쇼트와 페이드인 및 페이드아웃 기법이 자주 사용되고 배우들의 연기가 그야말로 시니컬한 점 등, 셰럴과 태머라가 일을 하고 이런저런 일과를 보내는 장면들은 TV 시트콤과 다름없다. 셰럴의 다큐멘터리 장면들은 거의가 일부러 조금씩 흐릿하고 흔들리도록 촬영돼 있어, 시네마베리테의 미학을 환기시킨다. 그런 한편, 곳곳에 배치돼 있는 해설자가 화면에 등장해 말하는 인터뷰

connecting them to her Italian heritage. Diana's casual revelation that she's had three Black boyfriends, and that a relative of hers even dated an "ex-Panther" once, seems to confirm Cheryl's fears and leads to the disintegration of their relationship. Dunye doesn't adjudicate on these matters or make any generalizations about interracial love; instead, through the unsaid tensions that swirl around both Cheryl's and Fae's relationships, she paints an interior portrait of the complexities of dating while Black and queer.

A lovemaking scene between Cheryl and Diana, described by one critic as the "the hottest dyke sex scene ever recorded on celluloid," caused a stir when the film came out. The scene in question is a beautiful ode to queer desire: Diana and Cheryl's naked bodies, their caresses and their colliding flesh, are shot in sensuous close-ups, as Leslie Winer seductively croons on the soundtrack, "I ain't afraid of skin."

↓ *The Watermelon Woman*
〈워터멜론 우먼〉

와 비디오 일기는 보다 전통적인 다큐멘터리의 형식을 갖고 온 것이다. 페이 리처드가 나오는 가짜 영상들처럼, 영화는 시종일관 어느 부분이 연출된 것이고 어느 부분이 '실제'인지 불분명하게 진행된다. 리처드의 이미지가 모호하게 느껴지는 이유는 조 레너드가 창작한 이미지의 품질이 실제 같았기 때문이 아닌 관객이 무엇을 모르는지도 알 수 없기 때문이다. 존재한 적이 없는, 그러므로 좌표도 없는 것의 진위를 우리가 어떻게 알아낼 수 있을까? 영화의 나머지 부분들도 마찬가지로 어느 한쪽이라고 단정 짓기 어려운 특질을 보여 준다. 대부분의 시청자는 영화의 각 부분에서 기본적인 형식적 비유법을 인지할 수 있겠지만, 흑인 레즈비언의 시각에서 사용되는 형식적 비유는 본 적이 없을 것이다. (〈워터멜론 우먼〉의 촬영감독인 미셸 크렌쇼도 흑인 레즈비언이다.)

특히, 영화 속에서 셰릴의 시선—영화감독이자 한 개인으로서 자각—은 백인 여성의 시선과의 협상을 통해 발전해 나간다. 셰릴의 여정은 그녀가 레즈비언이었던 리처드의 인생에 대해 발견한 것들과 묘하게 공명한다. 리처드의 섹슈얼리티, 그리고 리처드와 마사의 관계는 미스터리와 음울함, 금기에 휩싸여 있다. 마사의 가족은 셰릴이 리처드와 마사의 이야기를 꺼내자 셰릴을 자신의 집에서 내쫓는다. 우연히 비디오 가게에 들른 다이애나가 셰릴에게 관심을 표하면서 시작됐던 두 사람의 관계 또한 의혹과 의구심에 직면한다. 태머라는 노골적으로 다이애나를 싫어하며 다이애나는 흑인이 되고 싶어 하고, 셰릴은 백인이 되고 싶어 한다고 비난한다. 셰릴과 다이애나 간의 인종적 역

The Michigan Republican Pieter Hoekstra denounced the scene as "patently offensive and possibly pornographic" and tried to get the $31,500 grants that Dunye had received for the project to be deducted from the budget of the National Endowment of the Arts. Though he didn't succeed, the controversy demonstrated another continuity between the fictional and historical story of Fae and the modern-day, real-life journey of Dunye: the ongoing struggles faced by Black and queer women who aspire to commit their lives and culture to the screen. The NEA grant was in fact a small portion of the film's shoestring $300,000 budget; the rest had come from donations from friends and a fundraiser that auctioned off some of the photographs of Fae that Leonard had created for the film. The film's production and endurance are a testament to June Walker's advice to Cheryl: "Our family will always only have each other." Born out of the grassroots efforts of Dunye and her community, *The Watermelon Woman* ensured that Dunye's work would mean to all the Black, women, and queer filmmakers who came after her what Fae's life means to Cheryl in the film. "It means hope, it means inspiration, it means possibility," Cheryl says at the end. "It means history."

Devika Girish

Devika Girish is a New York-based writer, editor, and programmer. She is the Co-Deputy Editor of *Film Comment magazine* and a Talks programmer for the New York Film Festival. She is also a contributor to *The New York Times*, *Sight & Sound*, *Reverse Shot*, *Criterion Collection*, *Village Voice*, *Cinema Scope*, and other publications, and has served on the selection committees of the Mumbai Film Festival and the Berlin Critics' Week. Her work has been recognized with a 2018 National Arts and Entertainment Journalism Award and a 2019 Southern California Journalism Award, among other honors.

학은 전년적이진 않지만 은근히 드러나는 두 사람의 계층적 차이로 인해 더욱 복잡해진다. 이제 막 시카고에서 필라델피아로 이사 온 다이애나는 커다란 창고형 스튜디오에 혼자 산다. 이사 온 까닭도 그저 삶에 변화를 주고 싶었기 때문이다. 또 셰릴은 자신이 다이애나에게 페티시의 대상일 뿐일지도 모르다는 불안감을 가진 듯 보인다. 이는 두녜이가 카밀 팔리아 — 이 영화에서 그녀는 자신의 패러디 버전을 연기한다 — 의 인터뷰 장면을 통해 중요하게 짚고 넘어가는 현실이다. 이 장면에서 카밀은 유모, 수박과 같은 아프리카계 미국인에 관한 비유들을 자신의 이탈리아계 유산과 연결 지으며 전용(轉用)한다. 다이애나가 자신이 지금껏 흑인 남자 친구를 세 번 사귀었고, 가까운 친척 한 명은 ‘전 블랙팬서당 당원’과 사귄 적도 있다며 생각나는 대로 무심히 털어놓음에 따라, 셰릴의 우려는 현실로 확인되고 두 사람의 관계는 와해로 이어지는 듯하다. 두녜이는 이 문제들에 대해 판결을 내리지도, 서로 다른 인종 간의 사랑에 대해 어떤 식으로든 일반화하지도 않는다. 대신, 셰릴과 리처드의 교제를 둘러싸고 소용돌이치는 표면화되지 않은 긴장을 통해 흑인 퀴어 여성이기에 겪는 연애의 복잡성을 내면의 초상으로 그려낸다.

셰릴과 다이애나가 사랑을 나누는 장면은 영화 개봉 당시에 논란을 불러 일으켰고, 한 평론가는 ‘영화 역사상 가장 뜨거운 레즈비언 섹스신’이라고 평했다. 문제의 장면은 퀴어인의 욕망에 대한 아름다운 서정시다. 두 사람의 벗은 몸, 그들의 애무와 부딪히는 살결이 감각적으로 클로즈업되고, 이 장면에 삽입

↓ Cheryl Dunye
세릴 두네이
©Cheryl Dunye

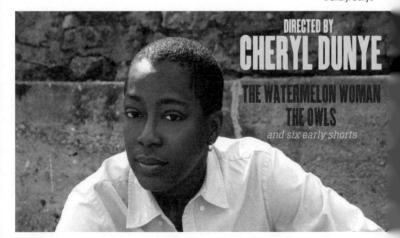

된 사운드트랙에서는 레슬리 위너의 매혹적인 목소리가 흘러 나온다. "난 피부색이 두렵지 않아." 미시간주 공화당 의원 피터 훅스트라는 이에 대해 "명백히 불쾌하며, 포르노로 볼 수 있는" 장면이라고 비난하며, 〈워터멜론 우먼〉을 찍으려는 두녜이에게 지급한 제작지원금 31,500달러만큼 NEA(The National Endowment for the Arts, 미국 국립예술기금)의 예산을 삭감해야 한다고 주장했다. 그의 노력이 성공으로 이어지지는 않았지만, 이 논란은 현대에 실제로 벌어지고 있는 두녜이 감독의 여정 또한 역사적이고 허구적인 리처드의 이야기와 연속선상에 있음을 입증한다. 즉, 자신의 삶과 예술적 의지를 영화에 헌신하고자 갈망하는 흑인 퀴어 여성들은 지금도 투쟁 상태에 놓여 있다. NEA 보조금은 사실상 〈워터멜론 우먼〉의 얼마 안 되는 제작비 300,000달러의 일부에 불과했다. 나머지 예산은 영화를 위해 레너드가 촬영한 리처드의 사진을 경매에 부치고 친구들의 지원을 받아 마련된 것이었다. 〈워터멜론 우먼〉이 제작 과정에서 또 이후에 겪은 시련은 "우리에게는 언제나 서로밖에 없다."라는 준 워커의 충고를 입증하는 듯하다. 두녜이와 동료들의 풀뿌리 노력으로 태어난 〈워터멜론 우먼〉이 분명히 보여주는 바, 두녜이의 작업은 그녀 이후의 모든 흑인, 여성, 그리고 퀴어인 영화제작자들에게 셰럴이 리처드의 삶에서 느낀 것과 똑같은 의미일 것이다. "그 의미는 희망이다. 영감이고, 가능성이다," 영화 말미에 셰럴이 말한다. "그리고 역사다."

데비카 기리시

데비카 기리시는 작가, 잡지 에디터, 프로그래머로 뉴욕을 중심으로 활동하고 있다. 현재 '필름 코멘트'의 공동 부편집자이자 뉴욕영화제 토크 부문 프로그래머다. '뉴욕타임즈', '사이트 앤 사운드', '리버스쇼트', '크라이테리언 콜렉션', '빌리지보이스', '시네마스코프'를 비롯한 여러 매체에 글을 실었으며, 베를린국제영화제 비평가주간과 뭄바이영화제 선정위원회 위원을 역임했다. 2018 내셔널 아츠앤드엔터테인먼트 저널리즘 어워드 및 2019 서던캘리포니아저널리즘 어워드를 수상한 바 있다.

Cheryl Dunye

1966 – childhood + Born in Monrovia, the capital of Liberia. Her mother is
an African-American, and her father is African, so she
calls herself "African-African-American". She gets used to
taking family pictures while living the life of a diaspora.
Her father's job at Polaroid plays a part in creating a
familiar environment for her to record her personal history
in images.

+ Moves to Philadelphia, the first city in the United States
where the black people called for freedom and liberation,
and the first city where the abolition of slavery was
passed. Instead of being identified as a single race, she
grows up experiencing the very different identities of the
black people.

1989 + While attending Temple University in Philadelphia,
Dunye cinematizes *Wild Thing* as her graduation project
which is a poem by Sapphire on the Central Park Five
case. A white woman who was jogging Central Park gets
gang raped, and the police identifies five black men in
their teens as the suspects. However, the DNA tests do
not match the semen found on the victim's body. In 2002,
it is found out that a white man named Matias Reyes
was the culprit. Dunye meets the black lesbian poet,
Sapphire, in New York, and interviews her about the case
and records her as she recites her poem. By mixing her
own story and images into it, she makes *Wild Thing:
A Poem by Sapphire*. This is her first journey in finding
her own style in filmmaking, as well as her identity as
a black lesbian woman.

1990 + Gets her Bachelor's degree from Temple University in
Philadelphia.

+ Thanks to a recommendation from a Temple University
professor who recognized Dunye's talents, Dunye
receives a scholarship from Art Matters Foundation to
admit to the art graduate school at Rutgers University.
The videos she makes there gets introduced in New York,
and Dunye steps into the art world.

+ In the fall of the same year, Dunye directs her short
experimental documentary, *Janine*. In a self-confessional
directing style, Dunye traces her memories of her

셰릴 두네이 연보

1966년부터 어린 시절	+ 라이베리아의 수도 몬로비아에서 출생. 어머니는 아프리카계 미국인이었고, 아버지는 아프리카인이었기에 스스로를 "아프리칸-아프리칸-미국인"이라고 명명함. 디아스포라의 삶을 살며 가족사진을 찍는 데 익숙했고, 아버지가 폴라로이드 회사에서 일한 것은 개인의 역사를 이미지로 기록하는 친숙한 환경을 조성하는 데 일조함.
	+ 미국에서 흑인들의 자유와 해방을 외쳤던 최초의 도시이자, 노예 폐지가 최초로 합법화된 역사를 가진 도시 필라델피아로 이주함. 하나의 인종으로서 규정되는 흑인이 아니라 매우 다양한 흑인들의 정체성과 다름을 경험하며 성장함.
1989년	+ 필라델피아 템플대학교 재학 당시 졸업 프로젝트로 만든 두네이의 작업은 '센트럴파크 파이브'라는 사건에 대한 사파이어의 시 '무법자들'을 영화화한 것임. 센트럴파크를 조깅하던 백인 여성이 집단 성폭행을 당하고 경찰은 십 대 흑인 남성 5명을 용의자로 지목하지만, 용의자 누구도 피해자 몸에서 검출된 정액과 DNA 테스트 결과가 일치하지 않았음. 2002년 범인은 백인 남성 마티아스 레예스로 밝혀짐. 두네이는 흑인 레즈비언 시인 사파이어를 뉴욕에서 만나 사건에 관한 인터뷰와 시 낭송 녹음을 함. 자신의 이야기와 이미지를 혼합해 단편 〈무법자들〉을 만듦. 흑인, 여성, 레즈비언으로서의 정체성과 영화 창작에서 자신만의 스타일을 찾아가는 첫 여정이었음.
1990년	+ 필라델피아 템플대학교에서 학사 졸업.
	+ 두네이의 재능을 알아본 템플대학교 교수의 추천으로 아트매터스재단의 펠로우십 장학금을 받아 럿거즈대학교 예술대학원에 진학. 그곳에서 작업한 비디오들이 뉴욕에서 소개되었고, 이에 두네이는 미술계에 발을 들이게 됨.
	+ 같은 해 가을, 단편 실험 다큐멘터리 〈재닌〉 연출. 고등학교 시절 같은 반이었던 재닌 소렐리와의 관계에 대한 기억을 자기 고백적으로 연출함. 두네이가 호감을 가지고 다가간 재닌은 백인 중산층 보수적 가정의 자녀로, 둘 사이의

relationship with Janine Sorelli who was in her class
during high school. Janine, whom Dunye was interested in,
was a child of a white middle-class family. Through
incidents between them, Dunye conveys the perceptions of
class, race, and homosexuality at the time. With self-
interview videos that alternate with videos of candles being
blown out, she figuratively illustrates her identity and the
change of emotions. This film reveals a personal and intimate
history to declare that one's identity is real although the
society does not respect it and denies it.

1991 + Directs the short experimental feature film, *She Don't
Fade*. A self-exploring feature film about the sexuality of
young black lesbians. A story in which Dunye plays the
protagonist and approaches various women in a humorous
manner without giving up in the realm of sexuality.

+ This is the time when the term New Queer Cinema is
coined by a film researcher named B. Ruby Rich, and
Christine Vachon and Todd Haynes are seen as key
figures. Nevertheless, no movies about lesbian African
Americans are found, and Dunye prepares a film in a way
that revealed herself. Since she majored in video art,
she didn't have a film degree, but she starts a production
based on her desire to express her identity.

1992 + Graduates from New Jersey state's Rutgers University's
Graduate School of Arts and Sciences.

+ Directs short experimental documentary, *Vanilla Sex*.
It reedits found pictures and footage. Still pictures of a
black woman and a white women performing are shown
vertically connected as if polaroid films are being
scrolled up. The footage is seen while Dunye's voiceover
leads us. It defines how the term "vanilla sex" is used
differently depending on one's sexual identity. Lesbians
have identical sexual identities, but the same term can
have very different meanings and contexts in black culture
and white culture.

1993 + Directs short experimental fiction film, *The Potluck
and the Passion*. A lesbian couple gets invited to a
couple's anniversary dinner, and the film dramatizes their
discussions on identity, sexual preference, and
sociopolitical issues. A potluck is a culture where

단적인 사건들을 통해 계급, 인종, 동성애에 대한 당시
시대 인식을 전달함. 셀프 인터뷰 영상과 촛불을 끄는
영상이 교차로 편집되는 이미지를 통해 정체성과
감정의 변화를 비유적으로 묘사함. 사회가 존중하지 않고,
존재하기를 부정하는 정체성에 대한 개인적이고
내밀한 역사를 드러내며 하나의 정체성이 실체임을
선언하는 영화.

1991년 + 단편 실험 극영화 〈그녀의 열정은 사라지지 않아〉 연출.
젊은 흑인 레즈비언의 섹슈얼리티에 대한 자기 탐구적
극영화. 두네이가 주인공을 연기하며 섹슈얼리티의
영역에서 포기하지 않고 다양한 여성에게 유머러스하게
접근하는 이야기.

+ B. 루비 리치라는 영화연구가에 의해 뉴퀴어시네마라는
단어가 생기고 크리스틴 바송, 토드 헤인즈 등이 대표
인물로 언급되던 시기였음. 그럼에도 레즈비언
아프리카계 미국인의 영화는 찾을 수 없었고 두네이는
스스로를 드러내는 방식으로 영화를 준비함.
비디오아트를 전공했기에 영화 학위는 없었지만, 자신의
정체성에 대한 표현 욕구를 기반으로 제작에 착수함.

1992년 + 뉴저지주립럿거즈대학교 예술대학원 석사 졸업.

+ 단편 실험 다큐멘터리 〈바닐라 섹스〉 연출. 사진과 영상
자료를 재편집한 파운드푸티지 작업 형식을 취하고 있음.
흑인과 백인 여성의 퍼포먼스를 찍은 스틸 사진들이
마치 필름을 검색하듯 세로로 연결되어 보여지고,
두네이의 내레이션에 따라 영상 푸티지가 보여지는 형식을
갖춤. 성 정체성에 따라 다르게 사용되는 '바닐라 섹스'라는
용어에 대한 다양한 정의를 설명함. 레즈비언이라는
동일한 성적 정체성을 가졌지만 흑인과 백인의 문화
속에서 하나의 단어가 매우 다른 의미와 맥락으로
사용된다는 것을 보여 줌.

1993년 + 단편 실험 극영화 〈포틀럭과 열정〉 연출. 한 커플의
기념일 저녁 식사에 초청된 레즈비언들이 정체성,
성적 취향, 사회정치적 이슈를 논하며 벌어지는

guests each bring their own food and share with others while socializing.

+ Directs *An Untitled Portrait*, a short video montage of Dunye's autobiographical story. She was fond of basketball since childhood, and she wanted to become like her father. Throughout her adolescence, she thought she wanted to be like a mother, but she now confesses that she wants to be herself through a voiceover over very personal Super 8mm home video images. A film that shows how emotions built up within people can reach other people's memories through the visual language.

+ *Janine*, *The Potluck and the Passion* and *She Don't Fade* participate in Whitney Museum of American Art's The Whitney Biennial in New York. Then her works are exhibited in festivals at San Francisco, Melbourne, and Berlin.

+ Invited to curate for the video section of the "Bad Girls" exhibition at New Museum, New York.

1994 + Directs the short film, *Greetings from Africa*, a humorous story about her experience as she tried to date again after her relationship of four years ends. Ted Hope and James Schamus, two key names in American independent film industry at the time, comes on board as executive directors on this film. Dunye who's used to working with the minimum number of staff experiences working with a film crew through this film. The film is produced with the support from the Mid Atlantic Arts Foundation of the National Endowment for the Arts.

1996 + *The Watermelon Woman* is shown at the Berlin International Film Festival and wins the Teddy Award. As the first feature film directed by an African-American lesbian,[1] it is an amalgamation of the narrative structure and the documentary-like format, creating a unique "dunyementaries" style which gets praised for expanding the boundaries of storytelling. Since she successfully made a film as a black lesbian female and was internationally recognized, she becomes an example that motivates the female queer community to actively work.

1999 + Participates in Walker-supported artist

[1]
As African-American lesbians, Michelle Parkerson was who made the first documentary, while Cheryl Dunye directe the very first feature film.

일화를 극화함. 포틀럭은 식사에 초대된 이들이 각자
가지고 온 음식을 함께 나눠 먹으며 친교의 자리를
가지는 문화를 칭함.

+ 두네이의 자전적인 이야기를 담은 단편 비디오 몽타주
〈제목 없는 초상〉 연출. 어린 시절부터 농구를 좋아하던
그녀는 아빠처럼 되고 싶다고 생각했고, 청소년기를
거치며 엄마처럼 되고 싶다고 생각했지만 이제는 내가
되고 싶다고 담담히 고백하는 내레이션이 흐르며 거칠고
사적인 슈퍼 8mm 홈비디오 이미지들이 펼쳐짐.
인간 내면에 응축되어 있던 감정이 어떻게 타인의 기억에
닿을 수 있는지를 영상 언어로 보여 주는 작품.

+ 〈재닌〉, 〈포틀럭과 열정〉, 〈그녀의 열정은 사라지지
않아〉로 뉴욕의 휘트니미술관 비엔날레에 참가하였으며,
샌프란시스코, 멜버른, 베를린의 축제에서 작품이 전시됨.

+ 뉴욕의 뉴뮤지엄에서 '배드 걸스' 전시의 비디오 부문
초청 큐레이터를 역임함.

1994년 + 단편 극영화 〈아프리카에서 온 인사〉 연출. 두네이의
4년간의 연애가 끝난 후 새로운 연애를 시도해 보며
겪었던 일화를 유머러스하게 풀어낸 이야기. 당시 미국
독립영화의 유명 인사 테드 호프, 제임스 섀머스가
이 작품의 총괄 프로듀서로 이름을 올림. 최소 인원으로
작업을 하던 두네이가 이 영화를 통해 촬영 스태프들과
작업하는 경험을 함. 영화는 미국 국립예술기금위원회
중대서양주 미디어아트 연구사업으로부터 일부
지원을 받아 제작됨.

1996년 + 〈워터멜론 우먼〉이 베를린영화제에서 공개되고
테디상을 받음. 아프리카계 미국 레즈비언이 감독한
첫 번째 장편 극영화로[1]
극영화 내러티브 구조와 사적
다큐멘터리 형식을 결합한
'두네멘터리(dunyementary)'라는
독특한 스타일을 창조했고
스토리텔링의 경계를 확장한 역사를
만들었다는 평가를 받음. 또한 흑인

[1]
미셸 파커슨이
아프리카계 미국인
레즈비언으로서
최초로 다큐멘터리를
만들었고, 셰릴
두네이가 첫 번째로
극영화를 연출함.

residency and works on the screenplay of her second feature film, *Stranger Inside*. As she did with the first film, she researches actual events and chooses to dramatize it in a modern way. Set in the harsh environment of a women's prison, this film depicts a young African-American woman who must put in effort to reunite with her mother whom she has never met. Inspired by historical events where slave families were forced to break up in the mid-1800s, it is a story of a mother-daughter reunion set in the 21st century.

+ While staying at the residency, Dunye conducts a screenplay workshop with twelve female prisoners in Shakopee Prison. On June 26, the last day of the workshop, Dunye's completed screenplay is recited.

2001 + With her screenplay, she challenges herself to directing a television film. HBO-produced *Stranger Inside* has its world premiere at the Sundance Film Festival. Starting with this film, she starts working on various works in the television industry.

2004 + Directs *My Baby's Daddy*, produced by Miramax.

2010 + Directs *The Owls*, produced by First Run Features. It gets invited to the Panorama section of the Berlin International Film Festival and has its world premiere.

2012 + Directs *Mommy is Coming*, produced by Jürgen Brüning Filmproduktion.

2013 + Co-directs *Valencia*, produced by Radar Productions.

2014 + Directs short film *Brother From Another Time*.

2015 + Directs short film *Black is Blue*, a story about a woman who gets a sex change operation to become a man, and this transgender man runs into a past lover. It gets screened at over 35 different festivals, and it wins the top short award at Frameline, an LGBT film festival, while being named as one of "5 Must-See Feminist Films" by the film magazine IndieWire.

2016 + For its 20th anniversary, *The Watermelon Woman*

여성 동성애자로서 성공적으로 영화를 만들고
국제적으로 인정받는 사례를 제시하며 여성 퀴어
공동체에 적극적인 작업 동기를 부여함.

1999년 + 워커 레지던시에 참가해 두 번째 장편 〈스트레인저
인사이드〉 시나리오 작업에 착수함. 첫 번째 장편과
마찬가지로 실제 있었던 사건들을 조사해서 현대적으로
극화하는 방식을 택함. 여성 교도소의 가혹한
현실을 배경으로 한 젊은 아프리카계 미국인 여성이
한 번도 만난 적 없는 어머니와 재회하기 위한 교도소
내의 노력을 그린 영화임. 1800년대 중반 노예 가족들이
강제로 헤어져야 했던 역사적 사실들에 영감을 받아
21세기를 배경으로 모녀 상봉의 이야기로 만듦.

+ 워커 레지던시에 머물며 두녜이는 섀코피 감옥에서
열두 명의 여성 죄수들과 시나리오 워크숍을 진행함.
워크숍 마지막 날인 6월 26일, 두녜이의 시나리오
작업 결과물이 낭송됨.

2001년 + 두녜이의 시나리오로 TV 영화 연출에 도전함. HBO가
제작한 〈스트레인저 인사이드〉가 선댄스영화제에서
월드 프리미어로 공개됨. 이 영화를 계기로 텔레비전
산업에서 다양한 작품 활동을 하게 됨.

2004년 + 미라맥스 제작 〈내 아기의 아빠〉 연출.

2010년 + 퍼스트런픽쳐스 제작 〈올빼미들〉 연출. 베를린국제영화제
파노라마 부문에 초청, 세계 최초로 공개됨.

2012년 + 위르겐브리닝필름프로덕션 제작 〈엄마가 간다〉 연출.

2013년 + 라다르프로덕션 제작 〈발렌시아〉에 공동연출로 참여.

2014년 + 단편 〈다른 시대에서 온 형제〉 연출.

2015년 + 단편 〈블랙은 블루〉 연출. 여성에서 남성으로 전환한
트랜스남성 주인공이 과거의 연인과 마주치는

becomes a part of The Museum of Modern Art's
(MoMA) permanent collection.

+ Selected as the grand winner in the Film – Video category
of the Guggenheim Fellowships.

+ Appointed as the member of the Academy of Motion
Picture Arts and Sciences in United States.

2018 + Starts writing the screenplay and shooting *The Wonder
of All Things*.

2019 + Founds production company Jingletown Films in
Oakland, California.

이야기를 담은 영화로 35개 이상 영화제에서 상영됨. 샌프란시스코에서 개최되는 LGBT영화제 프레임라인에서 최우수단편상을 받았으며, 영화잡지 인디와이어가 선정한 "반드시 봐야 할 페미니스트 영화" 5편에 이름을 올림.

2016년 + 〈워터멜론 우먼〉이 20주년을 맞아 뉴욕 현대미술관(MoMA)의 영화 컬렉션에 영구 소장됨.
+ 구겐하임 펠로우십 영화 부문 대상자로 선정됨.
+ 미국 영화예술과학아카데미 회원으로 위촉됨.

2018년 + 〈모든 것의 경이〉 각본 및 제작 착수.

2019년 + 캘리포니아 오클랜드에 위치한 제작사 징글타운 필름을 세움.

알베르티나
카리

Albertina Carri
Director, Producer, Media artist

Albertina Carri (1973 –) directed *Los Rubios* (*The Blonds*, 2003), which follows her investigation of what happened to her parents who were abducted by the Argentine military junta. By this film, which asks the question of how memory works, Carri drew attention as a representative of New Argentine Cinema. In her shorts and feature films, she has described the ugliness of patriarchy and power as well as gender violence and trauma resulting from it. Carri has served as the artistic director of the Asterisco International LGBTIQ Film Festival since 2014.

알베르티나 카리
영화감독, 프로듀서, 미디어아티스트

1973 –. 감독의 실화를 바탕으로 부모님이
군사정권에 납치되고 실종된 희미한 기억을
추적하는 영화 〈금발머리 부부〉(2003)를
연출했다. 기억의 작동에 대한 질문을 던지는
이 작품을 통해 뉴아르헨티나시네마의
대표 감독으로 주목받았다. 카리는
단편영화부터 가부장제와 상류층이라는
권력의 추함과 이로 인해 발생한 젠더 폭력과
트라우마를 묘사해 왔다. 2014년부터
아스테리스코국제LGBTIQ영화제의
위원장으로 재직 중이다.

©Albertina Carri

Albertina Carri

©Albertina Carri

Together in the eye of the storm

By Lucía Salas (Film Critic)

> Consider the darkness and the great cold
> In this vale which resounds with mystery.
> – Bertolt Brecht, *The Threepenny Opera*

Argentinians are profoundly lucky. It is hard to find a filmmaker or critic that doesn't know this Walter Benjamin quote by heart: "There is no document of civilization which is not at the same time a document of barbarism." When one person says it, the other nods. We all know about that storm that we call progress. But there are a few particular objects, certain films that seem to have been born right in the eye of the storm. Objects that were concerned with "brushing history against the grain," as Benjamin wrote, and by doing this, they transform the course of events. This is the case of Albertina Carri's *Los Rubios* (*The Blonds*, 2003), a film made from the tornado that was Argentina at the turn of the millennium.

The year 2003 was one of our most explosive ones. After a profoundly neoliberal decade that stripped the country of the little resources that were left after the dictatorship's looting, the crisis made itself evident, people took to the streets and the president left the government house in a helicopter in December of 2001. The word on the street was that the whole political class was not to be trusted ever again. In April of 2003, the two candidates that were on top of the results held 24% and 22% of the votes, and they went to a second run. The most popular candidate was Carlos Saul Menem,

폭풍의 눈 속에서 함께
알베르티나 카리의 〈금발머리 부부〉

글: 루시아 살라스
(영화평론가)

어둠과 지독한 추위를 생각해 봐요.
비탄의 소리 울리는 이 계곡에서.
　— 베르톨트 브레히트, '서푼짜리 오페라'

아르헨티나인들은 매우 운이 좋다. "문명의 기록은 동시에 야
만의 기록이다."라는 발터 벤야민의 표현을 모르는 영화감독이
나 평론가를 찾기 어렵기 때문이다. 한 사람이 이를 언급하면
다른 사람이 고개를 끄덕인다. 우리는 모두 진보라고 불리는 폭
풍에 대해 알고 있다. 그런데 그러한 폭풍의 눈에서 태어난 것
같은 몇몇의 특정한 대상, 특정한 영화가 있다. 벤야민이 쓴 것
처럼, "결을 거슬러 역사를 솔질하기"와 관련 있는 그 대상들은
이렇게 솔질을 함으로써 사건의 흐름을 바꾸어 놓는다. 알베르

former president and responsible for most of this crisis. The runner-up is Nestor Kirchner, a fairly unknown politician from the far south, a former member of the leftist youth in the 70s. Menem resigned from the election and Kirchner became the president with 22% of the votes. The rest is known recent history: Kirchnerism, a complex popular force that brought the conversation about politics back to everyday life, centering in collective memory and class conflicts.

Albertina Carri is the daughter of Ana María Caruso and Roberto Carri, who were members of Montoneros, a guerrilla organization active during the last dictatorship. They were kidnapped from their home, sent to a concentration camp, and murdered when Albertina was 4 years old, in 1977. *Los Rubios* interrogates this past and the effects it had not only in later history and Argentinian society but also on her own identity. It is a film that tries to find out what happened to her parents, tries to trace their last steps by asking institutions, their former colleagues, and even the neighbors to find answers, like an investigative documentary, it tries to reconstruct a memory that has been lost. Being very conscious of this loss, *Los Rubios* becomes also a film about the impossibility of full reconstructions. Being almost a baby at the time of the events, everything accessible to her and a whole generation has been someone else's tales, fragmented by the faulty works of memory, the criminal concealment of the state, and sometimes even the protective gaps of the elder, who release information only when they consider that it won't increase the trauma. Narrations are shaped by their contexts and by affect, and that is what shapes this film also.

티나 카리의 〈금발머리 부부〉(2003)는 새로운 밀레니엄을 맞이한 아르헨티나라는 토네이도 속에서 제작된 영화이다.

2003년은 아르헨티나 역사에서 가장 폭발적인 시기 중 하나이다. 독재정권의 약탈로 얼마 남지 않은 자원마저 강탈해 간 신자유주의의 10년이 지난 뒤, 위기는 분명해졌고, 사람들은 거리로 나왔으며, 대통령은 2001년 12월 헬리콥터로 정부 청사를 떠났다. 다시는 정치 계급 전체를 신뢰할 수 없다는 이야기가 시중에 돌고 있었다. 2003년 4월, 대선 1차 투표에서 상위를 차지한 두 후보는 24%와 22%를 득표하여 2차 결선에 출마했다. 가장 표를 많이 얻은 후보는 전직 대통령이자 당시 위기의 대부분에 책임이 있던 카를로스 사울 메넴이었다. 차점자인 네스토르 키르치네르는 최남단 지방 출신의 잘 알려지지 않은 정치인으로, 70년대 좌익 청년 그룹의 멤버이기도 했다. 메넴은 선거에서 사퇴했고, 키르치네르는 22%의 득표율로 대통령이 되었다. 복합적인 대중 세력의 하나인 키르치네르주의가 최근 역사에 남겨 놓은 것은 집단 기억과 계급 갈등을 중심으로 한 정치적인 대화를 일상생활 속으로 가져다 놓았다는 것이다.

알베르티나 카리는 마지막 독재 시대에 활동했던 게릴라 조직 몬토네로스의 멤버인 아나 마리아 카루소와 로베르토 카리의 딸이다. 그녀의 부모는 집에서 납치되어 강제 수용소로 보내졌고, 1977년 알베르티나가 4살이었을 때 살해당했다. 〈금발머리 부부〉는 이러한 과거사와 그 이후의 아르헨티나 역사와 사회만이 아니라, 그녀 자신의 정체성에 미친 영향을 조사한다. 탐사

Together with this process, Argentinian cinema was also changing. After a new cinema law in the early 90s that made the Cinema Institute an autonomous entity, the considerations on how films were supposed to be like became much broader. Very independent works started not only to get financed but also shown in all the distribution networks. These were the years of what it is known as New Argentine Cinema, when people like Lucrecia Martel, Lisandro Alonso, or Adrian Caetano started making films. Cinema was dealing with problems of the present, such as the profound economic and state violence that was growing in the country, and the relationship that had with the crudeness of human interactions. They were films that dealt with reality as a subject matter, shaping situations into perceptions. By the year 2003 the increases in cinematic freedom had reached a mesmerizing point, giving us very rare, fragile and at the same time influential works such as Diego Lerman's *Tan de repente* (*Suddenly*, 2002), Ezequiel Acuña's *Nadar Solo* (*Swimming Alone*, 2003), Federico Leon's *Todo Juntos* (*Everything Together*, 2002). At the same time, the millennium mambo was hitting every country in its way. One of the biggest boundaries to get softer was that between documentary

← Albertina Carri on shooting
촬영장에서
알베르티나 카리
©Albertina Carri

다큐멘터리처럼 부모에게 무슨 일이 일어났는지 알아내고, 답을 찾기 위해 과거의 단체들과 동료들과 이웃들에게 질문을 하면서 부모의 마지막 발걸음까지 추적하는 이 영화는 상실된 기억을 재구축하려 한다. 이러한 상실에 특별히 관심을 두는 〈금발머리 부부〉는 완전한 재구축의 불가능성을 이야기하는 영화이기도 하다. 당시에 거의 아기였던 그녀와 모든 세대에게 접근이 허용된 기억은 타인의 이야기로 치부되었다. 학자들의 기억에 대한 작업이나 국가의 범죄 은폐는 트라우마를 키우지 않는 선에서 정보를 제공하는 노인들의 방어 심리로 조각난 것이었다. 내레이션은 맥락과 감정에 따라 형성되며, 바로 이것이 이 영화의 형식이기도 하다.

이러한 과정과 더불어 아르헨티나 영화도 변화해 갔다. 아르헨티나 영화협회를 자율적인 독립기관으로 만들었던 90년대 초반의 새로운 영화법이 제정된 이후, 영화가 어떻게 되어야 하는가에 대한 숙고가 훨씬 더 광범위하게 이루어졌다. 상당히 독립적인 작업들이 제작비를 확보하고 배급되기 시작했다. 바로 이때가 루크레시아 마르텔, 리산드로 알론소, 아드리안 카에타노와 같은 사람들이 영화를 만들기 시작했던 뉴아르헨티나시네마라고 불리는 시기이다. 영화는 이 나라에서 점점 심각해지는 경제적, 국가적 폭력이나 추악한 상호 인간관계와 같은 현재의 문제를 다루었다. 실제 상황을 인식하여 현실을 주제로 다루는 영화였다. 2003년이 되자 영화적 자유는 매혹적일 정도로 확대되어서, 디에고 레르만의 〈어느날 갑자기〉(2002), 에서키엘 아쿠냐의 〈혼자하는 수영〉(2003), 페데리코 레온의 〈모두 함께〉

and fiction, where everything was becoming more fluid.

In this turmoil, Albertina Carri makes her second feature. With all the weight of history on her shoulders, she is first and foremost a filmmaker, and her medium is cinema. This is why you will never find two Albertina Carri films to be the same, they all have a different feel of how they respond to a preoccupation, a desire to make a new film, a different film. In every possible shape, they all brush genres against the grain, by taking a conventionalized cinematic form and deconstructing it. In the case of *Los Rubios*, the conventions of documentaries are turned upside down to think about the possibilities of truth and facts, or even to ask if the truth is a possibility. They also always work collectively. From full fiction to full documentaries, are explorations of what it means to be together, be it a family, a film crew, a romantic partnership of more than two people, society, or a generation. In *Los Rubios*, Carri explores her personal history surrounded by her peers in filmmaking. Carri does not surround herself with other people in her same family situation, but with people who are filmmakers, to solve the questions of history through film.

Insubordination is at the center of this film: Its very first scene takes something familiar and makes it unfamiliar. A family house at sunset is viewed from the outside. Inside there is light and the table is set. A child comes close to the entrance riding a horse and is met by two adults at the door, who take them hand in hand inside. Everything is made out of plastic: the house, the animals, even the food on the table. The people are represented by Playmobil, little plastic dolls, roughly articulated. We could say this family is

(2002)와 같이 많지 않지만 매우 섬세하면서도 영향력 있는 작품들이 우리에게 도착했다. 그 시기에 '밀레니엄 맘보'는 새로운 시대정신으로 모든 나라를 강타했다. 가장 크게 유연해지고 있는 경계 중의 하나는 다큐멘터리와 픽션 사이의 경계이며, 그 위에서 모든 것이 더 유동적으로 바뀌어 갔다.

이와 같은 혼란 속에서, 알베르티나 카리는 두 번째 장편영화를 만들었다. 역사의 모든 무게를 어깨에 짊어졌지만, 그녀는 무엇보다도 영화감독이며, 그녀의 매체는 영화인 것이다. 그러한 이유로 관객은 알베르티나 카리의 두 편의 영화가 결코 같은 이야기라고 생각하지 못할 것이다. 새로운 영화, 다른 영화를 만들고자 하는 집념과 욕망에 응답하는 방식에 따라 그 영화들은 모두 다른 느낌을 준다. 가능한 모든 모습 속에서, 카리의 영화들은 전통적인 영화 형식을 취하여 다시 해체하는 방식으로 "결을 거슬러 장르를 솔질"한다. 〈금발머리 부부〉의 경우는 다큐멘터리 관습들을 뒤집어서, 진실과 사실의 가능성에 대해 생각해 보거나, 그 진실이 가능한 일인지 묻기도 한다. 또한 그 영화들은 항상 결합되어 작동한다. 픽션 전체에서 다큐멘터리 전체에 이르기까지, 가족, 영화제작진, 두 사람 이상의 낭만적인 파트너, 단체 또는 세대 등, 함께한다는 것이 어떤 의미인지를 탐구한다. 〈금발머리 부부〉에서 카리는 영화를 만들면서 동료들과 함께 자신의 개인사를 조사한다. 카리는 바로 그 가족의 상황을 여타의 다른 사람들과 함께하는 것이 아니라, 영화를 통해 역사의 문제를 해결하기 위해 영화인들과 함께한다.

a plastic one, as it is a fake family and also the image of a family, of what a family is supposed to be, and that sense of what a family should be is constantly interrogated throughout the film and in all of Carri's work. A family is a collective whose shape is usually imposed on itself, with definite roles that go beyond personalities. This is a burden in every sense, even an affective burden. Carri will ask: why did my parents do this? Why didn't they leave the country? And the Playmobil dolls will appear again, being abducted by aliens, or walking through the roads of the farm where she grew up. The nuclear family is heavy for representation, and she both parodies and searches for, looking for alternatives for it.

A woman reads *Isidro Velazquez – Formas Prerrevolucionarias de La Violencia* (*Isidro*

← *The Blonds*
〈금발머리 부부〉

영화의 중심에는 반항이 자리하고 있다. 첫 장면은 익숙한 것을 취하여 낯선 것으로 만든다. 해질녘 어느 가정집이 보인다. 그 집 내부에는 조명이 켜져 있고 식탁이 차려져 있다. 한 아이가 말을 타고 현관으로 가까이 다가가 문 앞에서 두 명의 어른을 만나, 그들의 손을 잡고 집 안으로 들어간다. 모든 것이 플라스틱으로 만들어져 있다. 집, 동물, 심지어 식탁 위의 음식까지. 사람들은 투박한 관절로 된 작은 플라스틱 인형인 '플레이모빌'로 재현된다. 이 가족은 가짜 가족이자 가족의 이미지, 즉 가족에게 기대되는 것에 대한 이미지이기 때문에, 우리는 이것을 플라스틱 가족이라고 할 수 있다. 그리고 가족이라면 그래야만 하는 것에 대한 의미는 이 영화 전편에서 그리고 카리의 작업 전체에서 끊임없이 추적되고 있다. 가족은 일반적으로 구성원들의 개별 성격을 명확한 역할과 함께 그 형태가 부여되는 집단이다. 이것은 모든 방향에서 부과되는 부담이며 심지어 정서적인 부담이다. 카리는 "나의 부모는 왜 이런 일을 했을까? 왜 이 나라를 떠나지 않았을까?"라고 묻는다. 그리고 플레이모빌들이 다시 나타나 외계인에게 납치되거나 그녀가 성장했던 농장의 길을 걸어간다. 핵가족은 재현하기에 버거운 것이기에, 그녀는 대안물을 기대하면서, 패러디하고 찾아다닌다.

한 여성이 『이시드로 벨라스케스: 혁명 전의 폭력의 형식』(2001)을 읽고 있다. 로베르토 카리가 쓴 이 책은 가우초족인 이시드로 벨라스케스와 같은 로빈 후드의 모습을 혁명 투사의 원형으로 분석하고 있으며, 그 속에서 카리 본인과 많은 사람들이 싸우다 죽어 가게 될 투쟁의 기원만이 아니라 그 원인도 발견할 수 있다.

Velazquez, Pre-Revolutionary Forms of Violence, 2001), a book by Roberto Carri which analyzes the figure of the robin-hood like gaucho Isidro Velazquez as a proto-revolutionary fighter, in which the struggle that Carri and many others would die fighting could find not only its origins but also its causes, looking at the landscape of structural violence that has always been the Argentinian North and in which Isidro Velazquez moved in. A book by her father, but also the theoretical basis of a movement that had an effect on many others. In a later film, *Cuatreros* (2016), Carry explores a failed project to make a film about Isidro Velazquez and tells an anecdote. In a screening of *Los Rubios* she meets a man who tells her he can't believe he is with Roberto Carri's daughter and that, when he was a teenager, he was being trained as part of the revolutionary army

← *The Blonds*
〈금발머리 부부〉

또한 구조적 폭력의 배경을 보여 주는데, 그곳은 언제나 아르헨티나 북부 지역으로 이시드로 벨라스케스가 이주했던 곳이다. 이 책은 그녀의 아버지가 쓴 책일 뿐 아니라, 많은 사람들에게 영향을 미쳤던 운동의 이론적 기초가 된다. 카리는 다음 영화인 〈가축 도축〉(2016)에서 이시드로 벨라스케스에 대한 영화를 만들겠다는 완수하지 못한 프로젝트를 분석하면서 하나의 일화를 전한다. 〈금발머리 부부〉의 상영회를 하던 중, 그녀는 로베르토 카리의 딸과 함께 있다는 사실이 믿기지 않는다고 말하는 남자를 만나게 된다. 그는 10대 때 바로 그녀의 아버지의 책을 통해 혁명군의 일원으로 훈련을 받았다고 한다. 〈금발머리 부부〉를 만들고 난 뒤 몇 년이 지나서, 카리는 그녀의 아버지와 함께 납치되어 살해되었던 영화감독 파블로 시르가 그 책을 바탕으로 만든 영화를 추적한다. 그 영화의 필름은 현재 사라졌지만, 조사하던 중에 시나리오를 발견하게 되고, 그 영화가 〈금발머리 부부〉와 얼마나 비슷한지를 알게 된다. 시르 감독의 〈벨라스케스〉의 시나리오도, 서로 나누는 이야기가 마치 가족의 일인 양, 영화제작에 대해 토론을 하는 영화 스태프들의 모습으로 시작된다. 현장에서 그리고 책 속에서, 카리는 이러한 수수께끼에 답하고 대응하기 위해 노력하고, 추적할 수 없는 정보와 아이디어와 프로세스를 찾아냈다. 그녀가 전혀 알지 못한 채 늘 가족과 친구들에게 이야기로만 전해 들은 부모는 또한 하나의 픽션이기도 하다. 그들은 용감하고 아름다우며 선한 부모이며, 최고의 부모이자 영웅들이다. 영원히 사라졌기에 스크린 위로 결코 나타나지 못할 두 사람에 대해, 알아야만 하는 것과 믿어야만 하는 것 사이에, 분노하는 것과 이해하는 것 사이에 지속된 긴장이 있다.

with no other instructions than her father's
book. Years after making *Los Rubios*, Carri will
try to explore a film made based on her father's
book made by Pablo Szir, a filmmaker that was
kidnapped and murdered with him. The film
is now lost, and at a point in her research, she
found the script of this film and realized how
much of this script resembled *Los Rubios*, as the
script of *Los Velázquez* (1972) starts with a
crew discussing the making of a film, as if this
digressions were a family affair, even without
discussing it. Both in the field and in the books,
Carri tries to both answer and confront these
enigmas. She gathers glimpses of information,
ideas, processes that cannot be traced.
The parents that she never knew and are always
narrated to her by family and friends become
also a fiction: brave, beautiful, good parents, the
best parents, heroes. There is a constant tension
between having to know and having to believe,
being enraged and being understanding with
two people who will never materialize on screen
because they are forever missing.

In the next sequence, a documentary crew walks
the streets of Hurlingham, a city in the Buenos
Aires province. They ask the neighbors about the
people who used to live on that street, and, in
mid-conversation, a woman recognizes Albertina,
who was 3 when she last saw her and is now in
her late twenties. The woman speaks to Albertina
about herself as a baby but uses the third
person as if she wasn't the person that she just
admitted she recognized, as if that baby could
never have been an adult but forever an anecdote.
Around them, people avoid the camera eye while
they do their chores. Everyone says the same:
we had nothing to do with anything, we were just
here and we don't know what happened. While in
this process of walking the streets, a woman

이어지는 시퀀스에서, 다큐멘터리 제작진이 도시 힐링엄의 거리를 걷고 있다. 그들은 이웃들에게 그 거리에서 살았던 사람들에 대해 물어보고 대화를 나눈다. 한 여성이 마지막으로 보았을 때 3살이었고 지금은 20대 후반이 된 알베르티나를 알아본다. 그 여성은 알베르티나에게 아기였던 그녀에 대해 이야기하는데, 마치 조금 전 그녀를 알아본 것을 인정했던 그 사람이 아닌 것처럼, 그 아이가 결코 어른이 될 수 없는 사람이고 영원히 하나의 에피소드인 것처럼, 3인칭을 사용한다. 주변 사람들은 집안일을 하면서 카메라의 눈을 피한다. 모두가 똑같은 말을 한다. "우리는 아무 상관이 없어요. 단지 여기에 있었을 뿐 무슨 일이 있었는지 모릅니다." 거리를 걷던 중에 카메라를 좋아하는 한 여성이 그녀가 기억하는 것을 그들에게 이야기해 준다. "어떤 사람들이 와서 부모와 소녀들을 데려갔어요. 부모는 젊었어요." 그리고 나서 덧붙인다. "그들은 모두 금발이었지요." 그녀의 부모는 금발이 아니었고, 알베르티나도 역시 금발이 아니었지만, 지속적으로 재픽션화되어 왔던 그녀의 부모에 대한 이미지는 이제 갑자기 완전한 픽션이 되어 버린다. 스페인어 원제인 '로스 루비오스(Los Rubios)'는 금발머리의 사람들을 의미한다. 이제, 거기서 질문을 하던 소녀는 그 가족의 일원이 아니며, 될 수도 없다. 그 소녀가 반쯤은 상상이고 또 반쯤은 지어낸 묘사에 맞지 않기 때문이다. 갑자기 그녀는 그 시절 그곳에 있던 아기가 아니다. 이야기나 내레이션, 가십 같은 것들은 누군가에게서 그들의 정체성을 빼앗아 버릴 수 있는 것이다.

이 모든 이야기와 거짓된 설명 속에서, 이미지에 리얼리티가 부

who does like the camera tells them what she
remembers: some people came and took the
parents and the girls. The parents were young
and then she says: they were all blonde. Her
parents were not blonde, neither is Albertina,
but now all of a sudden this constantly re-
fictionalized image of the parents becomes a full
fiction: *Los Rubios* means *The Blonds*. Now
that girl who is there, inquiring, can't be, won't
be a part of that family, because she does not fit
this half-imaginary, half-made-up description.
Suddenly she is not that baby that was there at
the time. A tale, a narration, a gossip, can strip
someone of their identity.

Within all these tales and false accounts, reality
imposes in the image. As they walk the streets
of Hurlingham the present of the street manifests.
Now new people live there, new people have
been born. Now there is a very specific economic
situation and that seeks through all the corners
of the inquiry, *Los Rubios* becomes also a
document of the crisis, and that confronts its
idea of the crisis of representation. As they walk
the streets you can see a horse carrying a cart,
perhaps for collecting cardboard to sell,
a *cartonero*. The children are dressed poorly,
the water from the rain accumulates in the street
showing a complete lack of infrastructure, and
everyone constantly mentions the shanty
town next by. As Carri asks the neighbors for their
memories of past violence, the effects and
continuations of this violence appear manifested
in the landscape. A process of an economical
debacle, crystallized in the late nineties and early
two-thousands, comes from the financial looting
the dictatorship officials committed. As Carri
looks for answers about the past both confronts
them and ties them together. Something filters
there, an idea that poverty can create indifference,

여된다. 헐링엄의 거리를 거닐면서 거리의 현재가 분명히 제시된다. 이제 새로운 사람들이 그곳에 살고, 새로운 사람들이 태어난다. 현재 그곳에는 매우 특수한 경제 상황이 있는데, 조사 대상인 구석구석을 샅샅이 찾아다니는 〈금발머리 부부〉도 경제 위기에 대한 기록물이 되어 표현의 위기에 직면하게 된다. 제작진이 거리를 걸을 때, 당신은 거리의 폐박스를 모으기 위해 수레를 끌고 있는 말을 함께 볼 수 있다. 제대로 입지 못한 아이들, 빗물이 거리에 고여 있는 장면은 사회 기반 시설이 취약한 현실을 보여 주며 영화에 등장하는 모두가 변두리 판자촌에 대해 끊임없이 이야기한다. 카리가 이웃 사람들에게 과거의 폭력에 대한 기억을 물을 때, 이 폭력의 영향과 지속이 풍경 속에 명백하게 드러난다. 90년대 후반에서 2000년대 초반에 분명해진 경제적 붕괴의 과정은 독재정권의 관리들이 저지른 재정적 약탈에서 비롯되었다. 카리가 과거에 대한 답을 찾아가면서 현재는 과거와 대면하고 결부된다. 그리고 빈곤이 무관심을 만들어 낼 수 있다는 생각이 스며들게 된다. 왜냐하면 빚에서 벗어나기 위한 지속적인 투쟁은 모든 관심을 흡수하고 모든 것에 대한 두려움도 일으키기 때문이다.

그러고 나서 픽션이 다시 시작된다. 이 영화를 소개하는 인트로 섹션의 말미에서 한 여성(오프닝에서 책을 읽던 여성이다)이 카메라 앞에 나와 이야기한다. "내 이름은 아날리아 꼬우세로입니다. 나는 배우이며, 이 영화에서 알베르티나 카리 역을 맡았습니다." 카리가 자주 인용하는 "육체는 무엇을 할 수 있는가"라는 스피노자적인 질문에 답하면서, 육체에 이러한 역사의

as the constant struggle to stay afloat takes all the attention and creates fear of everything.

Then fiction comes again. At the end of the introductory section of the film a woman (the woman who was reading at the beginning) appears in front of the camera and says: my name is Analía Couceyro, I am an actress and in this film, I represent Albertina Carri. To answer the Spinozian question what can a body do? Which Carri can often be heard quoting. To the burden of this history to the body, Carri multiplies hers in the body of an actress. Her background information is tied now to both, as they will both appear in the film, sometimes in conversation. She is someone liberated from the weight of having to perform the narrative actions of the film, and her part in the narration of recent Argentinian history. But the actress is not only a proxy for Albertina but a part of the collective interrogation. Analía will soon join the crew, a group of young people who ask themselves what this all means, every bit of a tale that they get, they constantly enquire about the relationship between history and memory. Then she will perform all the traditional tasks of a documentary: look at footage, take notes, search for pictures, write on the computer. She will also embody Carri's most literal ideas in the shapes of monologues, taking the weight of the pudour that literature can create. She will also be the one releasing the anger, as she will appear screaming in the middle of the field, screaming of frustration, of confusion, of anger. She will make the film scream, as performance is a cinematic tool for the film to produce sensations. To the fiction of her past, Carri opposes the performance of her present, a film that is always taking the shape of its conflict, *Los Rubios* will tackle an identity crisis by having

짐을 지우기 위해, 카리는 여배우의 육체 속에 자신을 증식시킨다. 카리와 여배우는 함께 그 영화에서, 때로는 대화를 나누며 등장하기 때문에, 그녀에 대한 배경 정보는 이제 이 두 사람 모두에게 연결되어 있다. 카리는 영화 내러티브 속의 연기나 아르헨티나의 최근 역사에 대한 내레이션에서 수행해야만 하는 자신의 역할의 무게로부터 벗어나 자유롭다. 그러나 알베르티나의 대리인이자 집단 인터뷰의 한 부분이기도 한 여배우 아날리아는 영화제작에 합류하여, 제작팀의 청년들과 함께 전해 들은 이 이야기의 모든 조각들이 무엇을 의미하는지 자문하고, 역사와 기억의 관계에 대해 끊임없이 질문을 던진다. 그리고 그녀는 다큐멘터리의 모든 전통적인 작업을 수행한다. 촬영된 영상을 보고, 메모하고, 사진을 검색하고, 컴퓨터로 글을 쓴다. 그녀는 또한 카리의 아이디어를 문자 그대로 독백의 형태로 구현하여, 문학이 만들어 내는 품격 있는 무게를 취한다. 또한 현장 한가운데에서 좌절, 혼란, 분노의 비명을 지르면서, 분노를 풀어놓는 사람이 된다. 연기는 영화가 감각을 생산하게 해 주는 영화적 도구이기 때문에, 그녀가 영화로 하여금 비명을 지르게 만드는 것이다. 카리는 그녀의 과거에 대한 픽션과 그녀의 현재에 대한 연기를 대비시킨다. 그런 식으로 계속해서 갈등의 형식을 취하는 〈금발머리 부부〉는 정체성의 혼란을 겪는 방식으로 정체성의 위기에 대응한다. 그런데 이 모든 것이 픽션인가? 아니면 모두 진실인가? 형상화가 때로는 사실적이면서 때로는 장난스러울 정도로 인위적이어서, 해체에 직면하여 비명을 지르면서 동시에 소리내어 웃는 아날리아의 얼굴에는 진지함마저 비친다.

its own identity crisis: is it all fiction? Is it all true? Even seriousness is confronted, as the embodiment is sometimes realistic and sometimes jokingly artificial, with Analía having making faces, both screaming and laughing in the face of deconstruction.

The answer to the identity crisis of the self is in the collective, this film seems to also be saying. Not in the ways that they were pre-determined by others, but in their own terms. The responsibility of the collective is to define itself against external, forced definitions. The collective in *Los Rubios* is a cinema crew that becomes its own family until, in the very end, they embody the fiction of the Carri family: on the last shot of the film, at sunset, four members of the crew (Albertina included) walk away from the camera wearing blond wigs. They have become the blondes, they have fabricated them and they have become them for the sake of the film. They are their own kind of blond, evidently fake, make no effort to look like a dad, a mom, three girls, but they seem to be asking: what is a dad? What is a mom? What is the self, floating in history? It is all about belonging together, self-defined, ever-thinking, even in the fog.

Lucía Salas

Lucía Salas is an Argentinian film critic, programmer, and filmmaker based in Spain whose work navigates cinema, past and present. She is one of the editors of *La vida útil magazine* and the co-host of *We Can't Go Home Again*. Her writing has been published by *Con Los Ojos Abiertos*, *Jugend ohne film*, *Cahiers du Cinèma*, and more. As a part of La Siberia Cine, she made the films *Implantación* (2016), *Los exploradores* (2016) and *Implantación* (short, 2011). She studied Image and Sound Design at the University of Buenos Aires, MA in Aesthetics and Politics at CalArts, and is currently a Ph.D. candidate at Universitat Pompeu Fabra.

자아의 정체성 위기에 대한 해답이 집단 속에 있으며, 이 영화도 다른 사람들에 의해 사전에 정해진 방식이 아니라 그들 나름의 방식으로 이를 말하는 것처럼 보인다. 집단의 책임은, 외부로부터 강요된 의미에 반발하여, 집단 사람들이 스스로 정의하는 것이다. 〈금발머리 부부〉에서 집단은 영화제작진이며, 결국 카리 가족에 대한 픽션을 끝까지 구현할 때까지 그들이 가족이 된다. 이 영화의 마지막 쇼트에서, 해질 무렵 알베르티나를 포함한 4명의 스태프들은 금발 가발을 쓴 채 카메라에서 멀어진다. 그들은 금발이 되어, 위장을 하고, 영화를 위해 가족이 되었다. 그들은 그 가족 고유의 금발머리를 하고, 분명 가짜이기에, 아빠, 엄마와 세 딸처럼 보이려 노력하지도 않는다. 그러나 그들은 질문을 하는 것 같다. "아빠가 무엇일까? 엄마는 무엇일까? 역사 속에서 떠도는 자신은 무엇인 걸까?" 그것은 안개 속에서도 함께 연대하고, 자신들에 대해 직접 규정하고, 끊임없이 생각하는 것과 관련된 모든 것이다.

    루시아 살라스
루시아 살라스는 스페인에서 활동하는 아르헨티나 출신 영화평론가이자 영화제작자로, 영화와 더불어 현재와 과거의 길을 추적하고 있다. 영화전문잡지 '라 비다 우틸'의 편집인과 팟캐스트 '위 캔트 고 홈 어게인'의 공동 진행자이며, '콘 로스오호스 아비에르토스', '유겐 오네 필름', '카이에뒤시네마' 등의 잡지에 기고하고 있다. 또한 영상제작집단 '라 시베리아 씨네'의 일원으로 〈이식〉(2016), 〈탐험가들〉(2016), 〈이식〉(단편, 2011) 등의 작품을 제작했다. 부에노스아이레스대학에서 이미지사운드디자인을 전공한 뒤, 칼아츠에서 미학과 정치학 석사학위를 받았고, 현재 스페인 폼페우파브라대학에서 박사과정을 이수하는 중이다.

Albertina Carri

1973 + Born on April 7 under mother, Ana María Caruso, and
father, Roberto Carri, a sociology professor at the
University of Buenos Aires and an essayist.

1977 + On February 24, Carri's parents get abducted by the
military for being active members of the Peronist guerilla
group, Montoneros. Carri moves to her grandparents'
in Barrio Norte and lives with her two sisters. Although the
method was never revealed, Carri stays in contact with
her parents for some time before they lose touch.

1979 + Carri moves to her uncle's in the countryside. While
living in comfort and stability close to nature, she relieves
the shock she experienced from to her parents' incident
and takes the time to accept. This is when she gets inspired
to make a feature film about the rural life in *La Rabia*
(*Anger*, 2008).

1983 + After returning to Buenos Aires, she attends a high
school run by nuns. For several years, she studies
literature in the Faculty of Philosophy and Literature before
she drops out and begins studying film.

1991 + Carri is admitted to a film school Universidad del Cine,
FUC that teaches humanities and emphasizes practical
filmmaking, located in San Telmo, Buenos Aires.

1998 + In May, she completes her short, *No quiero volver a casa*.
In order to make a feature length film of the same title,
she begins writing the screenplay with her sister, Paula
Carri, and completes it in three weeks.
    + Directs *Niños*.

2000 + Feature film *No quiero volver a casa* (*I Won't Go Back
Home*) has its world premiere at the Buenos Aires
International Festival of Independent Cinema (BAFICI),
then it also gets invited to Rotterdam, London, and
Vienna among other major film festivals around the world.
It's a black and white thriller, and Carri uses the genre to
portray different families in different social levels. She
secured funding in an independent way, and instead of

알베르티나 카리 연보

1973년 + 4월 7일 출생. 어머니 아나 마리아 카루소와
부에노스아이레스대학교 사회학 교수이자 수필가였던
아버지 로베르토 카리의 딸로 태어남.

1977년 + 2월 24일, 페론주의자로 도시 게릴라 단체인
몬토네로스에서 활동하던 부모님이 군사들에게 납치됨.
바리오노르테 지역에 위치한 조부모 댁으로 이동해
자매 두 명과 함께 거주함. 방법은 밝혀지지 않았으나 얼마간
서신으로 부모님과 연락을 주고받았고 이후 연락이 끊어짐.

1979년 + 시골 삼촌 댁으로 이사. 자연 속에서 편안하고 안정적인
생활을 하며 부모님의 사건이 준 충격을 완화하고
이해하는 시간을 가짐. 이때의 전원생활은 장편영화
〈분노〉(2008)에 영감을 줌.

1983년 + 부에노스아이레스로 돌아와 수녀회가 운영하는
고등학교에 다님. 몇 년간 부에노스아이레스대학교
문학철학과에서 문학을 공부하다 중퇴하고 영화에 입문함.

1991년 + 부에노스아이레스 산텔모 지역에 위치한 인문학 교육과
제작 실습을 강조하는 영화학교(FUC)에 입학.

1998년 + 5월, 단편 〈집에 가기 싫어〉 완성. 자매인 파울라 카리와
동명의 영화를 장편으로 만들기 위해 시나리오 작업에
착수하고 3주 만에 완성함.
 + 〈아이들〉 연출.

2000년 + 극영화 〈집에 가기 싫어〉는 부에노스아이레스독립영화제
(BAFICI)에서 최초로 공개된 후 로테르담, 런던,
비엔나 등 세계 주요 영화제에 초청됨. 흑백 스릴러라는
장르를 통해 사회계급이 다른 가족들을 묘사한 작품.
독립적인 방식으로 자금을 확보했고, 스튜디오의
고전영화나 사회주의 리얼리즘 영화가 아닌 실제
부에노스아이레스의 강력한 이미지를 선보이는 장소에서

shooting at a studio like classical films or social realist films, she shot her scenes at places where the strong image of Buenos Aires could be seen.

2001 + Directs several shorts including *Excursiones*.
     + Directs *Aurora*
A stop-motion animation made out of still images. Using a telenovela directing style, it is a satire on excessive advertisements that claim their products can change your life.

2002 + Directs the short film *Barbie también puede estar triste* (*Barbie Can also Be Sad*).
A stop-motion animation made up of Barbies and sketches. Barbie, who symbolizes Caucasian bourgeoise heterosexual women, expresses sexual desires here, breaking the concept of gender identity as well as the innocent image it has as a toy for young girls. Using a telenovela approach to develop the story, the film sarcastically shows how macho men are full of deceit and violence against their families, while showcasing a Barbie doll who is devoted to her sexual desires beyond class and gender.

2003 + Her second feature length film and documentary, *Los Rubios* (*The Blonds*), wins the Jury Special Mention and Audience Award at the Buenos Aires International Festival of Independent Cinema (BAFICI). Following that, the film gets invited to Locarno, Toronto, Rotterdam, and Göteborg, among many other distinguished film festivals around the world, snatching all the awards. Carri becomes recognized as one of the most talented young Argentinian filmmakers of the time. This film questions what memories mean while tracking Carri's parents' case who went missing after they were abducted by the military. Carri starts to receive attention as a representative director of the New Argentine Cinema.
     + Directs a television short, *Fama*.

2004 + Directs *De Vuelta* (*Returned*).

2005 + Despite having a controversial theme, her third feature, *Géminis*, gets selected for Cannes Film Festival's

촬영된 삭품이었음.

2001년 + 〈현장학습〉 등 다수의 단편 연출.
  + 〈오로라〉 연출
  스틸 사진을 스톱모션 기법으로 표현함. 텔레노벨라
  스타일의 연출을 통해 '삶을 바꾸는 제품'이라는
  과대광고의 속성을 풍자함.

2002년 + 단편 〈바비도 슬플 수 있어〉 연출.
  바비 인형과 스케치 이미지로 구성된 스톱모션 애니메이션.
  백인 부르주아 이성애자 여성의 상징인 바비 인형이
  성적 욕망을 표출하는 캐릭터로 묘사되어, 고정된 젠더
  관념과 소녀들의 장난감이라는 순수한 이미지를 파괴하는
  작품. 저급 문화로 치부되는 텔레노벨라의 전개 방식을
  취해 마초 남성의 가정에 대한 기만과 폭력성을 전시하고
  계급과 젠더를 넘어서 성적 욕구에 충실한 바비 인형을
  풍자적으로 그림.

2003년 + 두 번째 장편이자 다큐멘터리 영화 〈금발머리 부부〉는
  부에노스아이레스독립영화제(BAFICI)의 심사위원
  특별언급 및 관객상을 시작으로 로카르노, 토론토,
  로테르담, 예테보리 등 세계 유수 영화제에 초청되며 수많은
  상을 휩쓸. 당대 아르헨티나 젊은 감독 중 가장 뛰어난
  인물 중 하나로 인정받음. 실제 카리의 부모님이 군사정권에
  납치되고 실종된 사건을 추적하는 과정을 다루며 기억이란
  무엇인가에 대한 질문을 던지는 작품. 이 영화를 통해
  뉴아르헨티나시네마의 대표 감독으로 주목을 받기 시작함.
  + TV 방영 단편 〈명성〉 연출.

2004년 + 〈귀환〉 연출.

2005년 + 세 번째 장편 〈쌍둥이자리〉는 논쟁적인 주제에도
  칸영화제 감독주간에 선정되며 아르헨티나 극장개봉까지
  이어짐. 외부 세계와 소통이 힘든 남매가 근친상간의
  관계를 맺고 있다는 걸 발견하는 과정에서 공허하고
  가식적인 아르헨티나 상류층을 묘사함.

Directors' Fortnight section and it gets a theatrical release in Argentina. Two siblings who have difficulty communicating with the outside world commit incest, and through the process of finding out their relationship, Carri portrays the Argentine upper class.

2007 + Co-directs television feature film *Urgente* with Christina Banegas.

+ *Los Rubios: Cartografía de una película* (*The Blonds: Cartography of a Movie*), the book is published by the Buenos Aires International Festival of Independent Cinema (BAFICI). The book includes unused scenes edited out from the final cut, the script, and documents to get funds from institutions. It also reveals some parts of letters from her parents in captivity to their daughter Albertina Carri and their sisters, Andrea and Paula.

2008 + With *La Rabia*, Carri wins the best director award at the Havana Film Festival, and the best director and best actress awards from Transilvania International Film Festival and Monterrey International Film Festival. Through the eyes of a young girl with speech impairment, *La Rabia* depicts violence in a family in Pampas, Argentina. The girl, who unconsciously identifies with her mother, shows strange symptoms and obsessive behavior by screaming animal sounds or getting undressed in public spaces due to the gender-based violence committed by her patriarchal and authoritative father. The mother's helplessness is reflected in the daughter's disability, and the trauma from the gender-based violence is reflected through the daughter's strange behavior in this film.

+ On November 17, her son Furio Carri Dillon Ros is born between her and Marta Dillon, an activist and a journalist. With their mutual friend and graphic designer Alejandro Ros, they form an alternative family.

2009 + Italy's Cinema Jove – Valencia International Film Festival awards Carri with the Luna de Valencia, the achievement award.

2010 + Founds television show production company, Torta, with her partner and writer, Marta Dillon. Produces *Visibles*

2007년 + TV 장편영화 〈위급상황〉 크리스티나 바네가스와 공동연출.

+ 부에노스아이레스독립영화제(BAFICI)는 영화제작기가
포함된 『금발머리: 한 영화에 대한』을 출판함. 책에는 최종
편집본에는 사용되지 않은 장면, 대본, 기타 기관에서 자금을
조달할 때 사용된 영화에 관한 증빙 자료들이 포함되어
있음. 특히 부모님이 포로 상태로 딸 카리와 자매 안드레아,
파울라에게 보낸 편지 일부가 공개되었음.

2008년 + 〈분노〉로 아바나국제영화제 감독상, 트란실바니아영화제,
몬테레이영화제 감독상과 여우주연상 수상. 언어장애를
가진 어린 소녀의 눈을 통해 광활한 초원이 펼쳐진
아르헨티나 팜파스의 한 가정에서 벌어지는 폭력을 묘사함.
무의식적으로 어머니와 동일시하던 소녀는 가부장적이고
권위적인 아버지가 어머니에게 가하는 젠더 폭력으로 인해
동물 소리를 지르고, 공공장소에서 옷을 벗으며 강박적인
행동을 하는 이상 증상을 보임. 어머니의 무력함을
딸의 장애로, 젠더 폭력으로 인한 트라우마의 결과를 딸의
이상 증세로 치환해서 보여 주는 작품.

+ 11월 17일, 활동가이자 기자인 마르타 딜런과의 사이에서
아들 푸리오 카리 딜론 로스가 태어남. 둘 사이 공통된
친구인 그래픽 디자이너 알레한드로 로스와 대안적인
형태의 가족을 꾸림.

2009년 + 이탈리아 발렌시아국제영화제에서 루나데발렌시아
공로상을 수상함.

2010년 + 파트너이자 작가 마르타 딜런과 TV 프로그램 제작사
토르타를 설립함. 〈보이는〉과 이후 공개된 〈23쌍〉(2012),
〈아름다운 숙제〉(2013) 등을 제작함.

+ 단편 〈남겨진 것들〉 연출.

2011년 + 아르헨티나 언어·도서 박물관의 요청으로 〈언어의 일부〉
제작. 살아남기 위해 고군분투한 아르헨티나 원주민
언어와 식민지 역사의 과정을 거치며 구전 및 문어 전통이
변화한 결과로서의 모국어에 대한 작업.

(2010), *23 Pares* (*23 Pairs*, 2012), and *La Bella Tarea* (*The Beautiful Tas*k, 2013) among others.
+ Directs short film *Restos*.

2011 + Produces *Partes de Lengua*, a work about the native language of Argentina that had to struggle to survive through the changes in oral and written traditions through the course of colonial history, due to the request from Mariano Moreno National Library.

2014 + Appointed as the chair of the Asterisco International LGBTIQ Film Festival held in Buenos Aires for its inaugural year, and is still currently active.

2015 + Carri makes the video installation *Operation Failure and the Sound Recovered* in the Parque de la Memoria in Buenos Aires. An audiovisual sample consisting of five works. Investigation of *Cuatrerismo*, *Cne Puro* and *Allegro*, three works that circulate around the first book of her father. And the works *Punto Impropio* and *A Piacere*, which cover the non-work of Albertina Carri's mother, Ana María Caruso.

2016 + *Cuatreros*, an essay documentary made up solely of archival images, is premiered at the Mar del Plata International Film Festival and is invited to the Forum section of the Berlin International Film Festival the following year. A project inspired by the first book by her sociologist father, the film follows the footsteps of Isidro Velazquez, a cattle thief, believed to be Argentina's last gaucho. It was recorded that he was killed by the police in 1967 on charges of stealing cattle several times in the Chaco region of northern Argentina, but the more the investigation went on, the records on Velázquez, who is seen as a hero of the people, becomes faint. The story unfolds with Carri's voiceover as they search for the lost history. The collage of fragmented archival images presents contradictory historical records and the discontinuation of history.

2018 + *Las hijas del fuego* (*The Daughters of Fire*) has its premiere at the Buenos Aires International Independent Film Festival and wins the Best Argentine Film Award.

2014년 + 부에노스아이레스에서 개최되는 아스테리스코
국제LGBTIQ영화제의 위원장으로 위촉되어 첫해의
포문을 열었으며 현재까지 활동 중.

2015년 + '작업 실패와 복구된 소리'라는 제목 아래 5개의
작품으로 이루어진 설치작업을 부에노스아이레스 기억의
공원에서 전시함. 카리의 아버지가 집필한 첫 번째
책에 대한 세가지 작품 (〈콰트레리스모〉, 〈쎄에네에
푸로〉, 〈알레그로〉)과 어머니 아나 마리아 가루소에 대한
없는예술(non-work) 두 작품 (〈푼토 임프로피오〉와
〈아피아체레〉)으로 구성되었음.

2016년 + 에세이 다큐멘터리이자 아카이브 이미지로만 구성된
〈가축 도축〉이 마르델플라타국제영화제에서 최초
공개되었고 다음 해 베를린영화제 포럼 부문에 초청됨.
사회학자였던 아버지의 첫 번째 책에서 영감을 받아
시작된 프로젝트로 아르헨티나의 마지막 가우초로
추정되는 가축 도둑 이시드로 벨라스케스의 발자취를
따라가는 영화. 아르헨티나 북부 차코 지역에서 여러 번
소를 훔친 혐의로 1967년 경찰에 의해 살해된 것으로
기록되었지만 민중의 영웅으로 추대되는 벨라스케스의
조사를 진행할수록 기록된 사실에 대한 확신이 옅어지며
잃어버린 역사를 찾는 과정을 카리의 내레이션으로
보여 줌. 단편적인 아카이브 이미지의 콜라주는 모순된
역사 기록과 역사의 비연속성을 이미지로 제시함.

2018년 + 부에노스아이레스독립영화제에서 최초 공개된
〈불의 딸들〉이 최우수아르헨티나영화상 수상. 이후
산세바스티안, 로테르담, 비엔나, 함부르크 등 유수의
주요 국제영화제에 초청됨. 가족을 방문하고픈
한 여자와 레즈비언 포르노 영화를 찍고 싶은 여자가
아르헨티나 남부 파타고니아로 여행을 떠나며 우연히
만난 여자들과의 관계와 교차되는 삶을 보여 줌.
사회의 기준과 표준에서 벗어난 여자들은 두려움, 수치심,
후회로부터 벗어나 인간으로, 여성으로서 자신의
존재와 삶, 관계를 탐구함.

아이 엠 인디펜던트 — 알베르티나 카리

After that, it's invited to major international film festivals such as San Sebastian, Rotterdam, Vienna, Hamburg, and among many others. A woman who wants to visit her family and a woman who wants to shoot a lesbian porn film travel to south Argentina's Patagonia and meet by chance. The film shows their relationship and their lives in alteration. The women who escaped from the society's standards and the norm are also able to escape from fears, humiliation, and regrets while exploring their beings, lives, and relationships as women and as humans.

↗ *The Blonds*
〈금발머리 부부〉

아이 엠 인디펜던트 — 알베르티나 카리

I am Independent – Beyond Mainstream: 7 Women Film Directors

아이 엠 인디펜던트 — 주류를 넘어, 7인의 여성 독립영화 감독

Index

찾아보기

April 29th, 2021

Publisher
Lee Joondong
JEONJU International Film Festival

Editor
Sung Moon

Co-editors
Stella Hwang, Hojin Kim

Advisor
Kim Kwangchul

Book Design
Park Yeounjoo

Design Cooperation
Lee Jinwha

Translation
Dahee Kim, June Kim,
Jeong Ayoung, Kyunghee Cho,
Joo Eunjung

Translation Supervision
Joo Eunjung

Proofreading
You Suyoung

Management support
Jang Seongho, Eom Eunjeong,
Yang Jiwon, Kim Kyoungsoo

Support (Jeonju City)
Choi Rak-ki, Seo Baewon,
Jeon Yong-geun, Yun Seon-a

Production
ThreeSteps

ISBN 978-89-98143-74-9

JEONJU International Film Festival
(54999) 2F, JEONJU Cine Complex,
22, Jeonjugaeksa 3-gil,
Wansan-gu, Jeonju-si, Jeollabuk-do,
Korea
Tel +82 (0)63 288 5433
Fax +82 (0)63 288 5411

propaganda
61-6, Yangwha-ro 7gil, Mapo-gu,
Seoul, Korea
Tel +82 (02) 333-8459
Fax +82 (02) 333-8460
www.graphicmag.co.kr

Printed in Korea

I am Independent – Beyond Mainstream: 7 Women Film Directors

초판 2021년 4월 29일

펴낸이
이준동

펴낸곳
전주국제영화제

책임편집
문성경

경영지원
장성호, 엄은정, 양지원, 김경수

편집
황성원, 김호진

지원(전주시)
최락기, 서배원, 전용근, 윤선아

자문
김광철

제작
세걸음

디자인
박연주

ISBN 978-89-98143-74-9

디자인 협력
이진화

전주국제영화제
54999 전라북도 전주시
완산구 전주객사3길 22
전주영화제작소 2층
전화 (063) 288-5433
팩스 (063) 288-5411
www.jeonjufest.kr

번역
김다히, 김준, 정아영,
조경희, 주은정

영문감수
주은정

발행처: 프로파간다
서울시 마포구 양화로 7길 61-6
전화 (02) 333-8459
팩스 (02) 333-8460
www.graphicmag.co.kr

교열
유수영

아이 엠 인디펜던트 — 주류를 넘어, 7인의 여성 독립영화 감독

Material Source and Support

Archivio Cinema del reale
Albertina Carri
Barbara Loden Archives Foundation
Big Sur
Cineteca di Bologna
Diego Schipani
Erratacorrige
Fondo Mangini-Del Fra
Foundation for Filmmakers
Impact24 Public Relations
iranwire.com
Jingletown Films (Cheryl Dunye)
Malavida Films
Mariana Bomba
OfficinaVisioni (Paolo Pisanelli)
Seville European Film Festival
SND Films
Televentures Corporation
UCLA Film & Television Archive
Viennale (Eva Sangiorgi)

Asian Culture Center (ACC)
   Cinematheque
Forest of Literature
Experimental Film and Video Festival
   in Seoul (EXiS)
Yang Sup Shin
Jong-han Choi (Semyung University)
Korean Film Archive
Han Okhi

I am Independent – Beyond Mainstream: 7 Women Film Directors